ISBN 978-1-331-73478-9
PIBN 10227758

Similar Books Are Available from
www.forgottenbooks.com

THE THAMES

AND ITS TRIBUTARIES

OR,

RAMBLES AMONG THE RIVERS.

BY CHARLES MACKAY,

AUTHOR OF "THE HOPE OF THE WORLD," ETC

IN TWO VOLUMES.

VOL. II.

LONDON:

RICHARD BENTLEY, NEW BURLINGTON STREET,

Publisher in Ordinary to Her Majesty.

1840.

PRINTED BY SAMUEL BENTLEY,
Bangor House, Shoe Lane.

CONTENTS

TO THE SECOND VOLUME.

CHAPTER I.

CHAPTER II.

CHAPTER III.

CHAPTER IV.

CHAPTER V.

CONTENTS.

CHAPTER IX.

CHAPTER X.

CHAPTER XI.

CHAPTER XII.

ILLUSTRATIONS.

THE

THAMES AND ITS TRIBUTARIES.

CHAPTER I.

Ruins of Godstow Nunnery. — The Legends of Fair Rosamond. — The Monks of Ensham. — Woodstock Park and its Memories. — Rosamond's Bower. — Chaucer's House. — His Description of Woodstock Park. — Queen Elizabeth's Verses while a Prisoner. — The Ghosts of Woodstock. — Blenheim.

ASSING from Oxford into Berkshire, and on through Botley, we follow the windings of the Thames for about two miles, by the by-road, till we arrive at Witham, the seat of the Earl of Abingdon, and so on to the ancient site of Godstow Nunnery, famous for its legendary and poetic associations. Who has not heard the touching story of " Fair Rosamond ?" a story upon which

historians in later years have attempted to throw discredit, but which will ever hold its place in the popular heart. And here we are upon the scene of it. Here on this bank the "Rose of the World" passed the innocent years of her early girlhood; and here she was buried, with that insulting epitaph so well known—

Hic jacet in tumba, Rosa Mundi, non Rosamunda;
Non redolet, sed olet, quæ redolere solet;

inscribed however in later years, when her royal lover, so faithful to her memory, was no more.

How sweet are the lines of the neglected and almost unknown poet, Daniel, upon this subject! We quote his Complaint of Rosamond, premising, that the poet succeeded Spenser as Laureate, in the year 1599, soon after which the poem was published. After describing the grief of Henry II. on discovering the body of his beautiful mistress, he continues—

Thus as these passions do him overwhelm,
    He draws near to the body to behold it,
And as the vine married into the elm
    With strict embraces so doth he enfold it.
    And as he in his careful arms doth hold it,
Viewing the face that even Death commends,
On senseless lips millions of kisses spends.

"Pitiful mouth!" said he, "that living gavest
 The sweetest comfort that my soul could wish,
O be it lawful now that dead thou havest
 This sorrowing farewell of a dying kiss!
 And you, fair eyes, containers of my bliss,
Motives of love, born to be matched never,
Entombed in your sweet circles, sleep for ever!

"Ah, how, methinks, I see, Death dallying seeks
 To entertain itself in Love's sweet place,
Decayed roses of discoloured cheeks
 Do yet retain the hues of former grace,
 And ugly Death sits fair within *her* face,
Sweet remnants resting of vermilion red,
E'en Death itself might doubt that she were dead!

"Wonder of beauty! oh, receive these plaints,
 These obsequies, the last that I shall make thee,
For now my soul that now already faints,
 That loved thee living, dead will not forsake thee,
 And hastes her speedy arms to overtake thee.
I'll meet my death and free myself thereby,
For, ah! what can he do, that cannot die?

"Yet, ere I die, thus much my soul doth vow
 Revenge shall sweeten Death with ease of mind,
And I will cause posterity shall know
 How fair thou wert above all womankind.
 And after ages monuments shall find,
Showing thy beauty's title, not thy name,
Rose of the world! that sweeten'd so the same!"

The beauty of the quotation may plead excuse for its length, and some reader, perhaps
unaware that such a poet as Daniel ever wrote,

may be tempted to stray into his pages, where he will find much to reward him.

Rosamond's funeral was celebrated here with great splendour, as the poet hints; and King John afterwards bequeathed a considerable sum, that the holy virgins of Godstow might relieve with their prayers and pious masses the souls of his father and Fair Rosamond. Upon the interment itself, great sums were lavished by the disconsolate king, and the parents of the lady. The tomb was of the most exquisite and costly workmanship, but much of it was destroyed when priestly bigotry ordered the removal of the body, as too impure to be buried within consecrated ground. Hugh, Bishop of Lincoln, visiting the nunnery in 1191, two years after the death of Henry, and about twenty after the death of Rosamond, and observing a tomb covered with velvet, silk, and cloth of gold, and magnificently lighted up with wax tapers, perpetually burning, inquired whose it was, and being informed that it was Fair Rosamond's, he ordered that " the harlot should be taken thence, lest through her the Christian religion should be scandalized." It was, however, only removed from the church of the nunnery, and not from the precincts altogether. Speed says, " the chaste sisters gathered her bones from the chapter-house whence they had been conveyed, and put them in a perfumed leathern bag, enclosing them so in lead, and laid them again in the church, under a fair large grave-stone, about whose edges a fillet of brass was inlaid, and thereon written her name and praise." At the dissolution of the nunnery, Speed says that the bones were so found. Leland confirms this account, adding, "Rosamond's tomb at Godstow nunnery, was taken up of late : it is a stone with this inscription— 'Tumba Rosamundæ.' Her bones were enclosed in lead, and within that in leather : when it was opened, there was a sweet smell came out of it."

This nunnery, sacred to her affecting memory, was founded in the reign of Henry I. by Editha, a matron of Winchester, in consequence of a dream she had. It would appear, that this lady had long meditated the pious work of founding a nunnery, but was at a loss where to erect it, until she dreamed that the most fitting place would be on the bank of the Thames, to the west of Oxford. Her confessor persuaded her that the dream was an intimation of the will of Heaven, and the nunnery was founded at Godstow accordingly, Editha becoming the first abbess.

Two sides of the nunnery remained till about the year 1769, when they were blown down by a high wind. Part of the wall and the chapel still exist, and belong to the Earl of Abingdon. Keeping on the same side of the Thames, we pass by Godstow Bridge, and follow the course of the river for awhile to Swinford Bridge, which we cross, and proceed to the ancient village of Ensham—termed, like Kingston, "a famous place" even in the days of the Saxon Heptarchy. It once possessed an abbey, a small portion of the ruins of which still remain, founded early in the eleventh century, and dedicated to the Virgin Mary and St. Benedict. A singular custom formerly prevailed here on Whit Monday, as we are informed by Samuel Ireland in his "Picturesque Views." It was the privilege of the towns people to be allowed to cut down as much timber in the neighbouring wood, as could be drawn into the courtyard of the abbey by men's hands only, which timber was to be their own, if they could succeed in dragging it out again! This was a very "ingenious device" on the part of the reverend fathers: the timber once got in, they allowed very little of it to be pulled out again, as it was a part of the stipulation, that the monks and the servants of the abbey should place every impediment in the way of its exit that they were able.

From hence to Woodstock is a pleasant walk of about four miles, following part of the way the stream of the Evenlode, a petty tributary of the Thames. The town of Woodstock derives most of the interest attached to its name, from the magnificent palace of Blenheim; but its ancient interest springs from the park and ancient palace of the kings of England, which latter was pulled down by order of the great Duke of Marlborough. In this palace King Alfred translated " Bœtius on the Consolations of Philosophy;" the work which was afterwards the solace of the poetical James I. of Scotland, when a prisoner in Windsor Castle. In the time of King Etheldred, a parliament assembled at Woodstock, between which period and the reign of Henry I. the town fell somewhat into decay. The latter, the only one of the early monarchs who had a cultivated mind, or took any delight in the recreations which taste and a love of literature are so abundant in affording, was pleased with the beauties of the surrounding scenery, improved the palace, and added several suites of apartments to it, at the same time enlarging and replanting the park, and enclosing it with a substantial stone wall.   Here also, as we learn from Stowe, he established the first menagerie ever known in England: " the King, for his pleasure," says the annalist, " desired the wonderful things of other countries, as lions, leopards, lynxes, and camels, of the which England had none, craving them from kings.   He had a park called Woodstock, in which he kept them, and put there, among others, a beast called " Stryr," or otherwise called a " *Porpentine,*" sent him from William of Montpelier."   The same historian says the park was seven miles in compass, that it was the first ever enclosed in England, and that divers villages, churches, and chapels were destroyed to make room for it.

In the reign of Henry II, the palace of Woodstock was inhabited by the beautiful Rosamond.   Here the royal lover built her the celebrated bower in the midst of the laby-rinth, the theme of popular poets, and the delight of romance readers ever since.   To quote the most popular of all the ballads ever made upon it—

The King for her defence
Against the furious Queen,
At Woodstock builded such a bower,
The like was never seen.

Most curiously that bower was built
Of stone and timber strong,
One hundred and fifty doors
Did to this bower belong,

And they so cunningly contrived
With turnings round about,
That none but with a clue of thread
Could enter in or out.

Though the authorities differ upon the point, whether this fair lady was poisoned by Queen Elianor, all agree that the Queen discovered her retreat. Higden, the monk of Chester, whose account is followed by Stowe, says, "the Queen came to her by a clue of thread or silk, and so dealt with her, that she lived not long after." Holinshed says, "it was the common report of the people, that the Queen found her out by a silken thread, which the King had drawn after him out of her chamber with his foot, and dealt with her in such sharp and cruel wise, that she lived not long after." Speed says, that the Queen "discovered her by a clue of silk, fallen from Rosamond's lap as she sat to take air, and suddenly fleeing from the sight of the searcher, the end of her silk fastened to her foot, and the clue still unwinding, remained behind, which the Queen followed, till she had found what she sought, and upon Rosamond so vented her spleen, as the lady lived not long after." Upon the dissolution of the religious houses, her tomb at Godstow, as we have already stated, was examined, and attracted some attention, and a *cup* being found upon it, the popular notion that she was poisoned was either originated, or acquired additional strength. However this may be, it is certainly worth notice that none of the old historians attribute her death to poison, and that the oldest ballads and poems made upon her sad fate with which we are acquainted, only date as far back as the reign of Elizabeth.

The popular ballad of Thomas Delone, already quoted, appears not to have been published till 1612, as may be seen from the introduction to it by Bishop Percy, in his " Relics of Ancient Poetry :" Daniel's " Complaint of Fair Rosamond" was published somewhat earlier. There is this to be said in favour of the popular version, — found popular, and made still more so by the poets,—that there is nothing improbable in the story of her poisoning. Queen Elianor is allowed on all hands to have been a jealous, violent, and bad woman. Poor Rosamond had but one sin to answer for, but her rival Elianor had many. She led a life of promiscuous gallantry before her marriage with Henry, and afterwards excited his sons to rebel against him, and distract the kingdom.

No traces of this famous bower and labyrinth have existed for centuries, but the concurrent testimony of all the historians impel us to believe that they did exist as represented. Some slight remains of a bath, amid the groves on the northern part of the park, are pointed out, which are believed to have formed part of the bower of Rosamond.

In Woodstock park resided for many years the father of English poetry, venerable, well-beloved, most worthy Geoffrey Chaucer. Many have asserted that he was born in Woodstock. The learned Camden once countenanced this opinion, for, speaking of Woodstock, he says "having nothing in it else remarkable, it can boast of having produced our English Homer, Geoffrey Chaucer." Leland doubted whether he were born in Berkshire or Oxfordshire; but if we may judge from the poet's own words, that great honour belongs to the city of London. Speaking of the disturbances in London, when the mob destroyed the Savoy palace, where he long resided with his royal friend, John of Gaunt, he says, "The city of London that is

to me so dear and sweet, in which I was forth
grown, and more kindly love have I to that
place than to any other on earth, as every
kindly creature hath full appetite to that place
of his kindly engendering." However this may
be, Woodstock is nevertheless classic ground,
for if Chaucer were not born there, he resided
there. "His house," says Dr. Urry, "was a
square stone house, near the park gate, which
still retained its name in 1721. Many of the
rural descriptions in his poems appear to be
representations of the actual scenery of the
park. Thus,

> " And right anon as I the day espide
> Ne longer would I in my bedde abide,
> But unto a woode that was mee fast by
> I went forth myself alone and boldily,
> And held the way downe by a brooke side
> Till I came to a land of white and grene,
> So fair an one had I never in bene,
> The ground was grene, ypowdered with daisye
> The flouris and the grevis alike hye,
> Al grene and white was nothing ellis sene."

These lines appeared to Dr. Urry to be an
exact portraiture of the way from Chaucer's
house down by the brook side, through part of
the park to the vale, under Blenheim Castle.
The nightingale in that poem is represented as
saying to the sleeping bard that it would sing—

"The morrow after St. Valentine's day
Under a maple that is fair and grene,
Before the chamber window of the Quene
At Wodestocke upon the grene laye."

The scene of his poem of the Dream is also laid in Woodstock Park, where it appears, when not engaged in study, his favourite diversion was to walk. Yet perhaps these morning walks among the trees, which he describes in various parts of his works with such luxuriance of poetry, were the times when he studied most. He made acquaintance with nature in her solitudes, studied her sweet face in his early rambles, and was thereby enabled to paint her so well. Chaucer, from the busy life he led in London, being mixed up so intimately with all the affairs of the powerful John of Gaunt, shared naturally the evils of that prince's fortunes. In the troubles that ensued in London, after the citation of Wickliffe, and the arrest of Comberton, late Mayor of London, Chaucer became obnoxious to the King, and was obliged to fly to the Continent to avoid imprisonment. On his return, he determined to mix himself up no more in political questions, and John of Gaunt, being then absent on his expedition to recover the kingdom of Castile and Leon,

which he claimed in right of his wife, he had
an additional reason for keeping himself secluded from the world. He, therefore, retired to
Woodstock, and busied himself, in revising
and correcting his poems. The exact time of his
final departure from Woodstock to Donnington,
where he passed the last two years of his life,
is not known with certainty. We have already
in our account of the river Kennett given some
account of these years. So, farewell, Chaucer,
of whom we will say in the words of old Lyd-
gate—

> " My maister Chaucer, chief poet of Britayne,
> Whom all this landè shoulde of righte prefer,
> Sith of our language he was the load star,
> That madè first to distil and raine
> The gold dew drops of speech and eloquence
> Into our tonguè through his excellence."

In Woodstock Palace, the Princess Elizabeth was confined by her sister, Queen Mary,
for a short time, during which captivity, as we
learn from Hentzner, the German traveller,
she wrote the following lines with a piece of
charcoal upon her window-shutter, being denied the use of pens and paper. The lines
were first printed in Hentzner's book, and afterwards at the private press of Horace Walpole,
at Strawberry Hill, from whence they were

transferred into Percy's Relics. "In Hentzner's book," says Dr. Percy, "they were wretchedly corrupted," but were restored, as they now follow, by Horace Walpole.

> "O fortune, how thy restlesse wavering state,
>   Hath fraught with cares my troubled will,
> Witness this present prisonn, whither fate
>   Could bear me, and the joys I quit.
> Thou causedest the guiltie to be losed
> From bandes wherein are innocents inclosed,
> Causing the guiltless to be straight reserved,
> And freeing those that death had well deserved.
> But by her envy can be nothing wrought,
> So, God, send to my foes all they have thought.
>   ELIZABETH, prisoner."

" A. D. MDLV."

These lines are of little or no value in themselves, but they become of interest from the station of the writer, and the strait to which she was reduced for want of writing materials. Shenstone has written a poem upon the subject.

Woodstock Palace and Park, with all their poetical and romantic associations, have, in later years acquired a still dearer place in the hearts of the lovers of English literature, by the beautiful novel of Sir Walter Scott. It is impossible for any one who has read it, to wander in that park without conjuring up the remem-

brance of the gentle Alice, the doughty old
Sir Harry Lee, and his honest dog, and the
iron warriors, and canting hypocrites of that
day, with stern old Cromwell giving his orders
to batter down the walls that he might take
possession of that last stronghold of royalty.

Woodstock Park and Palace were also the
scene of that famous ghost story related so mi-
nutely in Glanvil's book of Witchcraft, in the
form of a continuation to his wondrous tales,
by Dr. Henry More, and entitled, " A Trans-
cription of a Narrative out of the Natural History of Oxfordshire, of the strange passages

that happened at Woodstock, Anno. 1649, when the commissioners for surveying the manor house, park, deer, woods, and other demesnes belonging to that manor, sate and lodged there." Their first act was to efface every symbol of royalty; and a noble old tree, which had stood for centuries in the park, was uprooted by their order, merely because it bore the, to them obnoxious, name of the King's Oak. Immediately their troubles began; fearful noises were heard in the chimneys, bricks, tiles, and stones, rattled about their ears at all hours of the day and night; invisible hands pulled the clothes off their beds; shrieks and groans, and the clanking of chains were heard; their lights were suddenly extinguished, no one knew how; and glasses and bottles broke mysteriously wherever they attempted to lay hands upon them. The bewildered commissioners betook themselves to penitence and prayer, and watched all night with Bibles and drawn swords to repel the evil spirits that so tormented them. But all in vain; when worn out with watching they retired to rest towards the morning, they found logs of wood in their beds instead of pillows, and were drenched unaccountably with green ditch-water, as they attempted to lie down. Their eyes became no less bewildered than their ears; their fear became so great that they indulged each other's dread with the marvellous, and swore to each other that they actually saw the devil scratching with his hoof upon a candle to put it out; that they saw legions of imps in every corner of the house; that Beelzebub walked up and down the great room every night, howling in a most fearful manner, and sometimes making a noise as great as if a whole park of artillery had been fired off. Finding that their prayers were inefficacious, and enjoying no peacé or rest for several days and nights, they finally determined to quit Woodstock altogether, which they did in the firm belief that it was the abode of the devil and ten thousand of his evil spirits. Some years afterwards it was discovered that the man who played the devil to such perfection on this occasion was one Giles Sharp, the clerk of the Commissioners, a pretended republican, but in reality a loyalist, who had passed his early years in Woodstock, and who resorted to this trick to frighten away these rude spoilers from the hallowed abode of the royalty of England. The credulity of the commissioners rendered his deception comparatively easy; their contagious fears carried it on for him; and, aided by a few dexterous cavaliers, the object was accomplished even beyond his hopes. The truth was not discovered till after the Restoration.

Woodstock manor remained unoccupied, or nearly so, for about fifty years, when it was granted by Parliament in testimony of the nation's gratitude for the brilliant exploits of the Duke of Marlborough. Sir John Vanburgh was employed to build a suitable edifice, and the palace of Blenheim was the result. Yet the hero for whom it was intended never had the pleasure of inhabiting it; and, as may be seen from an interesting chapter in Mr. D'Israeli's " Curiosities of Literature," it became a source of annoyance to him for the remainder of his days. Parliament neglected to provide positively and in a proper manner the necessary funds, which were always charged upon the civil list of Queen Anne until her death, when the workmen, whose wages had been long in arrear, were glad to accept one third of their claims. Sir John Vanburgh feared his total ruin : the Duke of Marlborough groaned in bitterness of spirit, lest he should be forced in some way or other to pay a penny out of his own pocket, for the expenses of a building which was to have been erected at a nation's cost, and ultimately died without enjoying his princely

abode, leaving his hostile Duchess and the archi-
teet to fight out the question of expense between them.

This fine building has been condemned by
some as too massive, while others have regarded its massiveness as its great beauty. The
north, or grand front, extends from wing
to wing three hundred and forty-eight feet;
and the centre is supported by pillars of the
Corinthian order. The southern front has a
handsome portico, surmounted by a colossal
bust of Louis XIV, taken from the gates of
Tournay by the victorious Marlborough. The
approach to the front of the mansion is over

a lofty bridge, which was originally built at the desire of the great Duke himself over a very narrow stream, which gave rise to the following epigram in allusion to his well-known parsimony :—

> The lofty bridge his high ambition shows—
> The stream an emblem of his bounty flows.

The stream, however, was afterwards widened by the celebrated Capability Brown, who is reported to have said that the Thames, envious of the nobler expanse of water which his art had formed, " would never forgive him for what he had done at Blenheim." Near the bridge stands a column one hundred and thirty feet high, the plinth of which is inscribed on the four sides with the exploits of the Duke of Marlborough. The interior of the mansion is fitted up with great magnificence, and contains a picture gallery with many fine pictures, some of which were presented to the Duke by the citizens of Antwerp and other towns in Flanders. The library is also a fine room, upwards of two hundred feet in length, occupying the whole range of the west front, and containing a collection of books valued at thirty thousand pounds. The park, of about two thousand seven hundred acres, is laid out, as the parks of English noblemen usually are, in a style of great taste, and true appreciation of the beauties of natural scenery. Where Nature is niggard she is aided by art, and where bountiful, turned to the best advantage. Two sycamore trees upon an eminence mark the site of the ancient palace of Henry II, which was pulled down by the first Duke of Marlborough, at the advice of Lord Godolphin, because he thought it would obstruct the view from the windows of Blenheim.

Having lingered a sufficient time at this historical spot, we must retrace our steps to the neighbouring banks of the Thames, and proceed onwards from Ensham or Eynsham to Stanton Harcourt.

CHAPTER II.

Stanton Harcourt. — English and French Epitaphs.—The River Windrush. — The Splendid Shilling. — A Poet's Whim.—Battle of Radcot Bridge.

THE village of Stanton, called Stanton Harcourt, from the residence of the Earls of Harcourt, before they removed to their more magnificent seat at Nuneham Courtney, is pleasantly situated within view of the Thames, about two miles from the bank, and derives considerable interest from the fact that Pope was for some months an inmate of the hospitable house of the Lord Chancellor Harcourt, in the year 1718, and that there he finished the fifth volume of his translation of Homer. In the tower of the chapel is a room still called Pope's Room, which is the one he occupied as his study during the summer of the year mentioned. The poet recorded the completion of

his fifth volume by writing the date with a
diamond on a pane of red glass, which was
afterwards taken out of the window by a succeeding owner of the mansion, and preserved
with great care as a relic of genius.   Mr.
D'Israeli, who mentions the circumstance in his
" Curiosities of Literature" in his chapter upon
" Literary Residences," states his belief that
the pane is still preserved among the treasures
of Nuneham Courtney.   The following is a
fac-simile of the writing, taken from " Ireland's
Picturesque Views," the author of which states
that the pane was lent to him by the Earl

In the year 1718
ALEXANDER POPE
finish'd here the
fifth Volume of **HOMER**

of Harcourt.   Gay was also a visitor in the
summer of 1718, with his brother poet, at
Lord Harcourt's; and they composed together, during their residence there, a poem
upon the tragical death of two lovers, who
were struck dead by lightning while at work
in a neighbouring hayfield.   The picturesque
church of Stanton, contains several ancient mo-

numents of the family of Harcourt, who have been settled in the place since the conquest.

Among others, a monument to the memory of Sir Robert Harcourt, and of Margaret, his wife, who lived in the reign of Henry VI, has excited considerable notice from the fact that both the husband and wife wore the insignia of the noble Order of the Garter, and are so represented on their tomb. There is a modern monument to the memory of the Hon. Simon Harcourt, son of the Chancellor, who died in 1720, and for which Pope, at the re-

quest of Lord Harcourt, wrote the following
epitaph:

> To this sad shrine, who e'er thou art, draw near:
> Here lies the friend most lov'd—the son most dear,
> Who ne'er knew joy, but friendship must divide,
> Or gave his father grief but when he died.
> How vain is reason—eloquence how weak,
> If Pope must tell what Harcourt cannot speak;
> Oh, let thy once loved friend inscribe thy stone,
> And with a father's sorrows mix his own.

Dr. Johnson, in his critical notices of Pope's
epitaphs, written for the " Universal Visitor,"
and afterwards appended to his Life of Pope,
objects to the last two lines, and wishes they
had been omitted, as " they take away from
the energy without adding to the sense;" of the
remainder the critic says, " It is remarkable for
the artful introduction of the name, which is
inserted with a peculiar felicity, to which
chance must concur with genius, which no man
can hope to attain twice, and which cannot be
copied but with servile imitation." This praise
is as ill applied as the previous censure. It
does not seem at all clear that because the poet
was obliged to tell the grief which the father
could not speak, that either reason was vain,
or eloquence weak. We might ask whose reason was vain, and whose eloquence was weak?

It may be said that the eloquence of the poet
was weak in telling such grief as the father
must have felt; but where is the vanity of
reason? The plain fact is, that Pope did not
write good epitaphs, to which we may add that
very few men can. In England especially we
are sadly deficient in taste, in this respect, and
might take example of the French, who are
generally content to express their grief in prose,
for real sorrow has no leisure to make rhymes.
What can be more affecting than the simple
words upon a tomb-stone in the cemetery of
Père la Chaise—

Oh mon fils ! mon fils !

No epitaph that poet ever wrote can equal
this.

We follow the still narrowing stream of the
Thames until we arrive at New Bridge, where
it receives the waters of its tributary, the
Windrush; the latter rises, like the Thames,
among the Cotteswold hills, enters Oxfordshire
near Burford, and passes by Witney, famous
for the manufacture of blankets, into the
Thames. It has been alleged that the superior whiteness of the Witney blankets arises
from the nitrous qualities of the water of the
Windrush.

The Thames runs through an uninteresting

country for ten or twelve miles, especially on the Oxfordshire side, until we arrive at Tadpole Bridge, where the scenery improves a little. At the distance of about two miles is Bampton, which can only be classed as a considerable village now, but was formerly a town of some consequence, and still claims that rank. It is seated on a little rivulet that runs into the Thames, and was a town of some note at the Conquest. Bampton gave birth to John Phillips, the author of the " Splendid Shilling," which for some time was the most popular poem in the English language ; but which has long been consigned to a fifth-rate place, though it still boasts its admirers. He was also the author of a poem called, " Cider," and of another called " Blenheim," the latter being written at the instigation of the Tory leaders soon after that great victory ; " probably," says Johnson, " with an occult opposition to Addison," who was celebrating the same victory for the Whigs. The father of Phillips was the Rev. Dr. Stephen Phillips, minister of Bampton, in the rectory of which the poet received the first rudiments of his education. It is related of him, that he was always remarkably fond of having his hair combed—a fondness which did not forsake him when he quitted the paternal roof at Bampton. When at school, at Winchester, instead of joining in the amusements of the other boys, he retired to his cham ber, where he would sit for hours together, enjoying the luxury of a combing, which he persuaded or paid somebody to perform upon him. He wore his hair long and parted in the middle, after the fashion of the portraits of Milton, of whom he was a most enthusiastic admirer. Upon this subject of combing, the following anecdote of Isaac Vossius is given as a note by the editor of Dr. Johnson's "Lives of the Poets," to account for the propensity of young Phillips. The book quoted is the treatise of Isaac Vossius "*De Poematum cantu et viribus Rythmi*," Oxen, 1672, p. 62. "Many people take delight in the rubbing of their limbs and the combing of their hair, but the exercises would delight much more if the servants at the baths, and the barbers were so skilful in this art, that they could express any measures with their fingers. I remember that more than once I have fallen into the hands of men of this sort, who could imitate any measures of songs in combing the air, so as sometimes to express very intelligibly iambics, trochees, dactyls, &c. from whence there arose to me no small delight."

Leaving Bampton and its rectory, we pass by the small village of Clanfield, to Radcot bridge, with Farringdon Hill rising behind it. There was a bridge over the Thames at Radcot, in the fourteenth century, as we learn from the old chronicles, which tell of a battle that was fought upon it, or near it, between Vere Earl of Oxford, the favourite of Richard II, and the Barons, who had assembled an army to resist his power and influence. The Earl of Oxford, then known by the title of Duke of Ireland, was at the head of five thousand men, and rode forth as Stowe says, "in stately and glorious array, thinking none durst have encountered him;" but when he came to the bank of the river, which it was his object to pass, on his way to London, where he was certain of support from the citizens, he found the army of the Barons drawn up on the Oxfordshire side, to oppose his passage. Being a coward, as royal favourites generally are, he no sooner saw their superior force than he fled, leaving his second in command, Sir Thomas Molineux, to fight the battle as he could. In the encounter that ensued Sir Thomas entered the Thames on horseback, and a fierce combat took place in the midst of the water between him and Sir Thomas

Mortimer, a captain in the army of the Barons. As Molineux was springing up to the bank, his opponent caught off his helmet, and struck his dagger into his brains, and he fell back a lifeless corpse into the stream. The Duke of Ireland galloped down the bank till he was out of sight, when he dismounted, took off his armour, and swam across. He ultimately effected his escape to Flanders, where he died in exile five years afterwards.

Farringdon Hill, surmounted by its grove, about two miles from the Thames, is a prominent object in the view for a great distance, and a sort of landmark for the four counties of Oxford, Gloucester, Berks, and Wilts. It rises by a gradual ascent from the Vale of the White Horse, and from the top there is an extensive view of one of the most fertile and luxuriant districts in England. Pye, the Laureate, wrote a poem in praise of its beauties, with which he was well acquainted, having long resided in the neighbourhood. His house, which he built for himself, became after his death, the property of Mr. Hallett.

The town of Farringdon stands on the western acclivity of the hill, and is a place of considerable antiquity. Its castle, of which there are now no remains, was built during the civil wars in the time of King Stephen. Its site was granted to some monks of the Cistercian order, who built an abbey upon it, which, at the suppression, was granted by Edward VI. to his ambitious uncle, Lord Seymour. Near Farringdon are the remains of a camp of a circular form, supposed to be of Danish origin. It is two hundred yards in diameter, and is surrounded by a ditch twenty yards wide. Antiquaries have conjectured that it was the camp of the Danes, who were defeated near this place by King Alfred. At the commencement of the present century, when the north rampart was levelled, quantities of human bones and coals were found; and the former are frequently dug up by the labourers, who search for peat in the swampy ground about a mile south of the hill.

From Farringdon, a walk of about four miles, by the side of the great Coxwell and Eaton woods and the domain of Buscot Park, leads us to the small market-town of Lechlade, in Gloucestershire, and St. John's Bridge over the Thames. The church, erected in the fifteenth century, is a handsome building with an embattled tower, and inspired Shelley to write some melancholy verses, when he lingered within its precincts one fine summer evening, in 1815,

when he came ashore from his boat in his pil-
grimage to the sources of the Thames.

At Lechlade and its neighbourhood there is
truly a " meeting of the waters." The Thames
before its arrival at this town is little better
than a brook; but it here receives the waters of
four small streams, the Colne, the Churn, the
Lech, and the Rey, which united first render
it navigable. From Lechlade to the source
there is not sufficient depth of water to be
serviceable to commerce, and a canal has been
formed by the side of it, whereby the navigation is carried on to the Severn.

Upon one of these streams, the Colne, is the
town of Fairford, at the distance of two miles
from Lechlade. It is celebrated for its elegant
church, containing a handsome painted window, founded by one John Tame, a merchant
of London, in the fifteenth century, and a
native of Fairford. Tame was the captain of
his own vessel, and captured in the high seas,
when England was at war with Spain, a Spanish vessel bound to Rome, containing, among
other valuable articles, a quantity of stained
glass, intended as a present to the Pope.
These are the windows that at present adorn
the church, and are generally considered as the
work of Albert Durer. The glass was taken

out and buried during the civil wars, and so
preserved from the violence of the bigots of
that day, and when all danger was over, the
windows were put up again, but not in the
same places as before. These windows, or compartments of windows, are twenty-eight in
number, and chiefly represent biblical subjects.
Connoisseurs doubt whether the windows were
the work of Albert Durer, notwithstanding
the general belief, and the alleged opinion of
Vandyck, who is reported, it is not known
on what authority, to have said, that "the
workmanship was so exquisite, no pencil could
exceed it." The church is visited by all travellers who pass in that direction, and a man
is appointed to show the paintings for a gratuity, without which nothing is to be seen
in England, if it has four walls to enclose
it. The church itself, independently of its
windows, is a handsome specimen of the archi-
tecture of the age in which it was built. It
consists of a nave, chancel, and side-aisles, with
a tower in the centre. The interior is well
finished, containing an elegant carved oak
screen, surrounding the chancel.

Returning again to the Thames, we pass the
large village of Kempsford, also containing a
handsome church ; near which there is a tradi-

tion, that John of Gaunt once had a residence; and from thence upwards, to Cricklade. At the latter place the water is occasionally not above fourteen inches in depth, and so narrow at some places as to offer but little difficulty to a vigorous leaper. It was once thought, that Cricklade was formerly called Greeklade, from a Greek college it is said to have possessed, and which was afterwards transferred to Oxford. Camden gives the weight of his authority to demolish this opinion, and it is now considered, by well-informed antiquaries, to have derived its name from two British words, *cricw* and *ladh*, signifying a stony or a rocky country, as it is about here. Cricklade is an inconsiderable place, though it was formerly notorious enough in the annals of elections, for the shameless venality of its inhabitants.

There are several places in the neighbourhood of Cricklade well deserving of a visit. The ancient town of Cirencester, upon the Churn, from whence it derives its name; and the magnificent seat of Lord Bathurst at Oakley Park. The pilgrim to the sources of the Thames will do well to leave the direct course of the Isis, as the people hereabouts persist in calling it, and follow the course of the Thames and Severn Canal towards Cirencester, and thus bring both those places within the circuit of his rambles. Then returning to Cricklade, he may trace the narrow stream up to the hills where it takes its rise, and drink the water at its fountain-head.

Cirencester is a clean, neat, quiet town, not so large or so important as it used to be, but still a very tidy, quiet, respectable place, putting one in mind of a *ci-devant* beauty, who in the course of tell-tale years has lost the freshness of her charms, and is no longer a reigning toast, but has become a decent spinster; still good-looking, somewhat prudish, very precise in her personal appearance, and remarkably well-behaved. Cirencester (its inhabitants, for brevity's sake, pronounce it something like the word *sister*) boasts of its Roman origin, and is put down in Antoninus' Itinerary under the name of Durocornovium. Remains of the Roman military way between it and Gloucester are still traceable. The site of a great part of the former city, for it was a city once, though but a small town now, has been converted into pasture or garden lands, or corn-fields; and many remnants of antiquity have been at various times turned up by the plough or the spade, such as pieces of mosaic pavement, rings, intaglios, coins, and carved stones. In the

year 1723 an entire mosaic pavement was dug
up, with a large quantity of coins. We learn
from Dr. Stukely, who bought several of the
relics discovered here, that one Mr. Bishop, the
owner of a garden in the town, dug into a
vault, sixteen feet long and twelve broad, supported by square pillars of Roman brick, three
feet and a half high. Several other vaults of a
similar form, but somewhat smaller, were discovered close by. They were thought by the
doctor to have been the foundation of a Roman
temple, there having been found in the same
place several stone shafts of pillars, six feet
long, and immense bases of rough stone. These,
with the cornices very handsomely moulded
and carved, with modillons, and the like ornaments, were converted into hog-troughs by
some man who had no reverence for antiquity,
and thought much more of his live pigs than
of dead Romans. Some of the stones of the
bases were fastened together so strongly with
cramps of iron that the workmen, failing in
drawing them asunder, procured the aid of
horses to accomplish the task. Dr. Stukely
had the front of his house paved with them.

It is supposed that the Emperor Constantine,
son of a British lady, was crowned King of the
Britons in this city. It suffered severely se-

veral times during the wars of the Danes and
the Saxons, as well as in the civil wars of the
time of King Stephen. Being a strong place,
and seated on a commanding line of road, it
was a position of some importance whenever
the realm was convulsed by internal commotion; and in the dissensions of Henry III. and
his Barons it was taken and retaken by one
or the other party.

In the first year of the reign of Henry IV.
it was the scene of events, which, in the hands
of a romance writer, might be turned to good
account. The Dukes of Exeter and Surrey,
Montague Earl of Salisbury, and others, adherents of the deposed King Richard II, formed
a design to murder Henry IV. at a grand tournament at Windsor, to which they had invited
him. Their design being discovered by the
Duke of Aumarle, one of the conspirators, to
his father, the Duke of York, and by him to
the King, the conspirators went from Windsor
to Abingdon, Farringdon, and Cirencester, leading about with them a priest, named Maudelen,
whom they represented to the country people
as King Richard. This man bore an extraordinary resemblance to Richard, then a prisoner in Pomfret Castle; and being in royal
armour, with the crown upon his helmet, all

the country round was deceived. They were lodged in the abbey of Cirencester for some days, when, imagining that they were suspected by the people of the town, who kept a strict watch over all their proceedings, and stationed a strong guard at the abbey doors, the Duke of Exeter employed some of his soldiery to set fire to the town, that in the confusion that would ensue they might all make their escape. The design failed; the flames were speedily extinguished, and the people of Cirencester were so enraged that they assembled in great crowds, broke open the abbey doors, seized the Dukes of Exeter and Surrey, and Lord Salisbury, and without form of trial of any kind, cut off their heads in the marketplace. Their adherents, to the number of about one hundred, were made prisoners. Twenty-seven of them were beheaded in one day at Oxford, three at London, and one at Bristol. King Henry, to reward the townsmen of Cirencester for the service they had done him, granted them all the goods of the deceased nobles and their adherents, with the exception of their money, plate, and jewels. He also ordered, that every season four prime does should be sent to the men, and six bucks to the women of the town, together with a hogshead of choice wine.   He also granted the town a charter of incorporation, which it enjoyed till the reign of Elizabeth, when it was annulled.

Cirencester suffered some damage during the wars of the Revolution, and became a parliamentary garrison in the year 1642.   Prince Rupert took it by storm, and made upwards of a thousand prisoners.

Oakley Park, near this town, the seat of Earl Bathurst, was described by Pope as the finest wood in England."   Addison, Gay, Pope, Swift, and many other of the literati of that day, were often the guests of Allen Lord Bathurst, the Mæcenas of his time.   To him Pope addressed his well-known epistle on the Use of Riches, more often quoted, perhaps, than any of his works, not even excepting his " Essay on Man."   The park is said to be twelve miles in circumference, and contains an ancient circular tumulus, called Grismond's Tower, so named from a Danish chieftain, conquered by King Alfred, and supposed to be buried here.   On opening it some years ago several urns were found, containing ashes and burnt bones.   In the park there is also a ruin called Alfred's Hall, where it is traditionally reported, that he signed a treaty with another

Danish leader, named Gothrum. The mansion is a spacious structure, and contains a good collection of paintings.

Within two miles of Cirencester is the source of the Thames—a clear fountain in a little rocky dell, known by the name of Thames Head. This is the little infantine stream—so great a giant when it arrives at its full growth· What reflections we might make upon human affairs in general, from the mere sight of this oozing well; what a homily we might preach upon this text—the small beginnings of great things, and what encouragement might be held out to humble genius from it. Truly, the course of a river bears no bad comparison with the career of an able man, who makes his own fortune in the world. How slight is his beginning! yet, how full of confidence he runs on in his career, dashing over some obstacles, and turning round others—obliged to take a tortuous course, that his waters may not be changed into an inland lake, or be dispersed in ponds over a marshy country; and that he may arrive at the sea of death, whither he must come at last, with a wealthy and powerful name! See, too, how he gathers tribute as he passes—how smaller minds bear homage unto his, and are content to obey his impulses, and run with him in a mingled stream! See, too, how by his well-acquired wealth he increases the wealth of others—how, by the judicious distribution of his capital, he affords employment, and consequent profit, to thousands.— Thus we have seen our Thames: here he is a little child at play, crawling timidly about, and ignorant of his own strength; by and by he becomes able to walk alone, as at Lechlade, where he is first navigable. Still gaining strength, and increasing in stature, he becomes like a boy, lingering in quiet nooks, and in woody places, and leading a happy life of it. Next we have him at Oxford, a youth at college—his mind filled with reminiscences of antiquity, and assuming a classical name which does not belong to him, half for frolic and half for ambition. Next, emancipated from college, we have him turning courtier at Windsor—dallying in the consciousness of his youthful grace to gain a smile from royalty, and push his fortune in the world by means of royal favour. This he soon discovers is an idle fancy; and his good sense tells him to trust to his own strength for success, and to make himself useful to the world at large, and not a mere hanger-on at a palace. He therefore quits the court, widening and deepening as he journeys on; his mind expands, as it were, while his physical strength increases. He now makes himself a reputation—his character is known over the world—he becomes concerned in mercantile speculations, in which he is universally successful, and so full of probity, that traders from all parts of the world give him unlimited credit. They would as soon believe any monstrous improbability, as his failure or bankruptcy. Now he is rich indeed; and his house (which may be called all London) becomes the mart of the world, and thousands of merchant princes attend every day at his levee. He spreads wealth wherever he goes; and a whole population live by him. This is his prime of life—his busy period—and he goes on, full of years and honour, till he is swallowed up in the dark ocean of death!

The little dell, whence issues the gentle stream, is, in hot seasons, perfectly dry; but the drought that stops the supply at the fountain head, has but slight effect upon the course of the stream. It has so many different feeders from various parts of the country, that at Lechlade and Cricklade it runs on its usual course, uninfluenced by the scarcity at the head. There is an amusing story told of a simple cockney, who, on his way from Bristol to London, turned aside to visit the source of the river he was so proud of. It was a warm summer;—there had been no rain for three weeks, and the spring was dried up:—"Good God!" said he, with an expression of the utmost alarm and sorrow, "what ruin this must cause at London! What ever will the poor people do for water!" and his busy fancy conjured up a direful picture of a thousand ills consequent upon the stoppage of the stream: no more ships arriving at London, laden with the wealth of the world—the bankruptcy of rich merchants—the shutting up of 'Change—the failure of the Bank of England —the anguish of ruined families—and the death of thousands in the agonies of thirst!

The Germans tell a similar story of a traveller who visited the springs of the Danube, and which, as we are upon this subject, may serve as a pendant to the story of our cockney. The traveller in this case was a Swabian, and whenever the Germans wish to palm off a joke, a Swabian is sure to be the butt. On noticing in what a small stream the water trickled at the source of that great river Danube, he formed the bold resolution of stopping it up! He put his hand across it; and as he fancied the various cities upon its course deprived of their supply of water by his deed, he exclaimed, in the pride of his heart, "What will they say at Vienna?"

Having now, O reader, traced with thee this glorious river, from London upwards to its fountain head—having diverged with thee sometimes to the right hand and sometimes to the left, in search of memorials of history and antiquity, and pleasant recollections of biogra-phy, romance and poetry; having lingered in leafy woods, by flowery hedge-rows, and in enamelled meads, wherever it was likely we might find quiet and seclusion, and food for meditation; traced footpaths leading into lonely spots, and wandered into unfrequented places, in search of health for the body and amuse-ment for the mind—we are now ready for another series of rambles in thy company, which we shall commence accordingly in our next chapter.

CHAPTER III.

E proceed, in pursuance of our original plan, to follow the Thames to the sea, and note his memorabilia in that more important part of his course. As London was our first point of departure, so it must be our second. We must again take ship at London Bridge; and as we sail through the narrow passage left by the all but innumerable vessels that are moored on either side, take a longer view, and consider at greater length than when our course was upwards, the mercantile glories of England.

It is a trite remark, that the world in general

does not appreciate either the beauties or the advantages which are continually in its sight. How few of the inhabitants of London are sufficiently aware how truly magnificent in every respect is the spectacle of this forest of shipping. Even to the eye how picturesque are these black hulls, reposing in the water, with their taper and elegant masts, adorned with the banners of every civilized nation, pointing upwards to the sky. But how much more beautiful the prospect becomes, when we reflect, how great the cultivation of the arts of peace must have been before such an assemblage of the engines of commerce could ever have been collected together. Were it not for these vessels, and the myriads that crowd the ports of England, how low we should be in the scale of nations, how little would be the progress of manufacture, of science, of art, and of literature. These heavy-looking hulls are the depositories of the national wealth, which they bring from every nook of the globe, to be afterwards distributed into the humblest cottages of the realm By their means the ploughman and the artisan of England fare better than the kings and nobles of a barbarous age ; having a more comfortable dwelling to keep out the wind and rain, and sleeping

upon a softer bed than the great men of antiquity. By their means also the shopkeeper
enjoys luxuries which all the wealth of a feudal
chief could never have purchased; and new
wants are continually created, all tending, in
the effort to supply them, to raise mankind in
the scale of civilization.

But before we sail downwards with the tide,
and get out of sight of the mass of buildings
composing ancient London, we must not forget
that many of them solicit our attention. We
shall have more to say of the shipping and its
wonders when we arrive at the docks. The
approaches to the new bridge have been the

means of clearing away many old historical houses on both sides of the river; but after all there is little to be regretted. Narrow, crooked, and filthy streets have been pulled down, and replaced by rows of palaces; and a stranger to London, who had seen it twelve years ago, would hardly recognize it again in these places. The old public buildings, however, have been suffered to remain. Of these the most conspicuous is the world-renowned Monument, built by Sir Christopher Wren in commemoration of the great fire of 1666.

On the other side, in Southwark, stands the venerable gothic church of St. Saviour, with the Ladye Chapel adjoining, which has lately been restored, by a public subscription, from the decay into which it was rapidly falling. The church abounds in curious monuments of the olden time. One of them is to the memory of John Gower the poet, who shares with Chaucer the merit of being one of the fathers of English verse. He is, perhaps, the earliest bard who makes mention of the Thames. He relates, in one of his quaint neglected poems, that being on the river in his boat, he met the royal barge containing Henry IV

As I came nighe
Out of my bote, when he me syghe (saw)

> He bade me come into his barge,
> And when I was with him at large,
> Amongest other thynges said,
> He had a charge upon me laid.

Gower was a rich man for a poet, and contributed large sums to the rebuilding of the church. It has been said, that it was wholly built with his money; but this is erroneous. Lest any modern stripling, too fond of the unprofitable society of the Muses, should take courage by the reflection that one of the earliest of English poets was able to build a church, we present him with the following epigram, which will explain the mystery.

> This church was rebuilt by Gower the rhymer,
> Who in Richard's gay court was a fortunate climber;
> Should any one start, 'tis but right he should know it,
> Our wight was a lawyer as well as a poet.

He was a " fortunate climber," not only in the court of Richard II. but of the Lancaster who deposed him. Like other poets, he worshipped the rising star; and his reward was, to use his own words, that the new King " laid a charge upon him." It is commonly supposed that he was laureate to both these princes; but the office, if he ever held it, was merely honorary. He was buried in this church, where his monument may still be seen.

From its proximity to the Globe Theatre and others on Bankside, many of the players of the times of Shakspeare who resided in the neighbouring alleys, found a final resting-place in this church when their career was over. Among others, unhappy Philip Massinger, steeped in poverty to the lips, died in some adjacent hovel, and was buried like a pauper at the expense of the parish. No stone was placed upon the spot; but in the parish register this entry was made — " March 20th, 1639-40, buried, Philip Massinger, a STRANGER."

The church is sometimes called St. Mary Overy's, or St. Mary's-over-the-river, by which name it was founded before the Conquest, for a priory, to the superior of which belonged, before the building of the bridge, the ferry over the river.

Leaving this ancient building and its poets, we turn to the other side of the stream, where Billingsgate, a more renowned spot, claims our attention. The contrast is certainly great enough between poetry and Billingsgate. Topographers, however, cannot help these violent transitions ; they do not make their subject, but take it as they find it. Billingsgate is a spot famous wherever English literature is cultivated, or its language spoken. The name has become synonymous over nearly one half of the civilized world with foul and violent language. It is the chief fish-market of London, and the peculiar phraseology, and the frequent quarrels of its female merchants, have procured for it this unenviable notoriety. The ward in which it is situated, and from which it takes its name, is one of the oldest in the city. Fabian, Grafton, and others, maintain it to have been built by and named after a British king, called Belyn, who reigned more than three hundred years before the Christian era. According to tradition, there was a pinnacle over the gate, surmounted by a vessel of burnished brass, in which the ashes of King Belyn were inclosed after his body had been burned, in conformity with the usage of those times. The place appears to have been known as a fish-market so early as the time of King Ethelred in 1016.

In the reign of Edward I. an ordinance was published, regulating the prices at which the fish might be sold. It may not be uninteresting to cite a few of the items. Twenty herrings were to be sold for a penny; a dozen of the best soles for threepence; the best mackerel a penny each in Lent, and one half-penny out of Lent Salmon and pike were exceedingly dear. From Christmas to Easter

the price of the best salmon was five shillings,
and after Easter three shillings. A pike was
sold for the lawyer's fee, six and eightpence.
Eels, lampreys, and oysters were cheap; a gal-
lon of oysters being sold for twopence, and eels
and lampreys from sixpence to eightpence a
hundred. Some further regulations with respect to Billingsgate were published in the
reign of Edward III, who claimed a variety of
taxes from every ship that discharged its cargo
at that place.

Adjoining Billingsgate is the Custom-House,
a long handsome building, which looks like
what it is. How few of the thousands whom
business attracts to it every day know, or

knowing, remember, that one of the first comp-
trollers of the customs for the port of London,
probably the very first, was no less a personage
than Geoffry Chaucer. This office, a very lu-
crative one, was bestowed upon him by King
Edward III. in the year 1375. The articles
chiefly under the superintendence of the poet
were wool and hides, with a proviso that he
should personally execute the office, and keep
the accounts of it with his own hand. In the
year after Chaucer's appointment great pecula-
tion was discovered in other branches of the
customs, and many of the offenders were discovered and prosecuted. Not a word of complaint, however, was ever breathed against the
father of English poetry. His biographers say
that he was not continued in his office after
the accession of Richard II. owing to the jeal-
onsy with which the King regarded all the
friends and dependants of John of Gaunt, the
great artificer of Chaucer's fortunes. But when
that ambitious prince regained the favour he
had lost, he was not unmindful of his friend
and brother, for they married two sisters, and
procured him a pension, and the annual grant
of a pipe of wine from the customs of London.

There appears to have been no Custom-
house, properly so called, in the time of Chau-

cer, for in the year 1385, after his dismissal—
if dismissed he were, which is a very doubtful
point—John Churchman, one of the Sheriffs of
London, in consequence of the general complaint of the merchants, erected a convenient
house for the collection of the customs. But notwithstanding this, vessels discharged their car-
goes at various other places on the river, and so
continued to do for nearly two hundred years.

In the year 1559, an act was passed to com-
pel all merchant vessels to proceed with their
goods for inspection at the New Custom-house,
which was built expressly for the purpose. This
edifice was destroyed in the great fire of 1666,
and another was shortly afterwards constructed
at an expense of nearly ten thousand pounds.
This building met the same fate as its predecessor, having been burned to the ground with a
hundred and twenty houses in Thames Street,
in January 1714. It was again rebuilt at the
expense of the government, and lasted till
February 1814, when fire for the third time
destroyed it. A larger and more commodious
edifice was then begun, which was not completed until 1817. The site was formerly
part of the bed of the river, and great expense
was incurred in making a sure foundation.
The builder contracted for a hundred and sixty-

seven thousand pounds, and twelve thousand
pounds additional for the piling; but, when
completed, the total charge amounted to three
hundred and forty-six thousand pounds, and
twenty-four thousand pounds for the piling.
Notwithstanding all this care and expense, the
foundation was insecure. The long room gave
way in 1824, when considerable damage was
done. A new front upon a safer foundation,
was shortly afterward completed, under the
superintendence of Mr. Smirke.

And now we have arrived at

> The towers of Julius, London's lasting shame,
> By many a foul and midnight murder fed;

at the place which, of all others upon the
Thames, merits the most notice. Could we by
any means read the true and intimate history
of this solemn edifice; could the dumb walls
speak, and tell us of the groans they had listen-
ed to, the prayers they had heard, the ravings
of remorse, or the wail of innocence that had
echoed within them when not a living soul
was near; could we force them to deliver up
their awful secrets of unmerited suffering,
blighting tyranny, and of guilt, misery, and
despair in all their various shapes; how harrow-
ing would be the recital, and what hitherto
unopened pictures of the human heart would

be spread out before us to cheat us of our sympathy for thousands who are now for ever beyond its reach. The Tower of London, of all
other dungeons in the world, would, perhaps,
tell the saddest tale. The dens of the Inqui-
sition may have witnessed more suffering; St.
Angelo of Rome, or the Bastile of Paris may
have had more victims; but it is not for the
mere greatness of suffering, or the number of
sufferers, that men in general weep; it is for
the glory, or the patience, or the beauty of a
few victims that they shed most tears. The

same individuals who hear with callous indif-
ference of the slaughter of ten thousand men,
or the burning of twenty cities, melt into tears
for the misery of one.   Hence the peculiar
interest that attaches to the captives of the
Tower, including so many who have left a
never-dying fame, whose names are household
words to us, and the leading incidents of whose
career are engraven upon our memory.   Who
does not remember the sad story of Wallace,
imprisoned in these cells?—of Henry VI,

> Whose place was filled, whose sceptre wrung from him,
> Whose balm washed off wherewith he was anointed?

Of Clarence drowned in the Malmsey butt? of
the royal babes smothered by the orders of the
bloody Richard? of the ambitious Bohun,
Duke of Buckingham? of the conscientious
Sir Thomas More?—the tender, and innocent
Anne Boleyn?—the guilty Catherine Howard?
—the mild and accomplished Cromwell, Earl
of Essex?—the chivalrous Earl of Surrey?—
the proud Duke of Somerset?—the quiet and
erudite Lady Jane Gray? — her sad spouse,
Lord Dudley?—the pious martyrs, Cranmer,
Ridley, and Latimer?—the amorous, and high-
vaulting Earl of Essex?—the accomplished Ra-
leigh?—and the forlorn Arabella Stuart?   But
we cannot go through the long list of victims,

which stretches out like Banquo's progeny. Crowned and mitred and coronetted spectres start up before our mental eye, in long array, making us, as we reflect upon their fate, thank God that the " good old times" are gone for ever, and that we live in an age when law reigns paramount, and the axe is idle, except for the hewing of wood and the breaking of granite.

The Tower was not always used as a dungeon. It was until the time of Elizabeth, a royal palace, in which it was customary for the sovereigns to spend the first few days after their accession. Much difference of opinion has existed as to whether it were built by Julius Cesar. It seems now to be generally acknowledged by those who are the best informed, that a fortress was erected upon the spot by the Romans, but that the present edifice, or great White Tower, is the work of William the Conqueror. Rufus expended large sums in adding to and fortifying the building. Henry III. imitated his example, and taxed the Londoners very sorely for the purpose. In his reign, the outer walls fell down, it is supposed, by an earthquake, " for the which chance," say the old historians, " the citizens of London were nothing sorry." A brick wall was built by Edward IV. as well as that part of the structure known by the name of the Lion's Tower The store-house was begun by James I, and completed in the reign of William III. The various bulwarks are named The Lion's Tower, Middle Tower, Bell Tower, Beauchamp Tower, Dwelling Tower, Flint Tower, Bowyer Tower, Martin Tower, Castle Tower, Broad Arrow Tower, Salt Tower, Well Tower, Cradle Tower, Lantern Tower, St. Thomas's Tower, Hall Tower, Bloody Tower, and Wakefield Tower.

It is now twenty years since it has been used as a state prison: the last prisoners being Thistlewood and his accomplices, committed in 1820. It is now chiefly famous for its beautiful armoury; its Jewel Room, containing the regalia of England and Scotland; and its Record Office, in the Wakefield Tower, containing the parliamentary rolls from the reign of King John to that of Richard III, a survey of the manors of England, a register of the ancient tenures of all the lands, a perambulation of forests, a collection of charters granted to colleges and corporations, and various other state papers. It formerly contained a menagerie, but the wild beasts have been removed within the last eight or nine years to the Zoological Gardens in the Regent's Park.

At the distance only of a few yards from the Tower, the stranger's eye will not fail to notice a large unseemly stack of buildings, numbered and lettered like a constable of police, and overlooking all the neighbouring structures by half its height. It forms the range of warehouses of the St. Katherine's Dock Company, and, with the docks adjoining, was opened with great pomp on the 25th of October 1828. The docks cover an area of nearly twenty-four acres, of which eleven and a half form the wet-docks. The canal leading from the river to the great basin is only one hundred and ninety feet long and forty-five broad, but is of such a depth, that ships of seven hundred tons burthen may enter at any time of the tide. The expenses of the under-taking amounted to the immense sum of one million seven hundred thousand pounds; and during the year and a half that the works were in progress, two thousand five hundred workmen were daily employed. Upwards of twelve hundred houses, in one of the most wretched parts of London, were pulled down to provide space, and among them the venerable church and hospital of St. Katherine.

Perhaps none but the antiquary, so enthu-siastic as to love not only the fine wrecks but

the rubbish of past ages, will regret the demolition of this district; especially when it has
been applied to uses so beneficial to the trade
of the first commercial emporium of the world.
There are, nevertheless, some incidents connected with its history, which it may be interesting to record.

St. Katherine's hospital was founded by
Matilda, wife of King Stephen, and dedicated to the patron saint in pure and perpetual
alms for the repose of the souls of her son
Baldwin, and daughter Matilda, who were
buried in her life-time in the church of Trinity
Priory. She reserved to herself the right of
nominating the master or *custos* of the hospital
upon every vacancy, a right which has ever
since been exercised by the queens consort of
England. Elianor, queen of Henry III, was
not satisfied with so small a jurisdiction. Offended at many abuses which had crept into
the administration of the hospital, and desirous
of wresting it altogether from the control of
the prior and canons of the Holy Trinity, in
which it had been vested by its original foun-
dress, she instituted proceedings in the civil
and ecclesiastical courts to dispossess them.
She was long unsuccessful in her object, but
she persevered, and after many struggles and

great expense, so intimidated the prior and canons, and so wore out their patience by vexatious prosecutions, that they were glad to surrender their rights into her hands. She thereupon dissolved the hospital in the year 1268, and founded another with the same name and for similar purposes, but to be governed in a different manner.

According to tradition, it was in this building that Raymond Lulli, the shining light of the Hermetic philosophy, took up his abode when he was invited to England by King Edward II. to make gold for him out of brass and iron. It is not certain however, that that alchymist was ever in England. There was another Raymond, a Jew of Tarragona, whom some writers have mistaken for Raymond Lulli, and who had an apartment in the Tower of London, where he tried some experiments in the prevalent delusion of gold making.

In the church of St. Katherine Cree, removed with the hospital, to which it was an adjunct, was buried the famous painter, Hans Holbein, the protegé of Erasmus and Sir Thomas More, and much employed by Henry VIII. and Edward VI.

For nearly two centuries a sermon was annually preached here under rather remarkable

circumstances.   Sir John Gayer, once Lord
Mayor of London, was shipwrecked on the
coast of Africa on his return to Europe after a
successful adventure to the East.   While be-
wailing his fate upon the shore, he perceived a
huge lion making his way towards him, on
which he fell upon his knees, and prayed fer-
vently that God would deliver him.   The animal, strange to say, turned round after taking
a good view of him, intending perhaps to eat
him another day, and a ship arriving in sight
shortly afterwards, perceived the signal of the
merchant, and carried him to Europe.   On
his return to London, he placed the sum of
£200 in the hands of trustees, the interest of
it to be applied for ever in the purchase of
bread for the poor, and twenty shillings annually to be paid to the minister of St. Katherine's upon the 10th of October, the day of his
deliverance, for preaching a sermon in commemoration of that event, and the mercy of
God towards him.

Upon the death of Sir Herbert Taylor in
1839, the last Master of the hospital, some misunderstanding arose as to whether a queen
dowager preserved the same rights to the appointment as she enjoyed when a queen consort.   It was decided that the right expired

with her husband, and is now in consequence merged in the Crown. The hospital has been removed to the Regent's Park since the demolition of the old edifice. It was somewhere in this district, the exact spot, alas! unknown, that the author of that divine poem "The Faerie Queene" was born. We indulge the hope that some happy rummager among ancient manuscripts, will yet discover the name of the street that was the birth-place of so great a man as Edmund Spenser.

We are now fairly in the middle of that narrow strip of water, left free for the navigation by the innumerable vessels on either side, which is called the Pool. To the left of us lies Wapping—low, dirty, smelling strong of pitch, and renowned in the songs of Dibdin; and to the right, Bermondsey and Rotherhithe, both well entitled to share with Wapping this character of filthiness. But squalid and mean as they look, they teem with wealth, no inconsiderable portion of it their own, and the remainder warehoused with them for the convenience of those who dwell higher up the stream.

The London Docks alone, which may be said to form part of Wapping, contain wealth enough to purchase the fee simple of a principality. They cover a space of nearly sixty

acres, and were about three years in construction, having been commenced in 1802, and
completed in 1805. The great dock is twenty-
nine feet deep, covers twenty-four acres of
ground, and is capable of containing two hundred sail of merchantmen at a time. Mighty
indeed is the trade of London, as the books
of this and the other docks might show.
There is sublimity in commercial accounts
when the items are millions of gallons of wine
or brandy, millions of hogshead of sugar, or
tens of millions of pounds of tea. The quantity of wine always in bond in these docks
averages, it is computed, five millions of gallons; and the cellarage which contains them
would, in earlier ages, have been esteemed a
wonder of the world. The average quantity
of pepper in bond, is estimated at ten millions
of pounds; of tobacco, unmanufactured, twenty-
three millions of pounds; and of tea, at the
East India Docks, further down the river, fifty-
one millions of pounds. The value of the
latter alone, at the very lowest calculation, is
5,000,000*l.* sterling.

What a pyramid it would make were it
piled in a heap! what bushes must have been
planted, and flourished, and been stripped of
their leaves to produce it! and what an area
it would cover if spread abroad upon the

ground! The wine annually brought into London, this huge den of living men, would form a lake where ships of war might ride; the rum, another; and the brandy a canal to join them together. The tobacco, were it distributed, would provide every man, woman, and child in our islands with a pound of poisonous weed; and the indigo annually imported would dye father Thames in all his course from Cotteswold to Gravesend, as blue as the skies above him. The number of ships and men that are employed in bringing all these commodities from every part of the world into the Thames is computed at nearly four thousand of the former, and seventy thousand of the latter, in addition to eighteen or twenty thousand coasting and smaller vessels which annually enter the port of London, laden with coal and grain, and other indigenous commodities, employing, at the lowest calculation, six men to each vessel. Besides these, nearly ten thousand men are constantly employed in loading and discharging vessels, and half that number of watermen in navigating barges, wherries, and other small craft. The gross amount of custom dues paid on the enormous traffic of London was, in the year 1834, no less than 8,692,298*l.* sterling, and in the following years until 1839, about 9,000,000*l.*

A traveller proceeding down or up the
Thames does not see one quarter of the navies
engaged in this surprising amount of trade.
Though on each side of him vessels, apparently
innumerable, are moored, choking up the very
stream by their multitudes, there are still greater
numbers of ships, richer and more bulky, almost hidden from the view in the snug basins
of the docks, stretching downwards into the
heart of thickly-peopled districts, and bringing
occupation and subsistence to many a swarming hive of amphibious labourers, living half
upon the land and half upon the water.

The man tempted, for the first time, to dive
into these far recesses, is astonished at the
number of canals and drawbridges, and basins,
that meet his sight; at the odour of tar and
pitch, that subdues every other by its poi-
gnancy, and at the clink of hammers, the creaking of cranes and pullies, the loud " Yo, yo!"
or the reckless curse of the sailor, which are
the only sounds that smite upon his ear. The
immediate vicinity of the docks upon the Middlesex shore of the Thames would form a city
of itself; and such a city! a city of floating
palaces, in which the only spires would be taper
masts; and the houses on land mere adjuncts
and outhouses to those upon the water; a city,
of which the inhabitant of the more lordly

districts of the west could hardly form a conception, without a personal visit.

The very population is different to that in other parts of London, and is composed of a motley multitude of all hues and nations. There may be seen lounging the slim, but fierce, Lascar; the brown Malay; the heavy Russian; the swarthy negro; with a less noticeable crowd of Americans, Hollanders, Germans, Swedes, Frenchmen, and Portuguese, who all seem in the streets to have nothing else to do but to swear, and sputter, and smoke, and drink, but who, once upon ship-board, are the very models of bustling activity and cheerful labour.

But the glories of our river are not only to be found upon its bosom and on either side, but underneath it. The mass of its waters rolls over a work, which is one of the most remarkable instances of what the ingenuity and enterprise of man can accomplish. This is the Tunnel, now almost completed, the admiration of civilized Europe, and to many a stranger from afar the most wonderful of all the curiosities of England, and the first place on his memorandum-book to be visited and examined. Some years ago a still bolder undertaking was projected: a tunnel underneath the Thames at Gravesend, where the stream is considerably wider, and the influence of the ocean tides more perceptible. It was commenced on the Gravesend side in the year 1798, and some slight progress was made; but the difficulties were found so great that the plan was abandoned.

The next tunnel was projected at Rotherhithe, in 1809, by Mr. R. Trevethick, and was intended for foot-passengers only. Some progress was made with the works, but, for want of encouragement, they were abandoned; and nothing more was heard of a tunnel until the year 1823, when the present undertaking was suggested by Mr. Brunel. An act of Parliament to form the company was granted in 1824; the foundation stone was laid with great ceremony on the 2nd of March 1825, and the works have ever since been continued, and have now [1840] reached beyond low-water mark on the opposite shore, so that the most difficult and dangerous portion has been completed. But this result has not been obtained without accident and loss of life. Father Thames has more than once rolled the large volume of his waters into the excavation; the first time in May 1827, when there were upwards of one hundred and twenty workmen in the shaft, who all escaped; and a second time in January in the following year, when six poor men were drowned. On both occasions the damage was soon repaired: bales of cotton or wool, and loads of impermeable clay were deposited in the bed of the river where the irruption took place, the leak stopped, the invading waters pumped out, and the works resumed. A third and a fourth time the Thames;—not like a strong marauder who breaks wildly through the fences set up to restrain him, but like an insidious foe;—has penetrated and oozed through the soft strata of his bed, and filled the tunnel. On the last occasion, in November 1837, one man, who had drunk too freely of strong drink, and had fallen asleep in the shaft, was drowned. All the other workmen, being awake and attentive, received due notice of the impending deluge, and escaped without any difficulty. The opening to the tunnel is on the Surrey shore, a little to the eastward of the church of St. Mary, Rotherhithe. The tunnel is thirty-eight feet in width, with a double road for carriages going and returning, with pavements for foot-passengers. The height of the arch is twenty feet, and the crown of it in its whole extent is protected by masonry the most solid that the art of man can make; and there is a thickness of fifteen feet of earth between it and the bed of the river. The length of the tunnel, when completed, will be thirteen hundred feet.

Again, upon the bosom of the river, we pass on the left, Execution Dock, noted as the spot where pirates were formerly hung, and Limehouse, full of sea-faring people, and mentioned by Shakspeare in his Henry VIIIth, as famous for its blackguards, and by Ben Jonson also for the same reason. Beyond, we catch sight of the steeple of Stepney, to which parish all seamen in the merchant service pay their monthly threepence for poor-rates, to raise a fund for the maintenance of such poor as are born at sea, and who are entitled to a settlement in Stepney, provided they have not obtained another anywhere else. On the wall of the church was formerly a stone, affixed there in the year 1663, which, if we may believe the inscription upon it, once formed a part of the renowned Carthage. It has since been removed into the vestry. Stepney Church is noted for a monument to the memory of one Dame Rebecca Berry, who died in 1696, and who is supposed to have been the heroine of the once popular old ballad of " The Cruel Knight, or the Fortunate Farmer's Daughter."

In the reign of King Edward I, a parliament was summoned to meet at Stepney, in the house of Henry Walleis, then Mayor of London. The Barons, who chiefly composed the assembly, demanded of the King the con-

firmation of the charter, which he had promised
them for their aid in his Scottish wars. After
certain delay, the King agreed, but when the
document was ready for signature, the King
inserted the words, " the rights of our crown
saved," upon which the Barons broke up the
conference and went away. Edward not wish-
ing to offend such dangerous personages, sent
for them again to Stepney some weeks afterwards, as we learn from Stowe, and struck out
the obnoxious words, which, had they been
allowed to remain, would have afforded continual occasion of dispute and ill-feeling.

On the other side of the river are Bermondsey
and Rotherhithe, or, as the latter is more commonly called, Redriff, the first place where docks
were constructed for the convenience of the
commerce of London. The great dry dock here
has existed for nearly two centuries. The great
wet dock was finished in the year 1700. After
the bursting of the South Sea Bubble, in 1720,
the directors took a lease of this dock, where
their ships, engaged in the whale fisheries of
Greenland, landed their unfragrant blubber.
The docks are still used for the same purposes,
and are known by the name of the Commercial
Docks. Adjoining are the Great East Country
Dock, and several smaller ones. It was at Rotherhithe that King Canute is said to have be-

gun his famous trench to Vauxhall, for the purpose of besieging London. The channel through which the tide of the Thames was turned in the year when London bridge was first built of stone, is supposed by Stowe and other writers to have taken the same course.

In the parochial church of St. Mary, Rother-hithe, is buried one with whose name and affecting history all the youth of England are familiar—Lee Boo, Prince of the Pellew Island, who died of the small pox in 1780, at the early age of twenty, after he had learned the manners, and studied the civilization of England, and formed the praiseworthy design of introducing them into his own country.

Still amid the multitude of ships, we arrive at the Isle of Dogs, famous for its spacious and convenient docks, for the reception of vessels engaged in the trade of the West Indies. They cover a space of two hundred and four acres, and comprise an Import and an Export Dock, the former covering an area of thirty and the latter of twenty four acres, and from twenty to twenty-nine feet deep. The warehouses are large, and adapted for the reception, to use a sailor's expression, of " the mountains of sugar and the rivers of rum," that are required for the tea and the grog of our immense population. A canal runs right across the neck of land formed by the winding of the river, and completes the circumference of water, which justifies the appellation of island. It is three quarters of a mile long, and two hundred feet wide, and was excavated at the expense of government, in the year 1799, under the powers of an act of Parliament for improving the port of London. It is a great convenience to vessels of heavy tonnage, as by its means they avoid the tedious navigation round the Isle of Dogs, about four times the distance. The Isle of Dogs is thought to derive its name from having been the place where the King's hounds were kept in the days of Henry VIII. This place acquired some notoriety in the year 1835, as the spot where the recruits for the British Auxiliary Legion in Spain assembled prior to their embarkation, and studied a little of the art of war which they were so soon to practise. They were contemptuously called the Isle o' Doggians.

Before we pass Rotherhithe, on the opposite side, we must not omit to point out to the reader's notice, Cuckold's Point, with the pair of horns affixed to the top of a pole. There is a legend connected with this matter, which we shall relate when we arrive at Charlton, a few miles further down the stream.

CHAPTER IV.

Deptford. — The Victualling Office. — The Dock-Yard. —John Evelyn and Peter the Great. — Peter and the Quakers. — The river Ravensbourne.—Tradition of Julius Cesar. — Early History of Greenwich and its Palace of Placentia. — Coronation of Anne Boleyn. — Festivities at Greenwich during the Reign of Elizabeth. — Flattery of the Poets.

COTTAGE covered with ivy, just before we arrive at Deptford, marks the boundary between the counties of Kent and Surrey. Adjoining is Deptford Dock-Yard, founded by Henry VIII. and esteemed one of the most complete repositories for naval stores in Europe. The yard covers about thirty acres of ground, and contains every convenience for making, repairing, and fitting out ships-of-the-line. Artificers in wood and in iron have here large ranges of workshops and store-houses, where the hammer and the axe are scarcely ever idle, even in peace, but where, in time of war, they are plied incessantly in the construction of those floating bulwarks for which England is renowned, and which carry a hundred and twenty guns and a thousand men, to guard her shores from the invader, or to bear her fame with her victories to the remotest seas of the ocean. The number of workmen employed here during the war was about two thousand; but it has since been reduced at least one-half. The Victualling Office for the navy adjoins the Dock-Yard. The site was purchased by the government in 1745, from the family of Evelyn, and a handsome range of buildings erected. They were burned down four years afterwards with most of their valuable stores. The present structure, upon a much more extensive plan than its predecessor, was immediately commenced. It contains storehouses of various kinds, a spacious cooperage and brewhouse, houses for curing meat and fish, slaughter-houses, bake-houses, and other buildings, including residences for the principal and many subordinate officers, among whom are the clerk of the cheque, the hoy taker, the clerk of the brewhouse, the clerk of the cutting house, the clerk of the dry stores, the chief brewer, and the chief baker.

In the river opposite was formerly moored the Golden Hind, the vessel in which Drake sailed round the world. Queen Elizabeth paid him a visit on board this vessel in the year 1581, upon which occasion she conferred the honour of knighthood upon her subject, who had conferred more honour upon her reign and nation, than it was possible for her or any other potentate to bestow upon him in return. An immense concourse of people assembled on both sides of the river to catch a glimpse of their sovereign; and a small wooden bridge, on which were stationed about two hundred people, broke down, and they were all precipitated into the river. Happily they were all saved. The Queen had passed over it a few minutes previously, and the rush of people caused it to break.

But the most interesting circumstance connected with the Dock-Yard of Deptford is, that it was the residence for a short period of the great northern reformer, the Czar Peter. The Czar being wearied of the monotony of London, sick of its crowds, and disgusted with the rudeness of the people, who forced themselves upon him, and paid money to the servants for permission to see him feeding " like any other wild beast," and anxious moreover to see the dock-yards of England, the chief cause of his journey to our shores, bethought himself of taking a house at Deptford.

Sayes' Court, immediately adjoining the dock, the property of the celebrated John Evelyn, so well known for his love of trees, was at that time rented by Captain, afterwards Admiral Benbow, and his term of occupancy being near its expiration, the government made arrangements that it should be taken for the Czar. Poor Evelyn had often complained of Captain Benbow that he was a very bad tenant, that he was not polite, that he did not take sufficient care of his darling shrubberies and neat hedges; but little did he think when he agreed that the Imperial Muscovite should succeed him, what a change for the worse he was making, and what a fell destroyer and Vandal among shrubs he was admitting to his grounds. Scarcely was the Czar installed, when the work of destruction commenced. A door-way was broken through the boundary wall of the dock, that he might pass at once from Sayes' Court to the yard, where, by the by, as everybody knows, he spent a great deal of his time looking at the workmen, talking to them, working with them, and perfecting himself in the business of a ship-builder. But though he was a

builder of ships, he was a destroyer of plants,
a knocker down of holly hedges, a rude tram-
pler upon gooseberry bushes, and one that cared
not for lilies and roses.   Sport to him, but almost death to his philosophic landlord, were
the doings at Sayes' Court.   In the first place,
the Czar required exercise, and as a garden
was the very spot for it, he amused himself
every morning by trundling a wheelbarrow
through a gap which he made in the very
hedge of holly that was dearest of all others
to the heart of John Evelyn.   But though he
might disfigure, he could not destroy it; it was
too strong for him;—too well made to be tram-
pled down; — a circumstance which Evelyn
thus commemorated in his "Sylva," after he
had got rid of the intruder.

"Is there under the heavens," said he, with
mingled melancholy and triumph, "any more
glorious and refreshing object of the kind, than
an *impregnable* hedge of about four hundred
feet in length, nine feet high, and five in diameter, which I can still show in my ruined
garden at Sayes' Court (thanks to the Czar of
Muscovy) at any time of the year, glittering
with its armed and variegated leaves, the taller
standards at ordinary distances blushing with
their natural coral? It mocks the rudest assaults

of the weather, *beasts*, or *hedge-breakers, et illum nemo impune lacessit!*"

It does not appear that the Czar ever found out the truth of the last observation, or that it could apply to him at all, unless he were scratched by the good man's brambles. He did just as he pleased, and no remonstrances were ever made, for it was part of the English hospitality shown him by the government, that they paid for all the damage he occasioned, knowing well that it was not done wantonly, but from the nature and habits of the man. The house did not fare better than the garden. Evelyn's servant, who seems to have been a sort of spy in his master's interest upon the actions of the Czar, thus wrote to him after Peter had taken up his abode in that once clean and comfortable mansion. "There is a house full of people right nasty. The Czar lies next your library, and dines in the parlour next your study. He dines (twice a day) at ten o'clock and six at night, is very seldom at home a whole day, very often in the King's yard, or by water, dressed in several dresses. The King is expected there this day: the best parlour is pretty clean for him to be entertained in. The King pays for all he has."

Though Saye's Court was let empty to the

Czar, and furnished for him by William III, and though he only occupied it for three weeks, a surveyor, appointed by the King, reckoned, in conjunction with Evelyn's gardener, that the damage done to his house and grounds was to the amount of a hundred and fifty pounds, which sum, it appears from Evelyn, was afterwards paid by the King.

Evelyn, in his Diary, under date of the 3rd of June 1658, mentions, that a large whale was killed in the Thames opposite his house :—" A large whale," says he, " was taken betwixt my land butting on the Thames and Greenwich, which drew an infinite concourse to see it, by water, horse, coach, and on foot, from London, and all parts. It appeared first below Greenwich, at low water, for at high water it would have destroyed all the boats. After a long conflict, it was destroyed with a harping iron, struck in the head, out of which spouted blood and water by two tunnels; and after a horrid groan, it ran quite on shore, and died. Its length was 58 foot, height 16, black-skinned like coach-leather, very small eyes, great tail, only two small fins, a peaked snout, and a mouth so wide that divers men might have stood upright in it; no teeth, but swathed the slime only as through a grate of that bone which we call whalebone; the throat yet so narrow as would not have admitted the least of fishes."

While at Saye's Court, the Czar received a visit from the great William Penn, who came from Stoke Pogis to see him, accompanied by several other Quakers. Penn and he conversed together in the Dutch language; and the Czar conceived from his manners and conversation, such favourable notions of that peaceful sect, that during his residence at Deptford he very often attended the Quaker-meetings, conducting himself, say his biographers, "with great decorum and condescension, changing seats, and sitting down, and standing up, as he could best accommodate others, although he could not understand a word of what was said." But the chief pleasure of Peter, when he was not in the dockyard, was to sail about in a small-decked boat on the Thames, accompanied by his favourite Menzikoff, and three or four others of his suite, whom he instructed in the art of managing a boat, he himself generally acting as the helmsman. After spending five or six hours at this work, they used to repair to a public house in Great Tower Street, near Tower Hill, where they smoked their pipes, and fuddled themselves on beer and brandy.

The landlord, flattered by the preference given to his house by his royal guest, had his head painted and put up as his sign. It remained till the year 1808, when a virtuoso, taking a fancy to it, gave the landlord a new sign, copied from the original, in exchange for it, where it remains to the present day.

Evelyn was at this time a hale, hearty old man, in the seventy-seventh year of his age. His son, also named John Evelyn, and a man of great literary accomplishments, and one of the commissioners of the revenue for Ireland, died at Saye's Court, the year after the Czar left it. He was imbued with tastes similar to his father's, and translated a poem on gardens from the Latin of Renatus Rapin. He also translated the Life of Alexander the Great, from Plutarch. He died in his forty-fifth year. His father lived to eighty-six.

No traces now remain of the house and gardens of this family. The former was pulled down in the year 1728, and the parish work-house now stands upon its site. And as for the garden, time, and the neglect, or convenience of successive ages, have proved enemies to it, more rude than the Czar. Part of it now belongs to the Government, and is covered by the slaughter-houses of the Victualling Office;

and on the small remainder potatoes and cab-
bages have taken the place of the impregnable
holly-hedges and vistas of tall trees, which
once, as Lord-keeper Guildford expressed it,
made the grounds look so pleasant and " so
boscaresque."

Deptford was formerly called West Greenwich, and is said to derive its present name
from the depth of the ford over the little river
Ravensbourne, which here discharges itself
into the Thames. The ford has long since
been superseded by a bridge. The latter is
memorable in history for the total defeat of
Lord Audley and his Cornish rebels in the
year 1497. Headed by that nobleman, Flammock a lawyer, and Joseph a blacksmith of
Bodmin, they had advanced from Taunton,
with the design of taking possession of London. The Kentish men flocked to their standard; and on their arrival at Blackheath they
amounted altogether to about sixteen thousand
men. Lord Daubeny, who had been sent
against them by King Henry VII, made a
furious attack upon them at Deptford Bridge,
and after great slaughter, put them to flight.
Lord Audley, Flammock, and Joseph, were
taken prisoners, and shortly afterwards executed
on Tower Hill, the latter boasting in his hour

of death, that he died in a just cause, and that he would make a figure in history. This little stream, which here is called Deptford Creek, rises on Keston Heath, near Hayes Place, and runs a course of about twelve miles, passing by Bromley, Lewisham, and the borders of Blackheath. An old legend is told, to account for its romantic name. It is said, that Julius Cæsar, on his invasion of Britain, was encamped with all his force a few miles southward of its source. The army was suffering a good deal for the want of water, and detachments had been sent out in all directions, but without success, for a supply. Cæsar observed, that a raven frequently alighted near the camp, and conjecturing that it came to drink, he ordered its arrival to be diligently noted. His command was obeyed; and the visits of the raven were found to be to a small clear spring on Keston Heath. The wants of the army were supplied, and the spring, says the legend, and the rivulet of which it is the parent, have ever since been called the Raven's Well, and the Ravensbourne. It is, as some poet in the Table Book calls it,

A crystal rillet, scarce a palm in width,
Till creeping to a bed, outspread by art,
It sheets itself across, reposing there;

Thence through a thicket, sinuous it flows,
And crossing meads and footpaths, gathering tribute
Due to its elder birth from younger branches,
Wanders, in Hayes and Bromley, Beckenham vale
And straggling Lewisham, to where Deptford Bridge
Uprises, in obeisance to its flood.

Small and insignificant though it be, it is nevertheless a stream which has a name in history. More than one tumultuous multitude
has encamped upon its banks, shouting loud
defiance to their rulers. Blackheath, its near
neighbour, bore Wat Tyler and the angry
thousands that followed in his train; and, in
the Ravensbourne perchance, many of these
swarthy artisans stooped down to drink the
limpid waters, when, inflamed by revenge, and
the hope of plunder and absolute power, they
prepared to march upon London. Jack Cade
and his multitudes encamped upon the same
spot, and the Ravensbourne, after an interval
of eighty years, saw its quiet shores disturbed
by men met for the same purposes, and threatening blood, because, feeling the scourge of oppression, they knew no wiser means of procur-
ing relief, and were unable to distinguish between law and tyranny on the one hand, and
freedom and licentiousness on the other.

Perkin Warbeck met his adherents on the

same place; and Flammock and his Cornish men were here hewed to pieces, as already stated, by the victorious captains of Henry VII. Nor are these deeds of blood and turmoil the only events that signalize the Ravensbourne. At Hayes Place, near the spot where it first oozes from the sward, lived the great Earl of Chatham, and there was born his renowned son, William Pitt.

Besides its dock and victualling yard, Deptford is noted for two hospitals belonging to the Corporation of the Trinity House, or pilots of London. A grand procession comes from London to these hospitals annually on Trinity Monday, accompanied by music and banners, and welcomed by the firing of cannon.

Among the most famous residents of this town, besides the Czar Peter and John Evelyn, already mentioned, were Cowley the poet, and the Earl of Nottingham, Lord High Admiral of England, and the victor of the Spanish Armada. The house he inhabited was afterwards converted into a tavern, called the Gun; and his armorial bearings, sculptured over the chimney piece of the principal apartment, were long shown to the curious.

But Deptford has a neighbour more magnificent and more renowned than itself—Greenwich

—the pride of England, by the great waters flourishing, and the glory of the Thames. The approach to it by the river, is in the highest degree beautiful and striking. Those to whom it is familiar, pass it by without emotion; but the stranger, and especially he that knows something of its history, never refrains from warm admiration. The homage is forced from him whether he will or no, by the splendour of the noble hospital, standing so proudly upon the brink, and the greatness of the uses to which it is applied.

Hail, noblest structure, imaged in the wave!
A nation's grateful tribute to the brave;
Hail, blest retreat, from war and shipwreck, hail!

No ostentatious charity raised that edifice to feed the hungry and clothe the naked, and be lauded for it; but national justice reared it and maintains it, and national gratitude will foster it evermore. And no great thanks to it either. Like the private gratitude spoken of by the diplomatist who studied the human heart so well, it burns brightly, not so much for past benefits, but from a keen sense of those which are to come. Kindness to the worn-out veteran is one of the surest means of raising up the race of the young and vigorous to succeed him; and our nation in maintaining this hospital, is but keenly alive to its own interest after all.

As Greenwich owes all its importance to its hospital—as that edifice is not only the chief beauty, but the distinguishing characteristic of the place, and that which singles it out not only from every other town in Great Britain, but in the world, it may naturally be expected that it should receive the first notice at the hands of the topographer; but, as it is of modern growth, and the successor only of palaces that existed before its time, we will begin at the beginning, and not speak further of Greenwich Hospital, prominent though it be, until we arrive at it chronologically.

The manor of Greenwich, called in the early

records, East Greenwich, belonged formerly to
the abbey of St. Peter at Ghent. At the dissolution of the alien priories, it was granted by
Henry V. to the monastery of Sheen, or Richmond. It remained in the possession of the
monks for a very short time, being seized by
the Crown upon the disgrace of the bishop of
Baieux. Henry VI. in the eleventh year of
his reign, granted it to his uncle, Duke Humphrey, that Humphrey, with whom, according
to the vulgar saying still in use, everybody
who has no dinner is supposed to dine. Being
pleased with the spot, the Duke built a palace, extending, with its various courts, from
the river to the hill on which the Observatory now stands : there is a good view of
it in Hasted's " History of Kent." It was
named Placentia, and sometimes the Plaisaunce.
Upon his death it became the property of the
Crown. Edward IV. enlarged the Park, and
restocked it with deer, and then bestowed it
as a residence upon his queen, Elizabeth Wid-
ville. Henry VII. occasionally resided in it;
and Henry VIII. at one period of his reign
was so much attached to it, that he passed
more of his time at Greenwich than at any
other of his palaces. He adorned and enlarged
it at considerable expense, and made it so mag-

nificent, as to cause Leland, the antiquary, to
exclaim with rapture unbecoming an antiquary,
as he gazed upon it—

> How bright the lofty seat appears,
> Like Jove's great palace, paved with stars!
> What roofs! what windows charm the eye!
> What turrets, rivals of the sky!

It should be said, however, that the antiquary
wrote his praises in Latin, and that these verses
are the translation of Hasted, the historian of
Kent.   Henry VIII. was born in the palace,
and there also was born his daughter Mary, as
well as his great daughter Elizabeth—the circumstance connected with Greenwich, that of
all others rendered it most dear to the mind of
Samuel Johnson, who exclaims in the introduction to his Satire upon London—

> On Thames's bank in silent thought we stood,
> Where Greenwich smiles upon the silver flood,
> Struck with the seat that gave Eliza birth,
> We kneel and kiss the consecrated earth,
> In pleasing dreams that blissful age renew,
> And call Britannia's glories back to view.

A great fallacy of the lexicographer as to the
age of either Henry or Elizabeth being a bliss-
ful one; but let that pass.   It was a merry one
for the aristocracy of the court in some respects,
especially during the time of Henry, and had
there been any safety for their heads, they at
least would have had but little to complain of,

whatever might have been said by the people. Tilts and tournaments succeeded each other with great rapidity while he wielded the seeptre. On Shrove Tuesday, 1526, the King, with eleven knights, fought against the Marquis of Exeter with the like number in Greenwich Park; upon which occasion Sir Francis Bryan, one of the combatants, had his eye poked out by the point of a spear. While the King was indulging himself with sports of this kind, he published an edict at Greenwich against the less costly amusements of his subjects. "Commissions," says Stowe, "were awarded into every shire for the execution of the same, so that in all places tables, dice, cards, and bowls, were taken and burned; but when young men were restrained of these games and pastimes, some fell to drinking, some to ferreting of other men's conies, and stealing of deer in parks, and other unthriftiness." But Henry was not an enemy to the amusements of the people, provided they were conformable to his own notions; and his tournaments were visited by thousands of his subjects, who had free ingress and egress while they lasted, and ample accommodation besides. His Christmas festivals which he held in Placentia, were no less splendid than his exhibitions of chivalric sports. Revels, masques, disguisings, and banquets right royal, distinguished them from all the entertainments of former sovereigns. So much admired for its magnificence was the banquet he gave to the French ambassadors at this place in 1528, that honest old Stowe is obliged to confess, that "he lacked a head of fine wit, and also cunning in his bowels," to describe it with sufficient eloquence. The great tilt-yard was covered over, and converted into a banqueting room. The Hampton Court banquet given by Wolsey to the same personages just before, was, says the annalist, a marvellously sumptuous one; yet this at Greenwich excelled it as much as gold excels silver, and no beholder had ever seen the like. In the midst of the banquet there was tourneying at the barriers, with lusty gentlemen in complete harness, very gorgeous, on foot; then there was tilting on horseback with knights in armour, still more magnificent; and after this was an interlude or disguising, made in Latin, the players being in the richest costumes, ornamented with the most strange and grotesque devices. "This done," continues Stowe, "there came such a number of the fairest ladies and gentlewomen that had any renown of beauty throughout the realm, in the most rich apparel that could be devised, with whom the gentlemen of France danced, until a gorgeous mask of gentlemen came in, who danced and masked with these ladies. This done, came in another mask of ladies, who took each of them one of the Frenchmen by the hand, to dance and to mask. These women maskers every one spake good French to the Frenchmen, which delighted them very much to hear their mother-tongue. Thus was the night consumed, from five of the clock until three of the clock after midnight."

After the King's marriage to Anne Boleyn, he took her to reside at Greenwich; and when it pleased him to declare the marriage publicly, and have her crowned, he ordered the Lord Mayor to come to Greenwich in state, and escort her up the river to London. It was on the 19th of May, 1533, and father Thames had never before borne on his bosom so gallant an array. First of all the mayor and aldermen, with their scarlet robes and golden chains, followed by the Common Councilmen in their robes, and by all the officers of the city in their costume, with triumphant music swelling upon the ear, and their gay banners floating upon the breeze, walked down to the water-side, where they found their own barges ready to receive them, and fifty other barges, filled with the various city Companies, awaiting the signal of departure. Then, amid the firing of cannon, and the braying of trumpets, the procession started. A foist, or large flat-bottomed boat, took the lead, impelled by several fellows dressed out to represent devils, who at intervals spouted out blue and red flames from their mouths, and threw balls of fire into the water. "Terrible and monstrous wild men they were," says Stowe, "and made a hideous noise. In the midst of them sat a great red dragon, moving itself continually about, and discharging fire-balls of various colours into the air, whence they fell into the water with a hissing sound. Next came the Lord Mayor's barge, attended by a small barge on the right side filled with musicians. It was richly hung with cloth of gold and silver, and bore the two embroidered banners of the King and Queen, besides escutcheons splendidly wrought in every part of the vessel. On the left side was another foist, in the which was a mount, and on the mount stood a white falcon, crowned upon a root of gold, environed with white and red roses, which was the Queen's device, and about the mount sat virgins, singing and playing melodiously." Then came the Sheriffs and the Aldermen, and the Common Councilmen and the city Companies in regular procession,

each barge, having its own banners and devices, and most of them being hung with arras
and cloth of gold. When they arrived at
Greenwich, they cast anchor, " making all the
while great melody." They waited thus until
three o'clock, when the Queen appeared, attended by the Duke of Suffolk, the Marquis
of Dorset, the Earl of Wiltshire her father,
the Earls of Arundel, Derby, Rutland, Wor-
cester, Huntingdon, Sussex, Oxford, and many
other noblemen and bishops, each one in his
barge. In this order they rowed up the
Thames to the Tower stairs, where the King was
waiting to receive his bride, whom he kissed
"affectionately and with a loving countenance"
in sight of all the people that lined the shores
of the river, and covered all the housetops in
such multitudes that Stowe was afraid to mention the number, lest posterity should accuse
him of exaggeration.

On the birth and baptism of the Princess
Elizabeth, in the month of September following, the people of London were gratified with
the sight of a similar procession to Greenwich
and back again. The royal couple continued
to reside alternately at the palaces of Placentia
and Hampton Court until the year 1536, when
poor Anne Boleyn became no longer pleasing

in the eyes of her lord. On May day, in that
year, Henry instituted a grand tournament in
Greenwich Park, at which the Queen and her
brother, Lord Rochford, were present. The
sports were at their height, when the King,
without uttering a word to his Queen or any-
body else, suddenly took his departure, apparently in an ill-humour, and proceeded to London, accompanied by six domestics. All the
tilters were surprised and chagrined; but their
surprise and chagrin were light in comparison
to those of Anne Boleyn. The very same
night, her brother and his friends, Norris, Bre-
reton, Weston, and Smeton, were arrested, and
conveyed up the river to the Tower, bound
like felons. On the following morning, the
Queen herself was arrested a few hours afterwards and conveyed to the same prison, where
on the fifth day of her captivity, she indited
that elegant and feeling epistle to her tyrant,
dated from " her dolefull prison in yᵉ Tower,"
which every one has read and hundreds have wept
over. The King had long suspected her truth;
and the offence he took at the tilting match
was, that she had dropped her handkerchief,
accidentally it would appear, but which he conceived to be a signal to a paramour. On the
nineteenth, the anniversary of her coronation,

and triumphal procession from Greenwich three years before, her young head was smitten from her body by the axe of the executioner, within the precincts of that building where she had received the public kiss, in sight of the multitudes of London! Alas! poor Anne!

When his next Queen died at Hampton Court, Henry was so grieved that he could not look upon that palace without shedding tears. He retired first to Westminster, and then to Greenwich, where he kept his Christmas in his mourning apparel. But the gloom was not of long continuance. Greenwich soon became as gay as ever, and on the public reception of Anne of Cleves it was a scene of great splendour and rejoicing. The park was adorned with banners and festoons of the most magnificent description, and filled with all the chivalry of England, attendant upon the Sovereign. Nobles, Knights, Bishops, and Ambassadors thronged in those ancient avenues, and free ingress was also permitted to the people, as Henry rode towards Blackheath, to meet his new bride. After him rode the Lord Chancellor, and then Sir Anthony Browne, (afterwards husband of Lord Surrey's fair Geraldine,) holding the King's horse of state by a

long rein of gold ; and then the multitudinous
array of pages, esquires, and men at arms, followed by the nobles and their retainers; and
the Lord Mayor of London, and all the dignitaries of the city, and the several companies
in their holiday attire.   Tilts and tournaments
were celebrated every day in the park; while
on the river opposite the palace, the water-
quintain and other aquatic sports of the age,
were exhibited for the entertainment of the
Queen, and the numerous retinue of foreigners
who had accompanied her from Calais.   The
nuptials were celebrated in the chapel of the
palace.

During the reign of the two succeeding
Sovereigns, Greenwich lost that renown for
gaiety which it had acquired from the festivals
and constant hospitality of Henry.   Edward
VI. occasionally visited Placentia, and there he
died in his sixteenth year.   Mary was also an
occasional inhabitant of the palace.   During
one of her visits, a singular accident occurred.
The captain of a vessel proceeding out to sea,
observing the banner of England floating from
the walls, fired the customary salute, in honour
of royalty.   By some oversight, the gun was
loaded, and the ball was driven through the
wall into the Queen's apartments, to the great

terror of herself and her ladies. None of them received any hurt.

With the reign of Elizabeth, the glories of Greenwich revived. It was her birth-place; the favourite residence of her unfortunate mother, and dear to her for that reason, and in the summer months, it became during nearly her whole reign, the favourite seat of the court. She did not spend so much money in it as her father, neither was she so fond of tilts and tournaments as he was, nor was she altogether so fond of show and ostentation : but she contrived somehow or other to live in continual gaiety, sometimes by giving entertainments, and a great deal oftener by accepting them. On the 2nd of July, 1559, the year after her accession, the citizens of London entertained her with a grand muster of their forces in Greenwich Park. Eight hundred pikemen in their corslets, four hundred arquebusiers in their coats of mail, and two hundred halberdiers, were escorted by the Lord Mayor, Sheriffs, Aldermen, and other dignitaries in their coats of velvet, and their chains of gold, over the bridge to the Duke of Suffolk's in Southwark, where they were reviewed by the Lord Mayor. They encamped that night in St. George's Fields, and early on the following morning, commenced their march to Greenwich. They stationed themselves in the park on their arrival, and there waited until five in the afternoon, when the Queen appeared in the gallery at the back of the palace, and the exhibition of their warlike skill commenced. Dividing themselves into two bands, they fired their shotless guns at each other, and a mêlée began, presenting all the outward appearances of a regular battle, except the spilling of blood. This lasted for about an hour, when the Queen thanked the Lord Mayor for his politeness in commanding the show, and withdrew into the palace. The bands then broke up, and amused themselves till night fall by tilting, running at the ring, the quintain and other sports, when they marched back again to St. George's Fields in the order they had come in. This warlike Lord Mayor, was Sir William Hewett, a cloth-worker, whose apprentice Osborne became the founder of the present ducal family of Leeds.

Within the same month, Elizabeth herself gave a grand entertainment; but she forgot to invite the Lord Mayor. A rural banqueting house was erected in the park, made of fir poles and birchen branches, with all their green leaves about them, and variegated with festoons of flowers, both of the field and the garden, the rarest that then grew, being intermingled with roses, lilies, gillyflowers, lavender, and marigolds, and every description of sweet smelling herbs and rushes in profusion. Besides this rural bower for the " Queen of Beauty and of Hearts," as she was called, and loved to be called as well as Queen of England, tents were erected in various parts of the park, for the accommodation of the visitors, in which there was abundant store of meat and drink for all who chose to partake. The sports began by a tournament. This was followed by a masked ball and a banquet, and the whole concluded with a display of fireworks, and a discharge of artillery.

The old annalists make constant mention of Elizabeth's proceedings at Greenwich. The following account of a ceremony observed on Maundy Thursday, in 1572, is given in Nichols's interesting " Progresses" of that Sovereign. The court being then at Greenwich, the Queen, according to ancient custom, washed the feet of the poor on that festival. Being in her thirty-ninth year, thirty-nine poor persons attended in the hall of the palace to receive the royal alms. Their feet were washed, first by the yeomen of the laundry with warm water and sweet herbs, and afterwards by the sub-almoner, then by the almoner, and lastly by the Queen herself, the person who washed, making each time a cross on the pauper's foot, above the toes, and kissing it. This ceremony was performed also by the Queen kneeling, attended by thirty-nine gentlewomen, after which clothes, victuals, and money were distributed to them by the almoner in the Queen's presence. James II. is said to have been the last Sovereign who performed this ceremony. The dole is still kept up: the number of recipients annually increasing with the age of the Sovereign.

The same year, as Elizabeth was proceeding down the Thames to Greenwich in the royal barge, a serious accident occurred. She was sailing with the French ambassador, the Earl of Lincoln, and her Vice-Chamberlain, and discoursing, says Stowe, " about divers weighty affairs," when, as she came between Deptford and Greenwich, she passed a small boat in which was one Thomas Appletree, servant to Master Henry Cary, who was amusing himself with a loaded arquebus, and shooting rashly at objects on the side of the river. Suddenly a shot was heard, and one of the watermen in the royal barge, who sat within a few feet of the Queen, fell into the bottom of the boat, crying out in the most piteous manner that he was shot through the body. His arms having been stretched out in the act of rowing, the shot had passed clean through both of them, and he bled profusely. " The Queen's Majesty," says the annalist, " showed such noble courage as was most wonderful to be spoken of, comforting the man, and telling him to˙ be of good cheer, for that every care should be taken of him." Appletree, the unfortunate cause of the accident, was apprehended, thrown into prison, tried, and sentenced to death on the fourth day afterwards. A tall gibbet was erected on the river side between Greenwich and Deptford, exactly opposite to the place where the waterman was wounded, and the man brought out for execution. The prayers for the dead were said, the rope was placed round his neck, and every one awaited the signal that was to send the poor wretch into eternity, when a messenger arrived from the Queen, with her free pardon for the offender. A cruel experiment after all, and anything but a just one.

Greenwich is constantly mentioned by the flattering poets of that day, and the river Thames is complimented on its great good fortune in bearing so lovely a Sovereign continually on its bosom in her progresses from her capital to her summer palace. As the age of the Queen increased, so did the flattery of the poetasters. One in particular, said that the very fish in the Thames raised their heads out of the water, to gaze upon her beauty. Sir John Davis, writing in 1599, when she was sixty-six years of age, has the following aerostic among a collection of about thirty others, all in the same strain. It is addressed to Flora.

> Empress of flowers, tell where away
> Lies your sweet court this May :
> In Greenwich garden alleys,
> Since there the heavenly powers do play
> And haunt no other valleys.
>
> Beauty, virtue, majesty,
> Eloquent Muses three times three,
> The new fresh flowers and graces
> Have pleasure in that place to be
> Above all other places.

Drayton in a poem published in " England's Helicon" in the following year, thus eulogizes the Thames, and flatters Elizabeth, under the name of Beta.

> O thou silver Thames, O clearest crystal flood,
> Beta alone the phœnix is of all thy watery brood,
>   The queen of virgins, only she,
>   And thou the queen of floods shalt be,

Let all the nymphs be joyful then
  To see this happy day,
Thy Beta now alone shall be
  The subject of my lay.

Range all thy swans, fair Thames, together in a rank,
And place them duly one by one upon thy stately bank,
  Set them together all a good
  Recording to thy silver flood,
  And crave the tuneful nightingale
    To help ye with her lay,
  The csell and the thrusslecock,
    Chief music of our May.

See how the day stands still admiring of her face,
And Time, lo, stretcheth forth his arms our Beta to embrace,
  The Sirens sing sweet lays
  The Tritons sound her praise,
  So pass on Thames, and hie thee fast
    Unto the ocean sea,
  And let thy billows there proclaim
    Our Beta's holiday.

We'll strew thy shores with pearls where Beta walks alone,
And we will pave her princely bower with richest Indian stone,
  Perfume the air, and make it sweet,
  For such a goddess it is meet;
  For if her eyes, for purity,
    Contend with Titan's light,
  No marvel then although they do
    So dazzle human sight!

Decker still more complimentary, as he thought, indulged in the following, in the prologue to his "Old Fortunatus." "Some call her Pandora, some Gloriana, some Cynthia, some Bel-

phebe, some Astrea; all by several names to
express several loves, yet all these names make
but one celestial body, as all these loves meet
but to create one soul.   We are of her country,
and adore her by the name of Eliza.—Blessed
name! happy country! Eliza makes the land
Elizi-um!"

Hentzner the German traveller, who saw
the Queen at Greenwich in 1598, tells the
plain truth of this goddess of beauty.   "Next
came the Queen," says he, "in the sixty-fifth
year of her age, very majestic; her face oblong,
fair but wrinkled; her eyes small, yet black
and pleasant; her nose a little hooked; her lips
narrow, and her teeth black (a defect, the
English seem subject to, from their too
great use of sugar)   She had in her ears two
pearls with very rich drops; she wore false hair,
and that red.   Upon her head she had a small
crown.   Her bosom was uncovered, as all the
English ladies have it till they marry, and she
had on a necklace of exceeding fine jewels.
Whoever speaks to her, it is kneeling, and now
and then she raises some with her hand.   In
the ante-chapel next the hall, petitions were
presented to her, and she received them most
graciously, which occasioned the exclamation,
' Long live Queen Elizabeth !' to which she

replied, ' I thank you, my good people!' "—
Bearing in mind this description and contrast-
ing it with the overflowing flattery of all the
poetasters, we may smile with Horace Walpole,
and exclaim with him, " What! all this worship offered to an old woman with bare neck,
black teeth, and false red hair!"

CHAPTER V.

Visits of Sully to King James I. at Greenwich.—Demolition of the Palace of Placentia. — Building of a New Palace. — Origin, and completion of the Hospital. — The Funeral of Nelson.—The View from the Hill.—The Legend of St. Alphege.—The humours of Greenwich Fair.

HE history of the old palace of Greenwich, after the death of Elizabeth, loses its chief attraetions. With her died its gaiety and splendour; the long processions by water, the rural pavilions in the park, the maskings and revellings by moonlight, the tilting by day, and the flattering verses of the rhymers, all ceased together;—and James, in the ensuing summer, took up his abode in Greenwich without ostentation, and without welcome. The new King did not like to hear of his predecessor. He frowned upon those who suggested the peacefulness or the splendour of her reign, and the name of Elizabeth was heard in her halls no more.

Soon after his accession, the sage Marquis de Rosni, better known by his subsequent title of Duke de Sully, complimented the King on the part of his great master Henry IV. Sully went by water to Greenwich in the barges of the King, accompanied by a hundred and twenty gentlemen of his household; the banks of the river being lined with the multitudes of London to witness the procession. " I was shown into a chamber," says the Duke in his Memoirs, " to partake of a collation, contrary to the usual custom of England, which is not to regale ambassadors, or offer them even so much as a glass of water. His Majesty having sent to request my presence, it took me a quarter of an hour before I could reach the foot of the throne—a delay which was occasioned as much by the crowd of courtiers who were there already, as by my having ordered my whole household to walk before me. The King no sooner saw me, than he came down two steps from the throne, and would have come down the whole of them, so eager was he to embrace me, had not one of the ministers (Cecil) whispered in his ear that he ought not to go any further. 'If I,' replied the King aloud, ' honour this ambassador more than I have done others, I do not expect that it should become a precedent. I bear him a peculiar love and esteem for the affection which I know he bears to me, for his constancy to our religion, and for his fidelity towards his master.' But I cannot tell," adds Sully, " all the flattering things he said of me." After this public audience, the King made him ascend to the highest step of the throne, where they had a long private conversation about various matters:—the virtues of Henry IV.—the designs of Spain—but chiefly about hunting, to which, as is well known, James was passionately addicted.

A few days afterwards Sully had a second audience, when the King led him away alone, through several apartments, into a little private gallery, meanly enough furnished, where they had another long conversation about the affairs of Europe. Sully's third visit to Greenwich was to dine with the King. It was on a Sunday, the 29th of June, 1603, and Sully arrived at ten in the morning, with all the gentlemen of his household. He first went to church with the King, and nothing particular passed till the service was over, and they had sat down to dinner, when James began to talk to him about his favourite diversion of hunting, and the state of the weather as influencing it.

Sully was surprised to see that the domestics all went upon their knees to serve the King— a piece of regal pomp which he had not been accustomed to in his own country. During nearly all dinner time the discourse was about hunting, when accidentally the name of Elizabeth was introduced. James spoke of her with contempt, and even went so far as to say, that long before the death of that princess, he in Scotland swayed her counsels, and disposed of all her ministers, by whom he asserted he was much better served and obeyed than she was. " He then," says Sully, " asked for wine, and his custom is never to mix any water with it, and holding his glass in his hand towards Beaumont and me, drank to the health of the King, Queen, and royal family of France. I acknowledged the honour, and proposed the royal family of England, making particular mention of his children, when the King bent down his head and whispered in my ear that he should propose as the next toast—the double union which he contemplated between the two royal families. I received the proposition with every outward sign of joy, and also whispered that I was sure Henry would not hesitate for an instant between his good brother and ally of England, and the King of Spain, who had

already made some overtures upon the same
subject."

At another audience a few days afterwards,
they had a private conversation which lasted
about four hours, the King with his own hands
shutting the doors as they passed through the
galleries, to make sure that they were alone,
and then kissing the ambassador twice before
discussing the weighty matters they had met
to talk about.   Before the farewell audience,
he said he would not give Sully the trouble
to come to Greenwich, but would come himself to London to receive him.   He did so;
and told Sully he was so grieved at his departure, that he was obliged to go out hunting
to forget his sorrow in that agreeable exercise.

During his residence at Greenwich, James
made some additions to the palace, erected a
new wall to the park, and commenced a sum-
mer-house, called the House of Delight.   He
did not live to complete the latter, which
was finished by Henrietta Maria, Queen of
Charles I. who employed Inigo Jones as the
architect.   The King and Queen did not reside so often at Greenwich as their predecessors
from Henry VIII. had done; and after the
consummation of the revolution by the behead-
ing of the King, the palace was for a long time

deserted. An order was issued by the House of Commons for the sale of the palace with the park and lands adjoining ; but it was not sold, having been presented along with Hampton Court as a residence for the Protector. Cromwell, however, seldom visited it, and the palace was allowed to fall into decay. After the Restoration it was found in so ruinous a condition, that Charles II. caused the greater part of it to be taken down, and a new palace erected in its stead. This edifice forms the western wing of the present hospital, and was built by Webb, son in law of Inigo Jones.

Charles II. also enlarged the park, and had it replanted and laid out in its present avenues and shady walks by the great philodendron, John Evelyn. He also erected the Observatory on the top of the hill, for the use of Flamstead the astronomer royal, furnished it abundantly with mathematical instruments, and made a deep dry well for the observation of the stars in the daytime. From this hill, all English, and most American astronomers, commence the calculation of the longitude. The expense of all these improvements was about thirty-six thousand pounds.

No progress was made in the palace, in the reign of James II, but, in that succeeding, the kindheartedness of the amiable Queen Mary, suggested an idea to her husband which totally changed the character of the building, and eventually rendered it that which we now behold it, not only the boast but the glory of England, and more truly magnificent than the most splendid palace that ever in this world was erected for the convenience or the gratification of Kings. At Mary's solicitations, a grant of a certain house, built by King Charles II, with the lands appertaining thereto, was made for the use of disabled English seamen and their children, and for the widows and children of such as had lost their lives in the service of their country. After her death, King William carried on her benevolent designs, appointed commissioners to aid the work, and solicited the contributions of his subjects for the same end, as the necessity of his own affairs did not permit him to advance the considerable sums which the undertaking required. Another wing was forthwith commenced, under the superintendence of Sir Christopher Wren, and the works being continued by every succeeding Sovereign, were finally completed in the reign of George II. In that of George I. the forfeited estates of the Earl of Derwentwater, amounting then to six thousand per annum, but of more con-

siderable value now, were appropriated for the
maintenance of the hospital. Besides the revenues from these estates, the Hospital has various sources of income; including a payment of
sixpence per month from all seamen and marines in the royal navy or merchant service;
the duties arising from the North and South
Foreland light-houses; the rents of the market
at Greenwich; various fines for fishing in the
Thames with unlawful nets and at improper seasons; and forfeited and unclaimed prize money.

The hospital consists of four distinct piles of
buildings, which stand on a noble terrace upon
the river's bank, extending about eight hundred
and sixty-five feet, and are called after their
founders, King Charles', Queen Mary's, King
William's and Queen Anne's buildings. In
Queen Mary's, to the east fronting the river, is
the celebrated chapel, to which all strangers
resort; and in King William's, the west wing,
is the still more celebrated Hall, painted by
Thornhill, and containing portraits of the most
celebrated naval heroes who have arisen in our
isle since we became supereminent as a sea-
faring, and a sea-conquering people; models of
ships of war, and, lastly, what may be considered
more precious than all, the identical coat, worn
by the great Nelson at the battle of Trafalgar,

carefully enclosed in a glass case from the touch
of the visitor; but bearing many too perceptible marks that no care can preserve it from
the destructive touch of time, and the tiny
tooth of the devouring moth, which together
have made sad inroads upon the hallowed
relic.

In the upper hall is preserved another relic—
the 'funeral car, in which the body of Nelson
was conveyed with all the pomp befitting the
gratitude of a great nation to the illustrious
dead, to St. Paul's Cathedral. Of all the pageantry that Greenwich has witnessed since it
became a town, this was, if not the most magnificent, the most grand and impressive. The
body, after lying in state for three days, in the
Hospital, during which it was visited by immense multitudes, was conveyed on the 8th
of January, 1806, up the river to Whitehall,
followed in procession by the City Companies,
in their state barges. The flags of all the vessels in the river were lowered half-mast high, in
token of mourning, and solemn minute guns
were fired during the whole time of the procession. The body lay all that night at the
Admiralty, and, on the following morning, was
removed on a magnificent car, surmounted by
plumes of feathers, and decorated with heraldic

insignia, to its final resting place in St. Paul's Cathedral. From the Admiralty to St. Paul's, the streets were all lined with the military. The procession was headed by detachments of the Dragoon Guards, the Scots Greys, and the Ninety-second Highlanders, with the Duke of York and his staff, the band playing that sublime funeral strain, the "Dead March in Saul." Then followed the pensioners of Greenwich Hospital, and the seamen of Lord Nelson's ship the Victory, a deputation from the Common Council of London, and a long train of mourning coaches, including those of the royal family, the chief officers of state, and all the principal nobility of the kingdom. When the coffin, covered with the flag of the Victory, was about to be lowered into the grave, an affecting incident occurred: the attendant sailors who had borne the pall, rushed forward, and seizing upon the flag, before a voice could be raised to prevent them, rent it into shreds, in the intensity of their feelings, that each might preserve a shred as a memento of the departed.

Greenwich Hospital now lodges about three thousand old and disabled seamen, to attend upon whom are upwards of a hundred nurses, widows of seamen. Each pensioner, besides a

liberal allowance of clothes and provisions, receives a small weekly sum for tobacco and other
indulgences to which he has been accustomed;
the sailors one shilling, the mates one shilling
and sixpence, and the boatswains two shillings
and sixpence.   A library is also provided for
their exclusive use.   It is a pleasing sight to see

them sitting in the sunshine in the porches of
their palace, or swarming about in the green
alleys of the Park, with their old-fashioned cock-
ed hats and coats; some feeding the deer, some
lying at full length upon the sward, others turning over under the trees the smoke-coloured
leaves of some well-fingered manual, and others

again, standing upon Flamstead Hill, with tele-
scope to their eye, watching the arrival or departure of some vessel, with her white sails spread,
careering swiftly through the waters of the
Thames, and soliciting the loiterer, for a penny
fee, to do likewise. The view from this hill is
most agreeable and noble. Right underneath
lie the glades of the Park, and the twin domes
of the Hospital, and the eye, taking a wide
range, roams to the right and left, over the
busy bosom of the river, covered with ships,
and boats, and steam vessels,' bearing wealth
and passengers to and from the great heart of
England. The latter itself is dimly visible to
the west, crowned with a corona of perpetual
smoke, from which the dome of St. Paul's Cathedral emerges grand and imposing, its gild-
ed ball glittering in the sunshine, while all below is dim and cloudy. Every variety of view
afforded by a flat country may be seen from
this hill; the busy town, the busy water, the
retired woodland, and the fine open country,
dotted with herds of cattle, and enlivened with
clumps of trees, from which village churches
peep modestly forth, farm-houses, villas, and
fields of waving grain.

Of the patron saint of Greenwich, to whom
in former days its church was dedicated, and

which still bears his name, an old legend is related, which we, as avowed lovers of traditions, must not fail to record. St. Alphege was Archbishop of Canterbury at the commencement of the eleventh century, and Greenwich having been occupied by the Danes in one of their predatory incursions in the year 1011, a detachment was sent from thence to Canterbury, who brought back the archbishop with them to Greenwich, where he was detained a captive for seven months. While mourning in his cell, the monkish legends say he was visited by the devil, who appeared to him in the likeness of an angel, and tempted him to follow into a dark valley. St. Alphege, deceived by the false glitter of the celestial glory which the arch enemy had assumed, followed him wearily over rugged stones that cut his naked feet, through stinging underwoods, and sharp brambles that tore his flesh, until they arrived at a deep mire, into which the devil soused him, and vanished in his real shape with an insulting laugh of triumph. A real angel immediately afterwards appeared, who assisted him out, and told him to go back to prison, and suffer martyrdom for the glory of the Lord, which had been decreed his high privilege in this world. The saint did as he was bidden; and shortly afterwards his captors, being enraged because his friends could not pay the exorbitant ransom which they demanded, set upon him and cruelly murdered him. His body after death worked miracles: a rotten stake that was driven through it, flourished and bore leaves and blossoms, by which many of his murderers were converted. The citizens of London hearing of the event, purchased the body, and removed it from Greenwich to St. Paul's Church, where they buried it with great magnificence. It was eleven years afterwards removed to Canterbury by order of King Canute. The present parish church of Greenwich is supposed to have been erected on the very spot where the murder was committed.

Twice in every year Greenwich becomes the grand resort of the populace of London—first at Easter, and afterwards at Whitsuntide. What man, woman, or child residing within a circuit of twenty miles of Greenwich, and belonging to those classes of society who do not think it derogatory to enjoy themselves at a fair, that has not at one time or other been present at the celebrated Saturnalia? Greenwich is then in all its glory, and becomes, as Chaucer characterized it four hundred years ago,

Grenwiche that many a shewe is in,

and affords plenty of amusement for the bois-
terous man to share, and the quiet man to look
at. It is then that the manners of a large
class of the people of England, and chiefly
those of the metropolis, which is of itself a
nation, may be studied to advantage. On
Easter Monday, as soon as the day dawns, the
approaches to Greenwich, if the weather be
favourable, teem with the population of the
capital; some bent on fun, some on mischief,
some on drink and riot, some on honest profit,
some upon thimble rigging, and very many
upon obtaining foul possession of other people's
pocket handkerchiefs and loose valuables. But
by far the greater number go for enjoyment;
servant girls, apprentices, and journeymen from
London; artisans, farm labourers, soldiers and
sailors from the surrounding districts—a motley, disorderly, drunken, jolly multitude. They
rise innumerable, like Pharaoh's host, or the
swarm of evil spirits described by Milton, pouring down every lane, filling every avenue,
streaming upon every vacant foot of ground,
and covering the land like the locusts of the
East. Greenwich that day receives an accession of at least a hundred thousand living souls;
some trudging on foot, some riding in carts
and vans and waggons, some whirled by the

rapid steam-car, and others by the steam-boat, packed closely together with their wives and children, and all bent upon spending their earnings, or cheating other people of theirs. It is an animated but strange sight that the philosophic observer may behold, if he will station himself at any snug window on the line of road from London to the fair. Horses and donkeys are overladen by living loads, sweating and toiling along the dusty way in long procession, their drivers urging them to a speed that is impossible with such burdens, and cursing foul curses at the inevitable delay. Gigs, coaches, vans, coal-waggons, and even dust-carts, all come into use that day; and turnpike keepers reap a harvest sufficient to keep starvation from their doors for a twelve-month to come. Pedestrians numberless trudge on either side, while houses of entertainment yawn wide at every step; or booths, erected in the course of the night by the way-side, invite them to linger and expend a portion of their superfluity ere they arrive at the goal. It is no exaggeration to say, that the very road is alive with them. As the day advances to-wards the noon, they come in thicker shoals, denser and denser still, singing and laughing, and shouting and swearing, hundreds drunk,

and thousands more determined to become so;
while

> Draggle-tailed sluts and shirtless men,
> And young girls lewd and crazy,

launch forth their vulgar wit at every convenient opportunity upon their fellow way-
farers. Nor is the river a scene of less bustle.
Steam-boats bearing each one its cargo of five
or six hundred souls, arrive every five minutes
at the pier, and discharge them into the narrow
lanes and low public-houses of old Greenwich.
Wherries and barges are as heavily laden in proportion to their bulk; while the railway trains,
smoking and steaming like the post-chariot
of Satan, bring their human cargo by thousands at a time, to swell the mass. Then almost every house in Greenwich becomes a
shop; while at every door is stationed a "bar-
ker," to invite the crowd to partake of tea or
coffee or dinner. Those who bring their own
tea may purchase hot water and the use of
cups and a kettle; and those unprovided, may
supply all their wants either at a reasonable
or an extravagant rate, according to the style
of accommodation they are accustomed to.
The once quiet glades of the Park stream with
the unmannerly multitude; the deer, disturbed

by the din, fly to their securest retreats; while
abandoned women and blackguard men roll
down the One Tree Hill, amid the laughter of
idle boys, and the obscene jests of striplings
always more obscene than full-grown men.
Quieter parties are formed upon the grass,
and cloths are laid and corks fly under the
trees, while cold beef and bottled ale pass
rapidly round, eaten without plate or fork,
and drunk without the intervention of a glass.
But it is not by day that the uproar is at its
highest; it is at night that "the mirth and fun
grow fast and furious," and that the fair appears the very paradise of the vulgar.

Let any man who does not care for a
squeezing, or a tread upon his corn, put on his
oldest hat and coat, leave his watch behind
him, and all his money but half-a-crown, and
then venture into the throng, and he will see a
sight unparalleled in the world, and learn a little
of the rough jollity of the English populace.
He will at first be almost stunned by the con-
glomeration of noises that smite upon his ear;
the braying of unmelodious trumpets, the heat-
ing of loud kettle-drums, and still louder
gongs; the squeaking of wheezy fiddles, the
sonorous invitation of showmen, the "buy,
buy," of gingerbread venders; the shrieks, and

filthy talk of abandoned women ; the oaths of
abandoned men, and the roar of the ever-
moving multitude.   After the lapse of a little
time, when his ear has been accustomed to the
uproar, he will be able to separate the noises
into their several elements, and learn, that each
is the representation of some peculiar vice or
folly, all met to keep holiday together.   If he
have no appetite for shows ; no delight in looking at giants, dwarfs, learned pigs, pig-faced
ladies, painted cannibals, and children with six
toes upon each foot, let him turn into the
booth set apart for dancing or theatrical representations.   In the first he will just be able to
discover, amid dense clouds of tobacco-smoke,
hundreds of men and women, dancing like the
warlocks and witches at Alloway Kirk,—

> No cotillons bran-new frae France,
> But hornpipes, jigs, strathspeys, and reels,
> Wi' life and mettle in their heels,
> They reel, they set, they cross, they tumble ;—

the men smoking all the while ; and the women, leaving off at short intervals the hot exercise to regale themselves with deep draughts
of rum and gin, and some of them, when tired
of dancing, lending their sweet voices to swell
the harmony of the fiddlers, that set so many
heavy feet amoving.   When he has had enough

of the smoke and the odour of rum in these
pavilions of an old and frowsy Terpsichore,
let him enter the theatrical booth, and he will
sup full of horrors, in the first piece, and be
treated, in the second, with farce as broad as
the previous tragedy was deep.   Murders, rape,
incest, despair, suicide, and the gallows, will
be the staple of the first; practical jokes, jests
of venerable antiquity, and coarse as the audience, will form the staple of the second.
There sallow-faced mechanics, bluff peasants
and soldiers, and blear-eyed journeymen, stamped with the brand of dissipation, sit, for the
pleasant excitement of either, now and then
varying the entertainments by hurling ginger-
beer bottles at the heads of the performers, or
extinguishing the lights by well-aimed cab-
bages and potatoes.

And this is Greenwich-fair, the most famous
festival of the Londoners; the wonder of foreigners; an eye-sore to the magistracy and all
orderly people; but an evil which our short-
sighted legislation, in matters of popular recreation, augments, instead of diminishing.   Singing and dancing are forbidden all the year in
places where the populace resort; the Solons
of the quarter-sessions will not allow them to
hear music, or to dance, lest they should get

drunk, forgetting that they can become sottish without the exhilaration of either. They enclose common lands, and curb their amusements by every means, as if they were slaves, born to toil, and precluded by some law of nature from any refined enjoyments, and then they complain that once a year, upon occasion of a fair, their pent-up jollity explodes, and that they run riot, and commit all manner of excesses.

Several attempts have been made to suppress Greenwich-fair, but in vain. It still remains the noisiest and most disgraceful holiday of the London mob, and probably ever will remain so till our magistracy have a little more consideration for the amusements of the poor; and put a few more opportunities for recreation in their way; until the legislature takes up the question upon high and philosophical grounds, and provides such facilities for harmless and exhilarating sports for the many, as will withdraw them from the silent and sottish corners in low public-houses, where they sit almost every night, ready, whenever the period of their saturnalia arrives, to make up for the past privations of the year, by indulgences which harm themselves, and afford excuses to their local tyrants to draw still tighter, upon other occasions, the bonds that bind them.

Before leaving Greenwich, we should not omit to mention the Dreadnought, one of the most prominent objects that meets the rambler's eye on proceeding thither by water. This fine old man-of-war, now used as an hospital ship for seamen of all nations, and supported by the voluntary subscriptions of the charitable, was, in the days of his youth, a formidable enemy of the French and Spaniards; a worthy successor of the Dreadnought of old, which fought against the Spaniards in the time of Queen Elizabeth. In the glorious victory of Trafalgar he bore his part bravely; and under the command of Captain John Conn, he captured (we speak of him in the masculine, as a man-of-war) the large Spanish three-decker, the San Juan, which had been previously engaged by the Bellerophon and the Defiance. The San Juan surrendered, after a stout affray, in which her hull was greatly shattered, her masts cut away, her captain slain, and nearly three hundred of her men killed and wounded. The loss on board the Dreadnought was seven killed and twenty-two wounded. From being stationed for so many years past in the river, within so short a distance of the metropolis, the Dreadnought was well known to the multitudes of London, and afforded, even in her mastless condition, an accurate notion, to those who had never seen any other ship of war, of the floating bulwarks by which Great Britain is defended. In the summer of 1840 a leak was discovered in her hold (we may now promote her to the feminine gender, considering her as a nurse to the sick), which rendered her removal necessary, for a short period only, till her repairs were completed, and she was towed down to Sheerness for that purpose by three steam-boats, appointed for that special service, amid the cheers of a great multitude, who assembled to witness her departure. In a few days afterwards she was restored to her former moorings, where she now remains.

CHAPTER VI.

White Bait Dinners at Blackwall.—Assault on London by
Falconbridge.—The East India docks.—The River Lea.
—Reminiscences of Isaac Walton.—Poetics of Hoddes-
don.—Want's Inn at Broxbourne.—Theobalds.—A Good
Appetite; a Story of Henry VIII. and the Abbot of Wal-
tham.—Epping Forest.—The Bell at Edmonton.—The
Tournament of Tottenham.—True Philosophy at Totten-
ham Cross.—Stratford-le-Bow and Bromley.

URNING from Greenwich to
the opposite bank of the river,
we pass that considerable bend
which forms the Isle of Dogs,
and, on its eastern extremity,
see the hamlet of Blackwall, famous for its
shipping in the records of commerce, and for
its luscious white bait in the modern annals
of gastronomy. Hither, during the season, resort numerous aristocratic parties to regale
upon the peculiar delicacies of the place; hither resort Privy Councillors, Ministers of
State, and Under-secretaries, with whom of late
, years it has become quite fashionable to dine

at Blackwall.   So great a delicacy are these
tiny fish esteemed, that many persons consider
a white bait dinner to be the most elegant entertainment that an amphitryon can bestow.
They were long thought to be peculiar to the
Thames; but they have lately been discovered
in the Frith of Forth.   The chief taverns of
Blackwall are famous for, and mainly supported by them, where they are served up to the
guests at extravagant prices, a few minutes
after they are caught.

When the Bastard of Falconbride, as he was
called, made his attack upon London, during
the disastrous wars between the partisans of the
Red and White Roses, he was repulsed from
Southwark by the citizens, and driven to
Blackwall.   His object was to release Henry
VI, at that time captive in the Tower; and
having sent about one half of his forces from
Southwark to the meadows beyond Greenwich,
they transported themselves across the river in
boats and rafts to Blackwall.   From thence
they marched to London once more, and
stormed it at Aldgate, while Falconbridge
himself made a second attack upon London
Bridge.   Both assaults were unsuccessful.   The
Blackwall party, to the number of six-hundred,
forced an entrance into the city, and were cut

to pieces by the citizens, who immediately closed the gate, and suffered not one to escape alive. The remainder, who had not forced an entrance, were all taken prisoners. At London Bridge, the Bastard was repulsed with great loss, and retreated to Rotherhithe, with only two or three hundred men of all his host. Shortly afterwards he was captured by the Londoners, and beheaded, with nine of his companions, whose heads long remained upon the bridge, a terrible example to all beholders.

The stranger who visits Blackwall and its numerous canals and docks may exclaim with Dyer in his " Fleece,"

———————————— Here lofty Trade
Gives audience to the world—the strand around
Close swarms with busy crowds of many a realm :
What bales ! what wealth ! what industry ! what fleets !

It is the grand depôt of the East India trade. The docks were completed at the expense of the East India Company, and first opened for shipping in the year 1803. The import dock covers an area of about nineteen acres, and the export about twelve. Until lately every ounce of tea consumed in the United Kingdom, proceeded in the first place from this immense repository ; but since the breaking up of the monopoly of the East India Company, London

is no longer the only port for vessels engaged
in this gigantic traffic.   Here also is the most
extensive private ship-yard in Europe, belonging to Messrs. Wigram and Green.   When
these docks were dug in the year 1790, a discovery was made, which had geology been so
well understood as it is now, would have attracted the attention of most of the learned
men of the age.   A subterranean forest, or,
more properly speaking, the remains of one,
were found in a state of great preservation ;
not scattered in confusion, but lying in regular
order, and all the tops of the trees turned towards the south, in which direction they must
have been swept by some great convulsion of
nature—some sudden whirlwind, or some rushing of mighty waters from the north.

Close to Blackwall the river Lea discharges
itself into the Thames, "the Gulfy Lea, with
sedgy tresses" of Pope ; and " the wanton Lea
that oft doth lose his way" of Spenser ; the
most famous fishing stream in the neighbourhood of London, and suggesting at every step
upon its green banks some agreeable reminiscence of the gentle craft professed by Isaac
Walton.   A day's walk towards its source
from Bow to Hertford, is one of the plea-
santest excursions a contemplative man can

take—whether he be an angler or a mere peri-
patetic in search of health among the green
meadows and "breezy hills." It takes its rise
near Luton, in Bedfordshire, whence it flows
obliquely to Hertford and Ware, and then
passes close by Amwell, where the New River
that supplies London with water begins to run
almost parallel with it, and close by Hoddesdon, Broxbourne, Cheshunt, Waltham Abbey,
Enfield, Edmonton, Tottenham, Walthamstow,
and Bow. At Enfield the New River parts
company with it a little way, and taking a
bend to Southgate, flows on to Hornsey and
Canonbury, to the New River Head at Isling-
ton, where it is afterwards swallowed by the
million mouths of animated London. Let the
reader only imagine that we have reached Hertford, *per saltum,* and we will trace this pretty
stream downwards with him to its junction
with the Thames, and gossip as we go, after our
usual fashion, about the by-gone worthies who
dwelt beside it and fished in it; and of the
memorable events that may have signalized
each spot upon its banks.

Hertford was a place of some note in the
days when the Romans held possession of Britain, and afterwards became one of the principal
towns of the East Saxons. Alfred built a

castle to protect it from the Danes, who had more than once set fire to it, and plundered the people. After the Conquest, the place became a royal domain; and the castle for many hundred years was the occasional residence of the sovereigns of this country. A few, but very few traces of the structure are still said to exist; but in this respect we speak from hearsay only. There are several humble seminaries for education in and near the town, the most important of which is Haileybury College, on the road towards Hoddesdon, for the education of young persons intended for the civil service of the East India Company in India. In the town there is a branch school for the junior children of Christ's Hospital in London, and a free grammar school, having scholarships at the University of Cambridge.

Ware is also a town of considerable antiquity. It was founded in the reign of Edward the Confessor, and is mentioned in Domesday Book, under the name of Waras. In the times when England suffered from the invasion of the piratical Danes, they used often to sail up the Lea from Blackwall, as far as this place, where they erected a fort, from whence they made frequent sallies to ravage Hertford and the neighbouring country. In the year 1408, the Lea overflowed its banks, and swept away all the frail wooden and thatched tenements of which they were composed. After this calamity, when the town was rebuilt, dams and weirs were constructed in the river to guard against future inundations, from which weirs Camden supposes it took its name of Ware; but "the nourrice of antiquitie," so seldom wrong, was wrong in this instance, as a reference to Domesday Book will show. It is now a busy, comfortable, substantial-looking place, well attended by " brothers of the angle," who love the stream by which it stands, and think with reverence upon the name of old Walton, whenever they "stretch their legs over Tottenham Hill towards Ware upon a fine, fresh, May morning."

From Ware to Hoddesdon, the New River runs within a very short distance of the Lea. Hoddesdon is a small place, chiefly famous for a curious fountain that has long stood in the market-place, and alluded to by Prior in his ballad of Down Hall. Down Hall itself, whither the poet retired, after he was discharged from prison, at the close of the year 1717, is in this neighbourhood, standing upon one of the tributary rivulets that feed the Lea near Harlow, where Locke is buried. He was wearied of the ups and downs of politics, and, if we may believe him, found in his retirement more peace and happiness than he had ever known before; as he himself sings—

> The remnant of his days he safely past,
> Nor found they lagged too slow, nor flew too fast.
> He made his wish with his estate comply,
> Joyful to live, yet not afraid to die!

This was the true philosophic frame of mind, but he did not live long to encourage himself in it. His health failed him in his darling seclusion, and he died in 1721. Of Hoddesdon and its inn, the Bull, still existing to receive the traveller, Prior makes the following mention in his ballad of Down Hall, wherein he ludicrously details his adventures on going to take possession of the snug villa which the kindness of his patron Harley provided for his declining years.

> Into an old inn did their equipage roll,
> At a town they call Hoddesdon, the sign of the Bull,
> Near a nymph with an urn that divides the highway,
> And into a puddle throws mother of tea.
> > Down, down, Derry down.

> " Come here, my sweet landlady, pray, how d'ye do?
> Where is Cicely so cleanly, and Prudence and Sue?
> And where is the widow that dwelt here below?
> And the ostler that sung about eight years ago?
> > Down, down, Derry down.

" And where is your sister, so mild and so dear,
Whose voice to the maids like a trumpet was clear?"
" By my troth," she replies, " you grow younger, I think;
And pray, Sir, what wine does the gentleman drink?
Down, down, Derry down.

" Why, now let me die, Sir, or live upon trust,
If I know to which question to answer you first.
Why things since I saw you most strangely have varied,
The ostler is hang'd, and the widow is married.
Down, down, Derry down.

" And Prue left a child for the parish to nurse,
And Cicely went off with a gentleman's purse;
And as to my sister, so mild and so dear,
She has lain in the church-yard full many a year."
Down, down, Derry down.

" Well, peace to her ashes, what signifies grief?
She roasted red veal, and she powdered lean beef;
Full well she knew how to cook up a fine dish,
For tough were her pullets, and tender her fish."
Down, down, Derry down.

" For that matter, Sir, be ye squire, knight, or lord,
I 'll give you whate'er a good inn can afford.
I should look on myself as unhappily sped,
Did I yield to a sister or living or dead!"
Down, down, Derry down.

As ample,—it would be unkind to say, similar,
—accommodation is still to be found at this
ancient inn; which the traveller may perhaps
feel an additional motive for patronizing, when
he remembers that it ever boasted so illustrious

a guest as the author of the "Nut Brown
Maid," and if he finds better fare than Prior
did, so much the greater will be his satisfaction.
The Thatched Inn, another old hostelrie, alluded to by Walton, has disappeared, no one
knows how long ago. In the original edition
of the "Complete Angler," Piscator replies to
Venator, "that he knew the Thatched House
very well, for he often made it his resting-place
to taste a cup of ale there, for which liquor
that place was very remarkable." It has been
supposed, that a thatched cottage, once known
by the sign of the Buffalo's Head, at the further end of Hoddesdon, towards Ware, was
the house alluded to; but doctors differ upon
the subject, and there is no certain light to
guide the steps of the reverential angler.

The Rye-House, so called from its contiguity
to the house of the same name, famous in the
annals of Charles II, is the favourite resort of
the anglers of the present day.

The Rye-House, not the little inn of which
we have given the opposite view, but the old
edifice, tenanted in Charles II.'s time by Rumbold, the maltster, has a melancholy celebrity
in English history, and its name conjures up
affecting remembrances of the good lives, and
untimely deaths, of Russell and Sidney, the
martyrs of liberty. Rumbold the maltster, and

other weak or bad men, who were bound up in
one common discontent, with the wise and
good, against the misgovernment of Charles II.
and the intrigues of his brother James, were
no doubt concerned in a plot against the
King's life; but Sidney and Russell were
never proved to have taken part in it. The
house stood on the high road to Newmarket,
and Rumbold, the tenant, thought how easily
the King might be shot there on his way to
the races, whither he went once a year. " He
laid a plan of his farm before some of the
conspirators," says Hume, " and showed them
how easy it would be, by overturning a cart,
to stop at that place the King's coach; while
they might fire upon him from the hedges, and

be enabled afterwards, through by-lanes and across the fields, to make their escape. But, though the plausibility of this scheme gave great pleasure to the conspirators, no concerted design was as yet laid, nor any men, horses, or arms provided; the whole was little more than loose discourse, the overflowings of zeal and rancour."

Who needs to be informed how the trials of Russell and Sidney were conducted, and how a "sweet saint," in the person of a wife, sat by the side of the former, under the judgment-seat? Denied all aid in his defence, Lord Russell asked, " May I have somebody to write to assist my memory ?"—" Yes," replied the Attorney-General, " a servant." — " Yes," added the Judge, " any of your servants shall assist you in writing anything you please for you."—" My wife," replied Russell, with the pride of love ; " my wife is here, my Lord, to do it." " In vain," says Lord Grey, in his History of the Rye-House Plot, " did Lady Russell, the daughter of the loyal and virtuous Southampton, throw herself at the royal feet, and crave mercy for her husband ; in vain did the Earl of Bedford offer a hundred thousand pounds through the mediation of the all-prevailing Duchess of Portsmouth, for the life of his son. The King was inexorable. And, to put a stop to all further importunity, he said, in reply to the Earl of Dartmouth, ' I must have his life, or he will have mine.'—' My death,' said Russell, with a consolatory prescience, when he found his fate was inevitable, ' will be of more service to my country than my life could have been '" These, and other circumstances of the life and death of this statesman, and his fellow-martyr, Sidney, may be well known ; but we should pity the man who could tread within the precincts of the Rye-House, and, having known them, have forgotten them.

What London angler knows not the next place, Broxbourne, and its green meadows by the New River and the Lea? Who knows not " Want's Inn," and its quiet snug parlour, hung round with those scaly reminiscences of the river deeps, which the angler delighteth to get a nibble from, if he cannot catch? Ever since, and perhaps long before the days of Isaac Walton, Broxbourne has been a favourite resort of metropolitan anglers. It is a pleasant romantic spot, and deserves the preference that has been shown it, not only for its sport, but for its quiet sequestered scenery.

Still rambling down the banks of the river,

we arrive at Cheshunt, on the great Roman highway called Ermin Street. This village and manor were once possessed by John of Gaunt, no king himself, but father of a long line of English monarchs.

A bit of scandal is related of the nuns that resided here shortly before the dissolution of the religious houses. One Sir Henry Cole, of Nether Hall, as we learn from Fuller's History of Waltham Abbey, having received notice that some of the monks of Waltham were harboured in Cheshunt nunnery, pitched a buck-stall in the meadow, and inclosed them as they were returning in the dark from the convent. He brought them next morning to Henry VIII, at Waltham, who observed, " that he had often seen sweeter, but never fatter venison." Some minute critic has objected to this story, that there was no Sir Henry Cole of Nether Hall at this time. However that may be, the joke sits ill in the mouth of Henry, himself as amorous as uncleanly, and as fat as any of the offending monks could have been.

Cardinal Wolsey resided at Cheshunt for a short time, and a less illustrious, but, in the true sense of the term, a greater man than he, afterwards took up his abode in the same place, forsaking the world and its strife-begotten dignities, to live to a green old age, and die at last in peace. Richard Cromwell, the son of the Protector, " less than his sire, yet greater—not so happy, yet happier ;" peaceable, unambitious, and inoffensive, as historians have universally designated him, and unwilling to purchase dominion by the shedding of blood, he resigned his power without a murmur or a regret, and retired to the privacy of a country life. He travelled for some years on the Continent—smiled in his incognito, when the Prince of Conti designated him in his own hearing a pitiful fellow, and thought, no doubt, in his own mind, that he, the nameless individual, was the wiser man of the two; and finally retired to Cheshunt, where, under the name of Clark, he lived on a decent competence, to the age of eighty. He died in 1712, universally regretted by his neighbours. At Cheshunt is a College for the education of students intended for preachers of Methodist doctrines.

The next place deserving of notice is Theobalds, occupying the site of the ancient palace of that name, and now the seat of Sir Henry Meux. The old palace has long since disappeared. It was erected about the year 1559, by the celebrated Burleigh, to whom Queen Elizabeth paid no less than twelve visits at this place, putting him each time to an expense of between two and three thousand pounds. On the death of Burleigh, his son Robert, afterwards Earl of Salisbury, took possession of Theobalds, and gave a grand entertainment to King James on his journey from Scotland to assume the English crown.

In the year 1606 the Earl gave a second entertainment to the King, who was accompanied by Christian IV. of Denmark. James took a liking to the place, and prevailed upon the Earl to give it him in exchange for the manor and palace of Hatfield. He afterwards passed much of his time here; and it became his favourite residence. Hither he retired when, in a fit of virtuous indignation, he took the solemn oath, kneeling in the presence of the assembled judges, never to spare any one concerned in the abominable murder of Sir Thomas Overbury; the oath which he soon broke, when he found his favourite Somerset was so deeply implicated. His perjury would seem, indeed, in the words of his own imprecation, to have brought down " God's curse upon him and his posterity for ever." James died in this palace, according to some accounts, of an ague, but not without suspicion of poison administered by order of his favourite Buckingham; a suspicion which the entertaining author of the Curiosities of Literature has striven, very successfully, to show was without foundation. The room in which the King expired used to be shown to the curious until the year 1765, when the remains of the old building were pulled down.

Charles I. occasionally resided at Theobalds; and there received the famous petition from Parliament, in the year 1642. Upon the temporary abolition of royalty, the palace, along with many others, was ordered to be sold. Great part of it was taken down; and the sum produced by the sale of the materials applied to the uses of the army. The small remnant of it, with the lands adjoining, was granted as a reward to General Monk, but, on the failure of his male lineage, it again reverted to the crown. It was granted by William III. to his countryman, Bentinck Earl of Portland, from whom, after various changes, it came into the possession of Mr. Prescott, who pulled down the remains of it in 1765, as already stated, and erected the present edifice upon its site.

On the left hand, journeying downwards between the two rivers, the natural and the artificial, we arrive at the ancient town of Waltham Abbey in Essex, the seat and burial-

place of the last monarch of England of the
Saxon line   From Waltham Abbey, Harold
proceeded to take arms against the Norman
invader of his realm, and lost his empire and
his life at the field of Hastings.   Here his
corpse was buried, and the tomb inscribed with
the simple and touching words, " *Harold infe-
lix.*"   The name of this time-honoured place is
derived from two Saxon words, signifying the
town in the forest, and the addition of Holy
Cross, by which it is sometimes distinguished,
had its origin in a cross bestowed upon it by
Tovius, a Dane, standard-bearer to King Canute, which was supposed to cure all the diseases of the faithful, and work many miracles.

The monks of Waltham Abbey were long a
rich and powerful body, and received constant
favours and benefactions from most of the
early monarchs of England.   Henry III, who
was generally in distress for money, sometimes
found it convenient to bestow upon these hospitable monks the honour of his company for a
month or so at a time.   To enable them and
the inhabitants of the town the better to bear
the burden, he granted the latter the privilege
of a weekly market and an annual fair of seven
days.   The abbots had the privilege of wearing
the mitre, and of taking their place among the

Barons in Parliament. The revenues of the abbey amounted, in the time of Henry VIII. to nearly a thousand pounds per annum.

Of the last-mentioned King and the monks, a pleasant story is told, perhaps apocryphal, but as a tradition worth preserving. Henry often visited Waltham, as historians inform us, for "his private pleasures," and to see some fair wench in the neighbourhood, whose name has been forgotten. But the tradition does not relate to his amours, but to his love of frolic. As the song says —

> Old King Harry was fond of canary,
>   Fond of good victuals and sack was he;
> But more than canary did old King Harry
>   Love a sly joke, with his hey derry dee!
>   Hey, down! ho, down! derry down dee!

Having heard much of the sumptuous style of living of the abbot, even upon ordinary occasions, when no distinguished guest was expected, Henry disguised himself in the dress of a yeoman of the guard, and sought admittance at the hour of dinner. He was allowed to enter, and take his place at the lower end of the table, where he ate so very heartily of beef and cabbage, and drank so plentifully of sack, as to attract the notice of the abbot at the other end. " Gramercy!" quoth

the abbot, " but thou hast a famous appetite. I would give a hundred pounds if I
could eat such a dinner of beef as thou canst.
My poor queasy stomach can hardly digest the
breast of a chicken." A few days afterwards
the pursy old abbot received a message from
the King, requesting his immediate presence in
London. The abbot obeyed; and was forthwith committed to close custody in the Tower,
where bread and water, and not much of either,
constituted his only fare for several days.
When he had fasted sufficiently, a sirloin of
beef, with a flagon of sack, were placed before
him; on both of which he made inroads which
would not have disgraced a farm-labourer in
the vigour of youth and health, and was just
finishing his meal, when the Majesty of England, in his own character, burst into the apartment, and demanded the hundred pounds for
the good appetite, and the dinner to stay it,
which he had given him. The story adds, that
the abbot was glad enough at so pleasant a
termination to his unpleasant imprisonment,
and that he paid the hundred pounds without
a murmur.

The remaining portion of this old abbey,
now used as the parish church, has a venerable
and interesting appearance, and abounds with

quaint and curious architectural antiquities. The abbey lands, on the dissolution of the religious houses, were granted by Henry VIII. to Sir Anthony Denny, on a lease for thirty-one years, renewable at the King's will. This family long possessed them; and there is a remarkable monument still existing, to the memory of one of them, erected by his wife, Jeanne Champernon, "out of mean fortunes, but no mean affection." It is a mural monument, near the east end of the south aisle, and represents Sir Edward Denny, son of the Sir Anthony above alluded to, in his plate armour, lying on his side, with his lady beside him in her ruff and bodice, and their ten children, four boys and six girls, kneeling in front. Inscribed are the following lines :—

> Learn, curious reader, ere thou pass,
> What once Sir Edward Denny was :
> A courtier of the chamber,
> A soldier of the fielde ;
> Whose tongue could never flatter !
> Whose heart could never yielde !

The river Lea, which here forms the boundary between Hertfordshire and Essex, separates itself into several streams, and forms a number of small islands. It is believed, that the river originally flowed in one stream only.

It is well known that King Alfred diverted it from its accustomed channel, and by that means left the piratical fleet of the Danes ashore on the green meadows between Ware and Waltham ; and the tradition is, that it was never afterwards diverted again into its proper bed, but allowed to wander in divided currents, as we now behold it.

The neighbourhood of Waltham Abbey, especially on the Essex side, is extremely beautiful. There lies the hoary forest of Epping, or the remains of that once secluded, and extensive wildwood. It once took its name from Waltham, but as the distance between that town and its outskirts was gradually increased by the forest-felling hatchet, it borrowed a name from a town more immediately in its thick recesses, and called itself Epping. Henry III. granted a privilege, in 1226, to the citizens, to hunt once a year at Easter, within a circuit of twenty miles of their city. This privilege in the course of time was, by degrees, abandoned, until their hunting restricted itself to Epping and Hainault Forests, whither, until very recently, the citizens proceeded at Easter to hunt a stag, turned out for their diversion. Many are the shafts that ridicule has aimed at them, in consequence, from Tom Durfey, in his " Pills to purge Melancholy," to Tom Hood, who, though he does not give such a medicinal name to his books, sells pills more effective in purging melancholy than Tom Durfey or any of his predecessors.

On the Hertfordshire side of the Lea is the village of Waltham Cross, celebrated for, and named after the cross, which the affectionate Edward I. raised to the memory of his dearly beloved Queen Eleanor. She died in Lincolnshire; and at every place where the funeral procession stopped, on its way to London, the King erected a cross. Only three of them are now remaining, namely, those at Geddington, Northampton, and Waltham. That at Waltham was originally a very beautiful structure, but time, the great enemy, has made sad havoc on its fair proportions, defaced its effigies, and eaten into the very heart of its sculptured heraldry. Charing Cross, another of these loving memorials of conjugal truth, disappeared in the tumults of the Revolution; and the bronze image of the chief victim of that revolution now stands upon its site.

Continuing our course down the stream, and keeping as closely as possible to the Lea, we leave Enfield and its celebrated Chace on our right hand, and after a pleasant walk, arrive at Edmonton, once noted for its fair, and famous for ever in the adventures of John Gilpin. The Bell Inn still courts the company of the traveller, where

> Gilpin's loving wife
> From the balcony spied
> Her tender husband; wondering much
> To see how he did ride !

and where, after he had been carried so sorely against his will to Ware, and back again, his wife still stood, and pulled out half-a-crown, as a reward to the postboy if he overtook him.

The youth did ride, and soon did meet
   John coming back amain !
Whom in a trice he tried to stop
   By catching at the rein.

But not performing what he meant,
   And gladly would have done,
The frightened steed he frightened more,
   And made him faster run !

Away went Gilpin, and away
   Went postboy at his heels !

And such a ride as was seen that day was never seen since Turpin rode to York, or since Mazeppa was carried into the deserts on his wild horse. Edmonton is now a busy, populous place, but contains little to arrest the progress of the rambler. If he be a lover of literature, however, he will remember that Charles Lamb died in the village, on the 27th of December 1834, and will stay to visit the churchyard, and read his epitaph, written by the Rev. H. F. Carey, the translator of Dante :—

Farewell, dear friend !   That smile, that harmless mirth,
No more shall gladden our domestic hearth ;
That rising tear, with pain forbid to flow,
Better than words, no more assuage our woe ;
That hand outstretched from small, but well-earned store,
Yield succour to the destitute no more !
   Yet art thou not all lost : through many an age,
With sterling sense and humour, shall thy page

Win many an English bosom, pleased to see
That old and happier vein revived in thee;
This for our earth; and if with friends we share
Our joys in heaven, we hope to meet thee there.

The next remarkable place on the banks
of the Lea is Tottenham, renowned in face-
tious poetry for its famous tournament in the
bygone days, when these sights were as fashionable as Lord Eglintoun, the Marquis of
Londonderry, and the Queen of Beauty have
desired to make them since. Who can enter
this village without a pleasing emotion, as he
remembers the quaint old ballad that celebrates it, and its rustic beauty, and its flail-
armed heroes. It is related of the French
soldiers who invaded Spain, committing all
manner of excesses, that they became sobered
down as they entered the city of Tobosa, and
forbore to indulge in any outrage upon the
spot so familiar to them as the birth-place
of the fair Dulcinea, for whose charms the
immortal Don Quixote waged fierce warfare
against all the world. Why should not we,
who lay claim to more refinement than a French
trooper, indulge in similar feelings at Tottenham, when we remember the lovely Tyb? It
is not precisely known when the old ballad
was written, but it was first published in 1631,

and its editor, the Rev. Mr. Bedwell, rector of Tottenham, supposed it to have been the composition of one Gilbert Pilkington, his predecessor in office, so early as the reign of Edward III. It is a pity that its uncouth spelling and obsolete words are so very uncouth and obsolete as to render it " caviare to the million," who are ignorant in consequence,

> Of Hawkin and Herry,
> Of Tomkyn and Terry,
> And them that were doughty and stalwart in deed,

upon that memorable high day in Tottenham, when, for the love of that bright rustic damsel, the daughter of Randal the Reeve, Hawkyn, Dawkyn, Perkyn, Tomkyn, Terry, Dudman, Bud, and the rest,

> Sowed them in sheepskins for they should not brast,
> Each one took a black hat instead of a crest,
> A basket or a panier before on their breast,
> And a flail in their hand, for to fight prest,
>   Forth 'gan they fare.
>   There was shown mickle force
>   Who should best fend his course ;
>   He that had no good horse,
>   He gat him a mare !

> Such another gathering have I not seen oft,
> When all the great company came riding to the croft ;
> Tybbie, on a grey mare, was set up aloft,
> On a sack full of feathers, that she might sit soft.

Then, as Bishop Percy says, did this parcel of clowns imitate all the solemnities of the tourney. There were the regular challenge, the appointed day, the lady for the prize, the formal preparations, the display of armour, the escutcheons and devices, the oaths taken on entering the lists, and last of all, the grand encounter ; at which

> They tuggéd and ruggéd till it was near night ;
> And all the wives of Tottenham came to see the sight ;
> With wisps, and candles, and rushes, there alight,
> To fetch home their husbands that were in woful plight.
>   And some brought great harrows
>   Their husbands home to fetch ;
>   Some on doors, and some on hech,
>   Some on hurdles, and some on crech,
>   And some on wheel-barrows.

At last the great **Perkyn** vanquished his opponents, and **Tybbie**, glorious prize, became incontestably his own.

> He took her with great mirth, and homeward did they ride,
> And were all night together till the morning tide.

As the date of this composition is uncertain, we cannot know what effect the ridicule thrown by the author upon the fashionable tournaments had upon the public opinion with regard to them. Bedwell, its editor, and one of the translators of King James's Bible, and author also of a history of this parish, lies buried in the churchyard of Tottenham. A simple stone, with a simple inscription, marks the spot.

This village takes the name of Tottenham High Cross from a cross which has stood there from time immemorial, and which many persons suppose was erected by King Edward, like that at Waltham, to mark the spot where the corpse of his beloved queen rested on its way to London. The opinion, however, is disputed. What reader of Izaac Walton, be he angler, or be he not, that does not remember the philosophic conversation that took place here, between the fisherman and the hunter? " Well, scholar," says Piscator, " I have almost tired myself, and, I fear, more than almost tired you : but I now see Tottenham High Cross, and our short walk thither shall put a period to my too long discourse ; in which my meaning was, and is, to plant that in your mind, with which I labour to possess my own soul, that is, a meek and thankful heart. And to that end, I have showed you that riches, without it, do not make any man happy. But let me tell you, that riches with them, remove many cares and fears, and therefore my advice is, that you endeavour to be honestly rich, or contentedly poor ; but be sure that your riches be justly got, or you spoil all. For it is well said by Caussin—' He that loses his conscience has nothing left that is worth keeping.' Therefore be sure you look to that. And, in the next place, look to your health; and if you have it, praise God, and value it next to a good conscience; for health is the second blessing that we mortals are capable of; a blessing that money cannot buy, and therefore value it, and be thankful for it. As for money, which may be said to be the third blessing, neglect it not: but note, that there is no necessity for being rich; for I told you, there be as many miseries beyond riches as on this side them; and, if you have a competence, enjoy it with a meek, cheerful, thankful heart. I will tell you, scholar, I have heard a grave divine say, that God has two dwellings, one in heaven, and the other in a meek and thankful heart; which Almighty God grant to me and to my honest scholar. And so you are welcome to Tottenham High Cross."

"Honest Izaac!" is a phrase that has fallen into disrepute, but we will say, Honest Izaac Walton! and leave Tottenham, with his quaint and pleasant lesson of life still lingering in our mind, and continue our stroll down the banks of his favourite river.

A little lower, on its other bank, are Walthamstow in Essex, swarming with tasteful and comfortable villas, and Leyton, the "town upon the Lea," which some antiquaries affirm to have been a Roman station. Many Roman urns have been found amid the clay of the churchyard, and on the side of a lane leading to Stratford-le-Bow. The upper part of the town is called Leytonstone, from a Roman milliarium that formerly stood there. In the churchyard are buried Strype, the well-known antiquary, the vicar of the parish, who held that office for sixty-eight years, and died here at the patriarchal age of ninety-four; and another antiquary, as well known, Bowyer, the learned printer, and partner of John Nicholls, the author of that very interesting work, "The Progresses of Queen Elizabeth."

Passing by Clapton, Homerton, and Hackney, once suburbs, but now component parts of the mighty metropolis, the Lea arrives at the ancient village of Bow, or Stratford-le-Bow, with its quiet, sedate, venerable-looking church, originally built in the reign of Henry II. The old bridge over the Lea, lately replaced by a more elegant modern structure, was long a delightful object to the eyes of the antiquary. It was built by Margaret, the benevolent queen of Henry I, to whom London and its vicinity were indebted for many other good works. She also built the bridge at Channel Lea, and bestowed a considerable sum for making and repairing the road between the two. Bow Bridge long enjoyed the distinction of being the oldest stone bridge in England, and from its curved form, acquired the name, which was afterwards extended to the village beside it. London Bridge was not built of stone till about one hundred years afterwards.

Bromley-le-Bow, named from the same bridge, is the last of the pleasant villages that ornament the Lea, which is then lost amid the ship-yards, manufactories, and long straggling outskirts of the shipping districts of the metropolis. Divided into several branches, aided by canals, polluted by gasworks, and other useful but unfragrant factories, it loses its character of a retired and rural stream. Its very name is taken from it at the end of its useful career, and it unites itself with the Thames, neglected and unhonoured, under the name of Bow Creek.

CHAPTER VII.

Shooter's Hill; its Robberies and Murders. — Henry VIII. and his May Games. — Charlton. — Horn Fair. — King John and the Miller's Wife. — Woolwich. — The Dock. yard. — Wonders of the Royal Arsenal.

NCE more upon the Thames, we see the woody eminence of Shooter's Hill, castle-crowned, rising boldly to the right, and remaining visible for many miles, the most beautiful and most prominent object in the view. It was once in contemplation to build a town upon its summit, and a finer site could not have been selected either for pleasure or traffic. The lovely views it would have commanded up and down the Thames, northward over Essex, and Southward over the green vales of Kent, recommended it for the first, and its situation on the great Dover Road, would have made it very advantageous for the second. The project how-

ever fell to the ground for want of encouragement.

Early in the sixteenth century a beacon was
erected on the hill, to aid the navigation of the
river, and a watch was appointed to guard
the hill itself, which had from a very early age
been notorious as the resort of highwaymen.
Travellers were constantly robbed and murdered
in its thickets; and in the reign of Richard II.
orders were issued that the trees and under-
wood on each side of the road should be cut
down, in order that they might not afford
shelter to the freebooters. But still the place
preserved its bad name, and in an old play
of the time of Elizabeth, it is called the Hill
of Murder. This name, however, was probably
bestowed upon it, not so much for its assassin-
ations committed by freebooters, as for a
murder which had a love story for its foundation, and which excited much interest in the
year 1573. One George Browne, enamoured
of Mrs. Sanders, the wife of a wealthy merchant of London, determined to kill the husband that he might enjoy the wife; and being
encouraged by the latter, and by another woman named Drury, he lay in wait for him
on Shooter's Hill, where it was expected he
would pass, on his return to London from

St. Mary's Cray. The merchant, accompanied
by his servant, passed the fatal hill at the expected time, and Browne, aided by a fellow
named Roger Clements, or "trusty Roger," as
the confederates called him, set upon them
with daggers, and left them both apparently
lifeless in the thicket. The poor merchant
never breathed again; but his servant, though
pierced with eleven wounds, revived a little
in the freshness of the morning, and crawled
to the nearest house on the road to Woolwich,
where he gave information of his master's murder. All the accomplices were shortly afterwards arrested. The two women and "trusty
Roger" were hanged at Smithfield, and Browne
on a high gallows erected on the spot where
his crime had been committed. The bad character of Shooter's Hill clung to it, and deserv-
edly, long after the time of Elizabeth. In the
reign of James I. it was said of the numerous
thieves by whom Kent was infested, that they
robbed at Shooter's Hill as if by prescription.
No great improvement took place until the
year 1739, when an act of Parliament was
passed to widen the road over the hill. It is
still a lonely spot, where thieves might find
convenient shelter.

But the history of Shooter's Hill is not

wholly composed of incidents of robbery and murder. Many of its associations are of a pleasanter character. Hither came the princes of the House of Tudor and all their court "a-maying;" and here for a time resided the rural poet Bloomfield. Hollinshed, and after him Strutt, have described the May festival of Henry VIII, in the days of his hot youth, upon the hill. The plan of the games was devised by the officers of his guards, who, to the number of two hundred, clothed all in Lincoln green, like Robin Hood and his men of old, waited for him at the bottom of the ascent. The captain of the guard played the part of Robin Hood, and had his Little John, his Friar Tuck, and his Maid Marian, all in their appropriate costume. The King, riding from Greenwich with his Queen Catharine of Arragon, and a brilliant assemblage of the handsomest youths and maidens of his court, was accosted by Robin Hood, who begged permission to show him the skill of his followers in archery. Permission having been granted, the sports commenced, and the foresters drew the cloth-yard shaft, and shot their arrows thick and strong, until the King had seen enough. Robin Hood then invited him to come into the merry green wood, and see how the hunters fared; when the King and Queen were led into an arbour in the middle of the thicket, all made of green boughs, and containing a hall, an ante-chamber, and a large saloon, hung round with festoons of flowers and various emblems of the sweet month of May. Excuses having been made that hunters generally breakfasted upon venison, the only meat they could get, the King and Queen, with their attendants, to the number of about a hundred, sat down to a bountiful supply of that viand, and brown bread, accompanied by large flagons of sack and canary. After the entertainment, another show was provided for their gratification on their return to Greenwich. Upon the heath the cavalcade met two splendid chariots, each drawn by five richly caparisoned horses. One chariot contained the " Lady of the May," and the other the goddess Flora, who both made some highly complimentary speeches to the King, and dropped roses and lilies upon his path. Each horse had its name inscribed upon its forehead, and a fair young girl riding upon its back. The name of the first horse was *Laud,* or *Praise,* and of its rider, *Humidity;* of the second, *Memnon,* and of its rider, the *Lady Vert;* on the third, called *Phaeton,* sat the *Lady Vegitive;* on the fourth, called *Rimphon*, sat the *Lady Plaisaunce;* and on the fifth, called *Lampace*, rode the " *Lady of the sweet spring odours.*"   These all turned back with the King, playing upon the lute, and singing pastoral songs until they arrived at Greenwich.

The castle of Severndroog, upon the summit of Shooter's Hill, was erected in the year 1784;

A far seen monumental tower,
To tell th' achievements of the brave,

as Bloomfield expresses it.   A broad tablet of stone over the entrance, narrates its history in the following inscription :—" This building was erected in the year 1784, by the representative of the late Sir William James, Bart. to commemorate that gallant officer's achievements in the East Indies, during his command of the Company's maritime forces in those seàs; and in a particular manner to record the conquest of the castle of Severndroog on the coast of Malabar, which fell to his superior valour and able conduct, on the 2nd day of April, 1755."

The castle of Severndroog belonged to a noted horde of robbers and pirates on the coast of Malabar, under the command of a powerful chief named Angria, who, with his predecessors, had long troubled the English commerce in those seas, and forced the East India Company to keep up a force to check them and protect the traffic at an annual expense of fifty thousand pounds. Sir William, then Commodore James, was placed at the head of the maritime expedition in the year above-mentioned, and reduced the stronghold of the pirates which had long been considered impregnable. The poet Bloomfield when he resided on Shooter's Hill for the benefit of his health, was much pleased with this castle and its neighbouring heaths and woods, and has left in his poems a record of his thoughts and feelings. "Thus," said that simple and unfortunate bard,

> To hide me from the public eye,
>   To keep the throne of Reason clear,
> Amidst fresh air to breathe or die,
>   I took my staff and wander'd here.
> Suppressing every sigh that heaves,
>   And coveting no wealth but thee,
> I nestle in the honey'd leaves,
>   And hug my stolen liberty.
>
> O'er eastern uplands gay or rude,
>   Along to Erith's ivy'd spire,
> I start, with strength and hope renew'd,
>   And cherish life's rekindling fire;
> Now measure vales with streaming eyes,
>   Now trace the churchyard's humble names,
> Or climb brown heaths abrupt that rise,
>   And overlook the winding Thames.

Nearer to the bank of the river than Shooter's
Hill, and about a mile before we arrive opposite
that eminence, stands the pretty rural village
of Charlton, with its simple church upon a
hill; its antique stocks, where criminal seldom
or never sits; its little old-fashioned inns, with
their sign boards creaking in the wind; and
its comfortable baronial mansion and park,
where the rooks keep up a dignified cawing
the live long summer's day. The manor-house,
now the residence of Sir Thomas Maryon Wil-
son, was built by Sir Adam Newton, precep-
tor to Prince Henry, in the reign of James
I. It was long called King John's palace, by
the country people, who confounded it with the
old palace at Eltham in the vicinity, which
now goes by that name, but which was not
itself in existence in King John's day. The
Charlton people, however, cling to King John,
and insist that their celebrated Horn Fair, held
annually on the 18th of October, was established by that monarch. Lysons in his " Environs
of London," mentions it as a vague and idle
tradition—and such, perhaps it is; but, as we
are of opinion that the traditions of the people
are always worth preserving, we will repeat
the legend, and let the reader value it at its
proper worth. King John, says the old story,
being wearied with hunting on Shooter's Hill

and Blackheath, entered the house of a miller at Charlton to repose himself. He found no one at home but the mistress, who was young and beautiful; and being himself a strapping fellow, handsome withal, and with a glosing tongue, he, in a very short time, or as we would say in the present age, in no time, made an impression upon her too susceptible heart. He had just ventured to give the first kiss upon her ripe lips, when the miller opportunely came home and caught them. Being a violent man, and feeling himself wounded in the sorest part, he drew his dagger, and rushing at the King, swore he would kill them both. The poet of all time hath said, " that a divinity doth hedge a king," but the miller of Charlton thought such proceedings anything but divine, and would no doubt have sent him unannealed into the other world, if John had not disclosed his rank. His divinity then became apparent, and the miller putting up his weapon, begged that at least he would make him some amends for the wrong he had done him. The King consented, upon condition also that he would forgive his wife, and bestowed upon him all the land visible from Charlton to that bend of the river beyond Rotherhithe where the pair of horns are now fixed upon the pole. He also gave him, as lord of the manor, the privilege of an annual fair on the 18th of October, the day when this occurrence took place. His envious compeers, unwilling that the fame of this event should die, gave the awkward name of Cuckold's Point to the river boundary of his property, and called the fair, Horn Fair, which it has borne ever since.

But olden records, more trustworthy than traditions, inform us that the fair was established by Henry III. in the year 1268. How long it has borne the name of Horn Fair is not known. Phillipot, who wrote in the year 1659, says, it was called Horn Fair in his day, on account of the great plenty of winding-horns, cups, spoons, and various utensils made of that material, that were sold in it. A burlesque procession used formerly to be made at Deptford, which passed through Greenwich to Charlton, each person wearing a pair of branching antlers upon his head, and thinking himself privileged for that day to play all sorts of indecent tricks upon the women. This was at length found such an intolerable nuisance, that it was suppressed in the year 1768.

The church of Charlton was repaired and beautified at a considerable expense, by the executors of Sir Adam Newton, out of funds

left by him for this purpose. Among the monuments is one to the memory of Mr. Craggs
the elder, so famous in his day for his participation in the South Sea scheme, and to whose
son, Secretary of State in 1720, and also implicated in South Sea transactions, Pope wrote
one of his poetical epistles. Hanging Wood,
between the churchyard and the Thames, is a
sequestered spot of woodland, affording many
fine views of the river, and the opposite shores
of Essex.

Woolwich, the next place that solicits attention on the banks of the river, raises its giant
cranes and its huge dock-houses, to proclaim
its character, and make it evident to the stranger
at the first glance. This busy and populous
town first rose into importance in the reign of
Henry VII. when its dockyard, afterwards
called, by Camden, the mother dock of England, was first established, but in what year
is uncertain. In the third year of Henry VIII.
a great ship, the greatest until that time seen
in England, was launched from Woolwich
Dock, and called the " Harry Grace de Dieu."
In the reign of Elizabeth, another large vessel,
which also bore the royal name, was launched
from the same place, the Queen honouring the
ceremony with her presence. Before this time

Woolwich was but a little fishing-village, liable
from its low situation, to frequent inundations
of the river. The lower part of the town is
still dirty and miserable; but on the common
and the heights towards Shooter's Hill, is clean,
well built, and agreeable. It is a common
saying of the people at Woolwich, that more
wealth passes through their parish than through
any other in the kingdom, which is explained
by the fact, that the parish comprises a considerable portion of land on the other side of
the river, and that consequently the Thames,
and all the multitude of vessels bound to the
port of London, pass through it.

Woolwich is chiefly famous for its dock, its arsenal, and its barracks. In time of war, like its rival at Deptford, the dock is a scene of great activity and bustle; but little is done in time of peace. There are generally, however, two or three ships of war upon the stocks, affording employment to several hundred workmen. The arsenal, the grand depot of military stores for England, and the foundry of its cannon, is an establishment more remarkable. The circumstances that led to its foundation are also extremely interesting.

Until 1716, the chief foundry of the ordnance, was at Moorfields, London. In that year it was determined to recast several heavy pieces of artillery, which had been taken from the French by the Duke of Marlborough. A public exhibition of the process was announced; scaffolding, for the accommodation of great numbers of people, was erected, and, on the appointed morning, crowds of ladies and gentlemen had assembled. Among other persons attracted to see the sight, was a young Swiss, named Andrew Schalch, a native of Schaffhausen, who was travelling in England, in conformity to a law of his canton, which obliges all artificers to visit foreign countries for instruction and improvement before they

establish themselves in their own.   He was on
the ground from an early hour in the morning, and soon discovered that the moulds in
which the cannon were to be cast, were not
sufficiently dry.   He saw the danger, and immediately sought Colonel Armstrong, the Sur-
veyor-general of the Ordnance, whom he warn-
ed of the terrible explosion that might ensue
if the fault were not remedied.   His warning
was disregarded; so telling all his friends to
leave the place, he took his departure.   His
prediction was but too fatally verified.   The
heated metal poured into the damp moulds, ge-
nerated a quantity of steam: the moulds burst,
and the burning iron flew about in all directions, tearing down the roof and galleries, and
killing many people, and maiming many more.

Upon the news of this calamity reaching
the government, George I. resolved that the
foundry should be removed to a distance from
London.   Colonel Armstrong, when it was too
late, remembered the warning of the stranger,
and determined at the same time to secure the
future services of a man who had so intimate
a knowledge of his profession.   Not knowing
his name, or where to find him, he caused an
advertisement to be inserted in the public jour-
nals, mentioning the circumstances of their in-

terview at Moorfields, and desiring the stranger to call at the Ordnance Office, in the Tower of London. Schalch saw the advertisement, and called accordingly. So favourable an impression of his ability was made upon the Colonel's mind by this interview, that he was commissioned by the Board of Ordnance, to make choice of a spot in the neighbourhood of London, where a national foundry might be most conveniently established, and promised, at the same time, the honourable office of superintendent.

Schalch made his survey, and finally fixed on a plot of ground to the east of Woolwich, then known as the Rabbit Warren. The site was approved,—proper buildings were immediately constructed, and increased from time to time, as circumstances required, and the present noble arsenal is the result. Schalch held the office of superintendent for sixty years, and died in 1776, at the advanced age of ninety. This establishment continued to be called by its old name of the Warren for many years, until it was visited by George III, who gave it the more befitting appellation of the Royal Arsenal. Many people in Woolwich, however, so inveterate is habit, persist in calling it by its old name.

The King of Brobdignag, when Gulliver explained to him the nature and the uses of gunpowder, exclaimed in the extremity of his wonder, what 'a destructive and ferocious little animal man was. Who would not confess the truth and justice of the satire, after a visit to this arsenal, where cannon balls piled up in pyramids are to be counted, not by thousands or tens of thousands, but actually by millions! In the centre of an extensive area are arranged guns, howitzers, and mortars, in long and imposing rows. Though at peace with all the world, we are ready for war at a minute's notice, and at Woolwich alone are laid up, fit for use, no less than twenty-four thousand pieces of ordnance, twenty-one thousand of them made of cast iron, and about three thousand of gun metal, the largest weighing ninety hundred weight, and the smallest about two and a half hundred weight, forming altogether two hundred and two separate assortments, into which they are divided by the length of the piece, or the width of the bore. The cannon balls, weighing from two pounds to thirty-six, are piled in tremendous pyramids to the number of three millions, each one only awaiting the impulse to fly through the air, laden with death and destruction. The labour of piling them,

which is very great, is performed by convicts,
with weights upon their legs, and who are
stationed in the hulks, moored off Woolwich for
the purpose. When the allied Sovereigns visited England after the peace in 1814, they
agreed that of all the wondrous sights they had
seen in England, these implements of warfare
were the most wondrous; and the Emperor
Alexander had his doubts at first whether
these piles of iron balls were not wood, painted
iron-grey, to deceive him into a false idea of
our immense resources.

The process of casting the cannon at the
Arsenal is curious. The mould, which is a
mixture of clay, loam, sand, and other materials, having been prepared of the requisite size,
and secured by strong iron hoops, is heated to
a red heat, in order to avoid all danger of any
latent humidity, which might cause an explosion like that predicted by Schalch. It is then
placed in the earth before the furnace, and the
liquid iron is poured into it. The gun is thus
cast in one solid piece. The next processes
are those of turning the exterior and making
the bore, which are both performed at the same
time by one machine. A large bit, of the requisite diameter, is firmly fixed, against which
the solid gun is made to revolve, cutting away

the metal in flakes until the bore is excavated, while the implement for turning revolves at the same time, and completes the outer surface. The touch-hole is then drilled, and the gun is finished. It then remains to be seen whether it is trustworthy and fit for service, for which purpose it is carefully examined with magnifying glasses, in every part, its interior reflected upon mirrors, and its relative proportions tested with mathematical accuracy. If any imperfection is discovered, the piece is at once condemned to the foundry again ; but, if all seems perfect, the last grand test is resorted to ; the gun is loaded and fired. If there is a flaw in it, it bursts to pieces. If not, it comes from the ordeal triumphant, and becomes from that day forth one of the recognised thunderers that guard the British Empire.

The arsenal is divided into five departments : the royal carriage department, the inspector of artillery, the laboratory, the engineers, and the storekeeper's. To the first appertains the construction of all military carriages, ammunition waggons, forge waggons, carts for small ordnance, and the building and repairing of every kind of carriage connected with military or naval artillery. The second department receives all artillery cannon, muskets, rifles, pistols, to prove and examine them, and keep them always in such condition as to be fit for immediate service. In the third department, are made all cartridges, and rockets for war, and all descriptions of fireworks for days of national rejoicing, or in honour of royal visits. The manufacture of Congreve rockets, which for greater security is carried on in separate buildings near the bank of the river, is also under the superintendence of the officers of this department. The fourth, or engineer's department, constructs and repairs all the works and buildings of the Board of Ordnance. And the fifth, has the charge of all the miscellaneous stores, used in military or naval warfare. Over each department is an officer, supreme in his own sphere, and responsible only to the Board of Ordnance, by whom he is appointed. In the storehouses of the last department there are generally kept complete outfittings for ten thousand horse, as well as swords and muskets, and every kind of accoutrement for their riders. Here also are kept various implements of war, such as pikes for seamen when boarding a vessel, grappling irons, anvils, hatchets, spades for mining, &c.; the whole arranged in the most exquisite order, the horses' bits with the curb-chains hanging from them, looking, as the Woolwich Guide informs us, " like the stalactites of some beautiful grotto!" Long may they hang in such beautiful order is our prayer ; long may the cannon grace the arsenal, and its millions of balls stand in trim pyramids, to surprise the beholder. The day that should call them from their repose would be a disastrous one for Europe, and for humanity.

CHAPTER VIII.

The Devil's House.—The river Roding.—Barking.—Green
Street House. — The Gunpowder Plot. — Rainham and
Hornchurch. — Edward the Confessor and the nightin-
gales of Havering atte Bower. — Dagenham Breach.
Erith. — Purfleet. — The National Powder Magazine.
The river Darent. — Holmsdale. — Thomas à Becket.
The Nightingales of Otford. — The Ford of Darent. —
Dartford. — John Tyler and Wat Tyler. — The Martyr's
Ashes.—The river Cray.

PPÓSITE to Woolwich, in the
marshes of the Essex coast, but
in the county of Kent, stands
a solitary house, called by the
vulgar the Devil's House. It
formerly belonged to the family
of Devall, whose patronymic has been thus
perverted by the populace. This plot of land,
consisting of about five hundred acres, has belonged to the parish of Woolwich and county
of Kent from time immemorial; and tradition
accounts for its severance from Essex in the
following manner :—The body of a man having

been cast ashore there by the tide, was found by a fisherman of Woolwich, who immediately gave notice to the authorities of Essex. The latter refused to bury it; upon which, that duty was performed by Woolwich, whose magistrates sued those of Essex, to recover the charges. The Essex magistrates were condemned to pay, but refusing to do so, the patch of land in question was seized by a royal order, and from that time incorporated with Woolwich. Tradition, in this instance vaguer even than it is wont to be, has not informed us of the name of the monarch, or given us any clue by which the date might be discovered.

A considerable rivulet, called the Roding, discharges itself into the Thames near this place, under the name of Barking Creek. It rises somewhere in the neighbourhood of Dunmow, a village familiar by name to most people on account of its gammon of bacon, given as a prize to the married couple who passed a whole twelvemonth without quarrelling, a custom of which so pleasant an account is given in "The Spectator."

Passing southwards, it gives name to a whole district of Essex, and to several villages, called after it, High Roding, Aythorp Roding, Leaden Roding, White Roding, Margaret's

Roding, Abbot's Roding, Beauchamp Roding, and Berner's Roding. One of these, Abbot's Roding, was the birthplace of the celebrated John Thurloe, Secretary of State to Oliver Cromwell, and so well known for his State Papers. His father, the Rev. Thomas Thurloe, was rector of the parish.

From the Rodings the stream flows to Chipping Ongar, an ancient market town, whose name is derived from *coopen* or *cepan*, the Saxon word *to sell*, and where there was formerly an ancient fortress, erected by Richard de Lacy, protector of England during the absence of King Henry II. in his Norman wars. It was pulled down in the reign of Elizabeth.

The river then passes by Kilvedon Hatch, Navestock, the ancient seat and burial-place of the Waldegraves, between the two villages of Stapleford Tarry and Stapleford Abbots; and through that fine country, lying between Epping and Hainault Forests, until it reaches Ilford. It thence flows to the town of Barking, where it receives a small stream of the same name.

Barking Church is just visible to the passenger on the Thames, lifting up its modest turret from the low rich pasture lands in which it is situated. It was originally one of the

most ancient in England, having been founded,
with a nunnery adjoining, shortly after the
introduction of Christianity into England.
Among the abbesses have been, Matilda, or
Maud, wife of Henry I. and so well known for
her benefactions in the neighbourhood of London; Matilda, the wife of King Stephen; and
Mary à Becket, sister of the famous Archbishop of Canterbury of that name. Upon the
dissolution of the abbey by Henry VIII. the
abbess and nuns received a small pension, and
the edifice fell to decay. Scarcely any vestiges
of it now remain. The church is a spacious
edifice, with an embattled tower, and contains
many ancient monuments   Among others,
one to the memory of Maurice Bishop of London, in the reign of William the Conqueror,
and successor to that good bishop, William,
whose memory is so dear to the Londoners.

In the low lands, lying in the district within
view of the Thames, are two remarkable buildings, Green Street House and Eastbury House.
The former was inhabited by Anne Boleyn
before her marriage with Henry VIII. From
the tower a fine view of the Thames is obtained from Greenwich to Gravesend. This part
of the edifice was built by Henry to please that
luckless lady; and was renovated by Mr. Mor-

ley, the proprietor, at the end of the last, or beginning of the present century. In a communication sent by Mr. Morley to the Gentleman's Magazine, vol. xciv. part i. he states, that Anne Boleyn, while riding here, received the first offer of the monarch's hand. She had been formerly betrothed to a young nobleman, who had died ten months before, and she was in mourning for him when the offer was made. As was the custom, she requested to complete the twelvemonth of mourning for her lover, before she gave her consent to another union; and Henry during the interval caused the tower to be built, to afford her gratification. It is erroneously said, that Anne, after the fatal fall of her handkerchief at the tournament of Greenwich, went over the water to Green Street, and was thence taken to the Tower of London. As we have already stated, in our account of the old palace of Placentia, the Queen was confined to her own room in that building until the order came to have her conveyed to London.

Eastbury House, just visible from the river, was the residence of Lord Mounteagle, by whose means the Gunpowder Plot was discovered. Several stories are circulated relative to this building. A generally received tradition states,

that Guy Fawkes and the other conspirators
held their meetings here, and that from the
roof they were to have enjoyed the pleasure of
seeing the British Parliament blown into the
air.   Another tradition states, that it was here
that Lord Mounteagle received the famous
letter which led to the arrest of Guy Fawkes.
Both of these traditions are erroneous.   In the
first place, Lord Mounteagle was not one of
the conspirators, and never lent his house for
the purpose ; and, in the second, he was not at
Eastbury House, but in London, when he received the letter.   It is stated in the continuation of Stowe's Chronicle, that " about ten
days before the Parliament should begin, the
Lord Mounteagle, son and heir to the Lord
Morley, being then in his own lodging in the
Strand, ready to go to supper at seven of the
clock, one of his footmen, whom he had sent
of an errand over the street, was met by an
unknown man of indifferent appearance, who
suddenly delivered him a letter, charging him
to put it presently into his Lord's hands."   This
was the letter that prevented all the mischief.

On the other side of the river, beyond Woolwich, is the rural village of Plumstead, passing
which, we traverse two reaches of the stream,
called Gallions, and Barking Reach.   Beyond

the latter, on the Essex coast, commences Dagenham Breach, at a place where several small streams, traversing a low marshy country, fall into the Thames. Two of these streams, the Ingerbourn and the Bourne Brook, rise in the beautiful neighbourhood of Havering atte Bower, from whence they run in tortuous courses for about twelve miles. That picturesque spot was the favourite retirement of King Edward the Confessor, who so delighted in its solitary woods, that he shut himself up in them for weeks at a time. Old legends say, that he met with but one annoyance in that pleasant seclusion—the continual warbling of the nightingales pouring such floods of music upon his ear during his midnight meditations, as to disturb his devotions and draw his thoughts from God. He therefore prayed, that never more within the bounds of that forest might nightingale's song be heard. His prayer was granted—and during his whole life, the sweet birds disappeared from the spot, and left him in peace to his unloving and austere devotions. Another legend connected with this place, and with the same king, is, that an old beggar came and asked alms of him, to whom he gave a small gold ring, as the only gift his poverty allowed him to bestow. This beggar was a departed saint;—no less a personage than St. John the Evangelist, who had assumed this disguise to put his charity to the test, and discover, whether he, a monarch, was indeed a despiser of the world's wealth, and so poor as to possess no coin.   Some years afterwards, two pilgrims presented themselves at his quiet bower in Havering, and gave him back the same ring, with an intimation that they were sent from heaven, to warn him that, within six months, he should be called from this world, to enjoy eternal felicity in the bosom of his God.

Dagenham Breach receives its name from the village of Dagenham, about two miles from the river.   In the year 1707, upwards of five thousand acres of marsh land were laid under water by the inundations of the Thames and of the smaller streams already mentioned.   The origin of the calamity was the breaking in of a small sluice made for the drain of the land waters, which being neglected during more than a year, gradually increased till the whole district was inundated.   The proprietors of the land spent large sums in the endeavour to reclaim it; but the sacrifices were so great, that they reluctantly abandoned the design as impracticable.   At length the legislature interposed; an act was passed to continue the works, and a small tax was levied upon every vessel entering the port of London, to meet the charges. A gentleman named Boswell contracted for the work for £16,500; but after much labour and great expense in vain, he was obliged, in self-defence, to reliuquish the undertaking. Captain Parry, who had been employed by Peter the Great in similar works, and in building the city of Veronitz upon the Don, undertook shortly afterwards to repair the Breach for £25,000. It took five years to complete the work. Difficulties, under which ordinary minds would have sunk, were one after the other met and surmounted, but at an expense of more than £40,000. Parliament afterwards voted the sum of £15,000 to Captain Parry, the difference between the contract and the actual expense: but that gentleman was no gainer by his perseverance, except of honour; a satisfactory reward, it is true, but still more satisfactory when it comes upon a man with profit—smiling companion — by its side. Within the embankment, a pool of about forty-five acres still remains, where, during the season, a club of anglers resort; they also keep up by subscription a small thatched cottage on its brink, called the Dagenham Breach House, for the purpose of a club-house.

Immediately beyond is seen the little spire of Rainham, about a mile from the river, standing in the midst of a celebrated grazing district, which breeds some of the finest cattle sent to the London market. This church was one of the pluralities of Cardinal Wolsey.

Adjoining are Hornchurch Marshes, also famous for their fine cattle. The village is so named from a pair of horns affixed to the church. The tradition is, that its former name, something like it in sound, but much uglier, was bestowed upon it, in consequence of its having been built by some noted courtezan of an early age, who had repented of her vices, and taken this mode of showing the sincerity of her contrition. A certain monarch, nameless as the courtezan, is said to have taken offence at the name, and given the church a pair of horns, to be affixed against the wall, as a fair pretext for the change of designation. This may be but an idle story, and as such, it is slurred over with a contemptuous notice by most topographers.

On the Kentish side of the river stands Belvidere, the elegant seat of Lord Say and Sele, formerly inhabited by the able and eccentric Sir Samson Gideon, Lord Eardley. Adjoining is Erith, the old hythe or haven, with the ivy-covered tower of its ancient church, rising in venerable simplicity, and remarkable as the place where commissioners met to draw up the condition of a treaty of peace between King John and his Barons.

The reach of the river commencing at this place, is called " the Rands," a name the etymology of which has puzzled many inquirers. The Essex shore assumes here a more romantic appearance than it shows anywhere along its line. Generally low, flat, and marshy, it rises about Purfleet in abrupt chalky cliffs, on the summit of which, during the alarm of the Spanish invasion, the standard of England was placed by Queen Elizabeth, along with a beacon corresponding with other signal fires around the coast. It is now a busy little village, forming a hamlet to the parish of West Thurrock, lower down the stream. It is chiefly remarkable for its extensive powder magazine, removed hither from Greenwich in the year 1762. The quantity of gunpowder at Greenwich in 1718, amounted to about eight thousand barrels, and the inhabitants in that year were so alarmed lest an explosion should take place, that they prepared a petition to the legislature, showing the danger of permitting such a quantity to continue any longer so near

the Metropolis, and within but a very few
yards of the magnificent hospital, and other
public establishments, and suggesting that the
depôt should be removed to some more solitary
and convenient spot. King George I. directed
the Board of Ordnance to take measures for
its removal, but as Parliament had not voted
the necessary sums to purchase land or build
another, nothing could be done. Further petitions continued to be presented until the year
1750, when George II. ordered that an esti-
mate of the probable expenses should be laid
before the House. It was four years before
this was done, and six years more before the
act was finally passed ; with so little perseverance was it urged, and by such feeble interest
was the measure supported. The magazine
at Purfleet was, however, commenced in 1760,
and completed in 1762. The buildings consist
of five parallel sections, each about one hundred
and sixty feet long, and fifty-two wide. The
walls are five feet thick, and arched beneath the
slated roof. The arch is three feet in thickness, and the ridge of the roof is covered with
a coping of lead, twenty-two inches broad.
The powder is kept in small barrels, piled within wooden frames, and every possible precau-
tion is taken to prevent a calamity. Nothing

of iron is admitted; the doors have hinges of copper and brass; and every one entering, leaves his shoes behind him, and puts on goloshes of India rubber or cloth. The immense quantity of thirty thousand barrels, or three million pounds of gunpowder have occasionally been deposited in this place, and, had an explosion occurred at such a time, it is calculated that London, though fifteen miles distant, would have suffered severely. The possibility of such an event by lightning was so forcibly impressed upon the Board of Ordnance in the year 1772, that they consulted the Royal Society on the best method of preventing it· A committee of members was accordingly appointed, who unanimously recommended the adoption of Benjamin Franklin's conductors, and each pile of building is now provided with one.

To us it seems very strange, and unaccountable that men should be kept in a state of continual alarm, and a whole district exposed to the danger of devastation, by an establishment of this kind above ground. The adoption of the· following very simple and unexpensive plan would effectually prevent all mischief. In the first place, let tanks of sufficient magnitude be made, the gunpowder placed into large stone bottles, or stone barrels, hermetically sealed, and then lowered into the water, to be only raised as they are wanted for use. The only objection that could be urged to this plan, would be the risk of the powder being spoiled by the water. If the stone vessels were properly closed, and everybody knows that is no difficult matter to accomplish, this sole objection would be removed.

Opposite to Purfleet, the united rivers the Darent and the Cray discharge themselves into the Thames, under the name of Dartford Creek. The Darent rises at Squerries, near Westerham in Kent, and being joined by another stream, from Titsey in Surrey, flows on to Brasted, Sundridge, and Otford, in the neighbourhood of the latter receiving five smaller rivulets. From Otford its course is to Shoreham, Lullingstone, Eynsford, Horton Kirby, Sutton at Hone, Darent and Dartford. It is commonly called the Dart. According to Leland, its name is derived from a word in the old British language, signifying clear. Upon its banks, near Dartford, King Alfred routed the Danish host, a circumstance alluded to by Pope in his enumeration of the tributaries of the Thames, in his poem on Windsor Forest:

The silent Darent stained with Danish blood.

Spenser, in the "Fairy Queen" also enumerating the rivers attendant upon the Thames, when hastening to his nuptials with the Medway, celebrates the Darent as —

The silver Darent in whose waters clean,
Ten thousand fishes play and deck his pleasant stream.

The Darent flows for a considerable part of its course through the valley of Holmsdale, the inhabitants of which are proud to this day of a fabulous achievement of their ancestors at Swanscombe, which will be more fully related in its proper place. At Montreal, near Sevenoaks, once the seat of Lord Amherst, and so named by him in commemoration of his successes in Canada, the following lines are inscribed upon the wall of the root-house, in reference to this boast of the inhabitants of the valley.

" *This winding vale of Holmsdale,*
Was never won, and never shall."
The prophecy ne'er yet has failed
No human power has e'er prevailed,
To rob this valley of its rights,
Supported by its valorous wights !
When foreign conquest claimed our land,
Then rose the sturdy Holmsdale band,
With each a brother oak in hand:
An armed grove the conqueror meet,
And for their ancient charters treat,

Resolved to die erethey resign'd
Their liberty and gavelkind.
Hence Freedom's sons inhabit here,
And hence the world their deeds revere ;
In war and every virtuous way,
A man of Kent still bears the day ;
Thus may our Queen of vallies reign,
While Darent glides into the main,
Darent whose infant reed is seen
Uprearing on yon bosom'd green ;
Along his widening banks may peace
And joyful plenty never cease,
Where'er his waters roll their tide,
May heaven-born liberty reside.

Both the Darent and the Cray are famous for trout; but those of the latter are generally allowed to be the finest. Both rivers flow through a beautiful country, abounding at every step with pleasant reminiscences to the man of extensive reading. And first of the Darent as the more important of the two. Westerham, near which it rises from nine small springs, behind the noble mansion of Squerries, was the birth-place of Wolfe, the gallant conqueror of Quebec. In the church is a handsome monument to his memory, although the hero is buried at Greenwich. Otford is a more noted spot, named from Offa's Ford, from a ford over the Darent, where Offa, King of Mercia, defeated Lothaire, King of Kent, in the days of the Saxon Heptarchy. There was formerly a con-

siderable palace belonging to the Archbishops of
Canterbury, in this village, and it is an old
tradition, that Thomas à Becket frequently, resided here. A story is related of him similar
to that told of Edward the Confessor and the
nightingale of Havering atte Bower. The
legend is; " As he walked in the old park, busy
at his prayers, he was hindered in his devotions by the sweet note and melody of a nightingale, that sang in a bush beside him, and
therefore, in the might of his holiness, he
enjoined that no bird should be so bold as to
sing thereabouts; and a smith, then dwelling
in the town, having made great noise in shoe-
ing of his horses, he enacted by the same
authority that from thenceforth no smith
should thrive in that village." It would be
curious to ascertain the origin of all these
stories. One very like the foregoing is told
of Thomas Aquinas and Albertus Magnus,
who also, by the aid, not of prayer but
of the devil, stopped the sweet bird's song,
that interrupted them in their study of the
secret sciences, and also placed an enchanted
horse-shoe under ground in the street of Co-
logne where they resided. By this means, no
horses could ever be prevailed upon to pass the
spot, and disturb with their clattering hoofs,

or the rumbling of wheels behind them, the pursuits of these famous alchymists and necromancers.

There is a clear well in this parish, called St. Thomas's Well, strongly impregnated with iron, and medical in many diseases, which before the Reformation was universally believed to have been miraculously called into existence by Thomas à Becket, whose name it bears. Having suffered from the want of water, says the legend, he struck his staff into the dry ground, and immediately the water welled up clear as crystal, and capable, with faith, of curing all diseases. The Archbishops of Canterbury, though proprietors of Otford, did not often honour it with their residence, but preferred the neighbouring palace of Knoll or Knowle, now the magnificent seat of the Duke of Dorset. Archbishop Warham, in the time of Henry VIII, preferred Otford, and expended considerable sums in beautifying and enlarging it. His successor, Cranmer, surrendered it to the Crown with all its possessions. From the ruins of the palace, which are still standing, and from the traces of the remainder, which may be distinctly discovered, it appears to have been a very extensive building.

Winding through a sweet pastoral district, ornamented with some noble villas, the Darent reaches the little village of the same name, but more commonly pronounced Darne. The antiquary will be delighted to spend a few hours in its ancient church, where there is a very curious font. "It is," says Hasted, in his History of Kent, "a single stone, rounded and excavated, composed of eight compartments, with columns alternately circular and angular, and semicircular arches. The figures and objects are in high relief, and rudely carved." Hasted imagined that the figures were for the most part the mere result of the fantasy of the artist; but Mr. Denne, who was incumbent of Darent, gives a description of the font in Thorpe's "Custumale Roffense," in which he says that all the carvings bear an allusion to the history of St. Dunstan, and his frequent contests with the devil. His elevation to the See of Canterbury, by King Edgar, and his baptism of the infant King Ethelred, who unluckily eased nature in the font, are both depicted. The monkish legends, in allusion to the latter, say that the infant was immediately dropped from the arms of the Saint, who pronounced that he should be accursed all his life for so vile a deed. Various other incidents in the fabulous history of Dunstan are recorded on this curious font; but the memorable punishment he inflicted on the Evil One, by pulling his nose with a pair of red-hot pincers, is not among them.

Dartford, or Darentford, was an ancient demesne of the Kings of England, and has been held by many noble and illustrious personages. It was granted by King John to Hugh, Count of St. Paul, who mortgaged it with the King's permission, for three years, to provide funds for a crusading expedition to the Holy Land. Edward II. granted the manor to his half brother, Edmund of Woodstock, whose sons, Earls of Kent, inherited it in succession, but died without issue. It then fell to their sister, Joan, the wife of that gallant soldier Edward the Black Prince, who resided upon it for a short time. After various changes, it came into the possession of the famous Guy Earl of Warwick, and on his death on the bloody field, devolved upon the duke of Clarence, [he of the malmsey butt,] in right of his wife, the daughter and sole heiress of the King-maker. The Countess of Warwick, in the reign of Henry VII, surrendered this and one hundred and fourteen other manors, to the crown.

James I. granted the manor to George and
Thomas Whitmore, who conveyed it shortly
afterwards to the well-known Sir Thomas Wal-
singham. It was sold in 1613 by the latter,
for so small a sum as five hundred pounds.
There is another manor at Dartford, formerly
in the possession of the Knights' Templars,
after whom it is still named, Temple Manor.

The town abounds in the remains of antiquity, of which the most interesting are the
ruins of a nunnery, supposed to have been originally the manor house, but converted into a
nunnery by Edward III, after the death of his
gallant son. Several ladies of high rank were
superiors of this convent, which was for a
prioress and fourteen sisters of the order of St.
Augustine, and among others, Bridget, daughter of Edward IV, who died within its walls.
At the dissolution of the religious houses, the
possessions of this were valued at upwards of
four hundred pounds per annum. Henry VIII.
at considerable expense, converted the building
into a palace for himself, but it was never inhabited as such by the Monarchs of England,
except by Elizabeth for two days, on her return to Greenwich after one of her progresses to
feast upon her friends in Kent and Sussex.
Small remains of it at present exist, but from

these it is evident the building must at one time have been very extensive.

It is generally supposed that the famous insurrection of the commons of England under Wat Tyler, began at Dartford, though Hume states that it began in Essex. It is curious to see how the old historians differ upon almost every point, however important, or however trivial. If we are to believe Stowe, the captain of the insurgents was Wat Tighler, of Maidstone, and there was another man, a tiler, in Dartford, commonly called John Tyler, whose daughter received the indecent outrage which caused the father to knock out the tax-collector's brains with a hammer. John Tyler of Dartford, soon found himself at the head of a considerable company, and marched forthwith to Maidstone, to join Wat Tighler, who was a blacksmith. Stowe further informs us that the more immediate cause of the outbreak happened before the insult of John Tyler's daughter at Dartford.

Sir Simon Burley challenged a tradesman of Gravesend as his bondsman, and though the inhabitants greatly interested themselves in the man's favour, Sir Simon fixed an exorbitant sum as the price of his manumission, and would not abate a farthing. People then be-

gan to ask why there should be bondsmen at
all ; the discontent which had been germinating
in the popular mind, suddenly burst forth, and
the insurrection was at a considerable height,
when it received an increase of strength by
the accession of John Tyler. Grafton, Frois-
sart, and other historians, relate the matter dif-
ferently, and at this distance of time it is impossible to say where the tumult began, and
whether Wat Tyler was a native of Maidstone
or of Dartford, or whether, as Stowe says,
there were two Tylers. The commonly received
opinion is that the name of the insulted father
was Walter Hilliard, that he was by trade a
tiler, and that he lived at Dartford. In
Southey's juvenile Drama upon the subject, he
adheres to another tradition, which makes the
man a blacksmith.

Among the earliest sufferers for conscience
sake in England, was the vicar of this town,
Sir Richard Wich. He was burnt for heresy
on Tower Hill, in June 1440, greatly pitied
by the people, who, after his death, came in
great numbers, secretly by night to the place of
execution, to collect his ashes and the ground
he had stood on, as holy relics. The crowds
at last became so numerous, that the Mayor
of London sent an armed force, and arrested

a great number of them, and among the rest
the vicar of Allhallows, Barking, who had encouraged the delusion for his own profit, the
people bringing him offerings whenever they
found a particle of the ashes of the departed
martyr. It was said of this vicar of Allhallows, that he had secretly mixed a quantity of
spice with the ashes of the dead man to deceive the people, and make them believe that
they smelt so fragrantly by miracle. He confessed the imposition when he was in prison,
and was condemned to die for it; but his
sentence was remitted.

Near Dartford is a large open plain, called
Dartford Brent or Brim, where a tournament
was held by King Edward III, on his return
victorious from his Norman wars, and where
also the Duke of York assembled with a considerable army, in the reign of Henry VI.
This town, standing on the high road to Canterbury and Dover, is a place of some traffic.
It is populous and thriving, and has some handsome public buildings.

The Cray, which joins the Darent below
Dartford, and flows with it into the Thames,
is a much smaller stream. It is beautifully
clear, and gives name to the four pretty villages of North Cray, St. Mary's Cray, Foot's

and Paul's Cray, and the small town of Crayford. It takes its rise near Orpington, and
runs through Bexley, and the villages above
mentioned. Several of these places are interesting to the rambler who loves to visit the
abodes of the great departed, or the scenes of
history. Orpington, at its source, was honoured with a visit from Queen Elizabeth, who
made a progress into the then newly-erected
mansion of Sir Percival Hart. On her arrival,
says the account in Phillipot, she received the
caresses of a nymph who personated the genius
of the house. Then the scene shifted, and from
several chambers which were so contrived as
to represent a ship, there was an imitation of
a sea-battle, with which the Queen was highly
delighted.

Bexley, a beautiful village, is chiefly remarkable for its manor, which once belonged to that
dear name in the literature of England, the venerable Camden, "nourrice of antiquitie," who
bequeathed it to the University of Oxford for
the endowment of a professorship of history.

Crayford is so named from an ancient ford
over the river. Considerable estates here once
belonged to the gallant Admiral Sir Cloudesly
Shovel, who has a monument in Westminster
Abbey, and also a monument in the church of

this place. In the churchyard is a gravestone with the following epitaph—a wretched attempt at wit.

" Here lies the body of Peter Isnell, thirty years clerk of this parish. He lived respected as a pious and mirthful man, and died on his way to church to assist at a wedding on the 31st of March 1811, aged seventy. The inhabitants of Crayford have raised this stone to his cheerful memory and as a token of his long and faithful services.

> The life of this clerk was just three score and ten,
> Nearly half of which time he chaunted *Amen*.
> In his youth he was married, like other young men,
> But his wife one day died, so he chaunted *Amen*.
> A second he married—she died, well? what then?
> He married and buried a third with *Amen;*
> Thus his joys and his sorrows were treble; but then
> His voice was deep bass as he sung out *Amen*.
> On the horn he could blow as well as most men,
> So his horn was exalted in sounding *Amen*.

How miserable this is. Some may laugh at the folly of it, but we pity the levity which could inscribe it on so solemn a place. Tombstone literature is at a very low ebb in England, with some rare exceptions. The continental nations, as we have already remarked, are infinitely before us; and such doggrel as the above, would not be permitted in their cemeteries.

The tomb is too solemn a place to be inscribed with any other words than such as are prompted by regret and love.

After their junction, the two rivers of Cray and Darent offer nothing to stay the step of the traveller. Even the angler avoids the muddy waters known as Dartford Creek, and, jogging on further inward amid the rural villages and green fields of Kent, visits them separately, and finds in the proper season to reward him for his pains, abundant store of,

"Swift trouts diversified with crimson stains."

CHAPTER IX.

GAIN arrived, after our ramble inwards, at the junction of the Darent with the Thames, we follow the course of the great river, and see beyond Dartford Creek, the remains of the venerable Castle of Stone, rising amid the foliage on the Kentish shore. It is generally believed that Stone Castle was built by King Stephen, and for many ages it belonged to the noble family of Northwood, one of whom distinguished himself under Richard I, at the siege of Acre. The square embattled tower is the only remains of its former grandeur. The church

embounded among the trees is also an ancient edifice. There was formerly a chime of musical bells in its tower, and the tradition is, that Queen Elizabeth, as she passed up and down Long Reach, as this part of the river is called, took great pleasure in hearing them. Ben Jonson in his Epithalamium for the marriage of his friend, alludes to the musical bells of the churches that overlook the Thames,

> Hark ! how the bells upon the waters play
> Their sister tunes from Thames's either side.

This church and its tower were struck by lightning in 1638, and since that time the chimes have not been replaced.

Greenhithe, situated on the bank of the river, has a ferry into Essex for horses and cattle, which formerly belonged to the nunnery at Dartford, but is now an appurtenance to the manor of Swanscombe, immediately behind it. The hamlet, at one time, was chiefly supported by the profits of its immense chalk pits, several of which are considerably below the level of the Thames. Great quantities of the chalk are consumed in the potteries of Staffordshire; the flints also which abound in the pits, are a profitable article of commerce, being collected and shipped for China, where they are used in the manufacture of pottery. The place is but a hamlet to Swanscombe. The latter is written Swinescamp in Domesday Book and was so named from Sweyn the Danish King, the father of Canute, who erected a castle here to preserve a winter station for his ships, during his piratical incursions into England. The remains of this castle were said by Phillipot, who wrote in the beginning of the seventeenth century, to be visible in his time.

Swanscombe was long a cherished spot by all the people of Kent, on account of a fabulous story related by a monkish historian, and too readily believed by the Kentish men, whose self-love was flattered by it. When William the Conqueror, says the tradition, was advancing from Hastings to London, he endeavoured to force himself through Swanscombe, (a place which was *rather* out of the direct line, it must be confessed), but was valiantly opposed by the men of Kent, who advanced towards him, each bearing leaves and branches of trees, so that their army appeared like a moving wood. Suddenly they threw down their leafy screens, to the great alarm of the Conqueror, and appeared an imposing multitude of warriors, well armed with arrows, spears, and swords, and demanded the confirmation of all their ancient

laws and privileges, before they would acknowledge him as their sovereign. William at once
consented, and in consequence, says TRADITION,
the men of Kent enjoy to this day the ancient
custom of *gavelkind,* almost peculiar to their
county, and inscribe on their arms the proud
motto " Invicta." The first writer who mentions this story, is Thomas Sprot, a monk of
Canterbury, who lived more than two centuries after the Norman invasion. It is not
until comparatively recent times that its truth
has been called in question. Like many other
common stories, it will not bear examination,
and is already exploded by all who have bestowed a thought upon the matter.

The white spire of Swanscombe church, about
a mile distant, is visible from the Thames at
high-water on a clear day. There was formerly an altar in the church famous for the
cure of madness, and to which vast numbers
of pilgrims were conveyed by their friends.
There are no monuments of particular notice.
In the nave are to be seen the relics of a rare
and affecting custom in this county, namely,
funereal garlands, which are borne before the
corpse of a virgin, placed upon the coffin during
the service in the church, and afterwards hung
up as memorials.

The manor originally belonged to William de Valence and his descendants, Earls of March. The representative of that noble house, ascended the throne of England in the person of Edward IV, the Rose of York, when the manor became vested in the Crown, and so remained till the reign of Elizabeth, who granted it to Anthony Weldon, clerk of the green cloth, in whose family it remained for many years. Sir Anthony Weldon, sufficiently known for his " Memoir on the Court of King James I," was grandson of the above-named gentleman, and like him resided at Swanscombe. The manor was sold in 1731, and has since been in the possession of the opulent family of Child, the bankers of London.

In a wood, situated partly in this parish, and partly in the parish of Southfleet, is a remarkable cavern, with cells, called *Clapper-Napper's Hole*, from a notorious robber, who is reported to have made it the place of his retreat, and whose name has been used as a terror to the infantile part of the community, from the days of King Alfred to the present time.

The church of Swanscombe is very ancient, with a square tower and octagon spire, which was struck by lightning on Whit-Tuesday, in the year 1802.

On the other side, passing Belmont Castle, an elegant modern mansion in the Gothic style, the seat of Richard Webb, Esq. we arrive at the pretty little market-town of Gray's, or Gray's Thurrock. It takes its name from the ancient family of Grey, the manor having been granted by Richard I. to Henry De Grey, ancestor of the families of Grey de Wilton, Grey de Ruthyn, Grey de Rothesfield, and others. It is a small place, carrying on some trade in bricks and corn.

The Essex coast about here is low and unattractive. The Kentish shore is more inviting, and more thickly studded with towns, villages, and country seats. The river too begins to widen as it approaches the ocean; and here the water first begins to taste brackish. Passing Ingress, or Ince-grice-hall, we arrive at Northfleet, a populous village, mentioned in Domesday Book, under the name of Norfluet. It is divided into two districts, upper and lower: the upper on the chalk cliffs, and the lower on the shore. The church contains many monuments and fragments of monuments, some as early as the fourteenth century. Among others are one to the memory of Richard Davy, keeper of the jewels to King Henry VI, and one to Edward Brown, physician to King

Charles II. and an eminent naturalist in his day.

Behind this village lies Southfleet, that formerly stood on a sheet of water, formed by the creek of the river, but now dammed up. It is on the line of the old Roman road, Watling Street, and is supposed by some antiquaries to be the *Vagniacæ* of Antoninus's Itinerary. It has belonged to the See of Rochester, from a period considerably anterior to the Conquest, and was a ville that had an extensive and peculiar jurisdiction of its own, embracing not only offences committed within its own bounds, but also all such committed in any part of the kingdom, if the criminal were apprehended within its limits. An instance of the exercise of this jurisdiction is given in Blunt's " Ancient Tenures and Customs of Manors." Two women, who had stolen some linen at Croindene, supposed to be Croydon, in the year 1200, were arrested at Southfleet, whither they had been pursued by the authorities of their own district. Henry de Cobham, Lord of Southfleet, refused to deliver them up, and immediately proceeded to try them for the offence. As they loudly asserted their innocence, they were allowed to prove it, by the then very common ordeal of fire. They accordingly delivered their arms to the attendant priests, who always superintended the foolish ceremony, when one of them was exculpated, and the other found guilty. The latter was then taken forth to a pool called Bikepool, communicating with the Thames, and her arms and legs having been previously tied together, she was thrown in and drowned. In later times, two men of Deptford were accused of defamation in the Consistorial Court of Rochester, for representing that three women of Southfleet were guilty of witchcraft. The only proof they gave of the charge was, that they each "kept a monstruous tode." Considering the age when the crime was imputed [1585], an age, when the chaplain of Queen Elizabeth openly prayed that her Grace might be preserved from the malice of witches, when James VI. of Scotland presided at trials for the same offence, and condemned women without scruple to the flames, and when all over the continent of Europe thousands upon thousands of victims were annually sacrificed at the shrine of this prevalent delusion, it is wonderful that these women escaped. Hundreds of women were executed in England upon charges as frivolous as this. Two of these were acquitted, and their defamers fined. In the case of the third, as she was somewhat suspected of witchcraft by her neighbours, and as she was moreover a notable scold, she was ordered to attend at the next court-day, with six good women for her compurgators, and likewise admonished to resort to the minister without fail every Sunday or holiday, to testify her faith in the eyes of all who doubted. This sentence, so mild and so sensible, stands alone in the annals of witchcraft at that period, and reflects lasting credit upon the humanity of the judges. Had Matthew Hopkins, witch-finder-general, been alive and thereabouts, the case would have been somewhat different.

A short distance beyond Northfleet, and between that village and Gravesend, a new town, entitled Rosherville, is in process of formation on the estate, and from the designs, of Mr. Jeremiah Rosher. There is also a zoological garden and pleasure-ground, for the resort of the numerous visitors from the metropolis, who flock to Gravesend and its neighbourhood during the summer season. The place, when completed, promises to become a great ornament to the bank of the river.

The spires, and numerous buildings of Gravesend, the most considerable town we have passed since leaving London, and the first port

on the Thames, now rise before us, and give palpable evidence of a thriving and populous place. Its piers, projecting far into the stream, are crowded with steam-boats, each crowded with passengers to and from the great city, with whose population Gravesend is the favourite and most convenient watering-place. There is an absurd opinion afloat among the immense multitudes, who never inquire for themselves, or who have not the opportunity of doing so, that Gravesend, or, the End of the Grave, was so called in consequence of the great plague of 1666, having stopped short of

that town. The name of the place in Domesday
Book is Gravesham, or the town of the Grave,
Graff, Earl, or chief magistrate, which in the
course of time has been altered to Gravesend.

Little mention of this town occurs in history
until the reign of Richard II, when the French
sailed up the river, burned and plundered the
town, and carried off some of the principal
inhabitants. To aid the town to repair its
serious losses on this occasion, the abbot and
brethren of St. Mary le Grace, on Tower Hill,
London, to whom the manor belonged, obtained of the King a privilege for the watermen of Gravesend and Milton, that they solely
should be permitted to convey passengers to
and from London. The fare was fixed at four
shillings for each boat, containing twenty-four
persons, or twopence a-head.

In the same reign, as mentioned in our account of Dartford, one Sir Simon Burleigh
excited a commotion in Gravesend, by seizing
one of the principal inhabitants for his bondsman, and refusing to liberate him under the
then exorbitant manumission of three hundred
pounds. The men of Gravesend, joined by
Wat Tyler from Maidstone, afterwards be-
seiged Rochester Castle, where the man was
confined, and set him at liberty, along with

several other prisoners. The Sir Simon Burleigh, the cause of this disturbance, and one of the men, whose overbearing pride and insolence helped to drive the people of England to that famous rebellion, was beheaded about seven years afterwards. He was concerned in the treasons of the Duke of Ireland, and Nicholas Brember, Lord Mayor of London, and expectant Duke of New Troy, found guilty, and sentenced to be hanged, drawn, and quartered. He was at the time Constable of Dover Castle and Chamberlain to the King, who, upon consideration of his high offices, dispensed with the ignominy of this punishment, and had him put to death by the more honourable mode, as it was considered, of decapitation, without the drawing and quartering. "He was," says Stowe, "an intolerable proud man, and a great oppressor of the poor."

From the time of Richard II, until the year 1819, passengers were conveyed between London and Gravesend in small sailing boats. The fare, originally twopence, was gradually raised to sixpence, and in the year 1779, there being covered, or tilt boats, the fare was raised to ninepence, and shortly afterwards to a shilling.

It may not be out of place to mention here, that at the same period the only water-conveyance to Margate was by the hoy, which left London once a week, sometimes performing the passage in eight or ten hours, but at others being beaten about for three days. The fare was two shillings and sixpence.

The first steam-boat from London to Gravesend commenced running in 1819, at which time there were but two boats engaged in the transit. There are now upwards of twenty; some of the largest of them being built to accommodate seven hundred passengers. There is a ferry across the river to Tilbury in Essex, for troops, horses, carriages, &c. We have already mentioned in our account of the Thames Tunnel, that it was in contemplation about the year 1798, to construct a tunnel at this place, to facilitate the communication. The undertaking, however, being attended with too much difficulty, was soon abandoned.

Gravesend is the limit of the jurisdiction of the London Custom House; and all vessels engaged in foreign trade, or coming from foreign ports, are boarded here by the officers of that establishment, who accompany them to the parent office in London. The Thames at this part is a mile in breadth, and the tide in its ebb and flow, rises and falls about twenty feet.

Great part of Gravesend was burned down in the year 1727, and Parliament, in the year 1731, granted the sum of five thousand pounds towards rebuilding the church. Milton, which joins Gravesend, was incorporated with that parish in the reign of Elizabeth, and the two were governed by a mayor, jurats, common-councilmen, and other officers, until the passing of the Corporation Reform Act in 1835, when some changes were introduced into that, as well as other corporations.

The manor of Gravesend was granted by William the Conqueror to his half-brother, Odo, the bishop. Upon his disgrace, the family of Cremaville came into possession; and in the reign of Edward II. the whole reverted to the Crown. Edward III. granted it to Robert de Ufford, Earl of Suffolk, an eminent warrior of that day, and one of the first Knights made by that sovereign on the institution of the order of the Garter. In the reign of Richard III. the manor was again in the possession of the Crown, by whom it was conveyed to the Abbey of St. Mary on Tower Hill. After the dissolution of the monasteries, it passed through several hands during the reigns of Henry VIII, Edward VI, and Mary, till it came into the possession of Dudley Earl of Leicester. He received Elizabeth's permission to sell the manor; and it was purchased by Sir Thomas Gawdye. The latter only retained it a few years, and sold it again to William Brooke Lord Cobham; upon the attainder of whose son, in the reign of James I, it once more reverted to the Crown. By him it was granted to his kinsman, Ludovick Stuart, son of the Duke of Lennox, and from him descended into the family of the Blighs, Earls of Darnley, in which it still remains.

Gravesend, as we learn from Mr. Jesse's entertaining " Memoirs of the Court of England during the reign of the Stuarts," was the scene of an adventure which befell King Charles I, when Prince of Wales, on the commencement of his chivalrous journey to Spain with the Duke of Buckingham in search of a wife:—

" On the 27th of February, 1623," says Mr. Jesse, " the Prince retired privately from court, and came to Buckingham's house, at Newall in Essex. From thence they set out on the following day (accompanied only by Sir Richard Graham, master of the horse to the duke), and arrived, though not without adventures, by way of Gravesend, at Dover They had previously disguised themselves with false beards, and adopted fictitious names; the Prince passing as Mr. John Smith, and the duke as Mr. Thomas Smith.

" The first accident which happened to them was encountering with the French ambassador (who was, of course, well acquainted with their persons) on the brow of the hill, beyond Rochester. Their horses, however, though merely hired at the last post, were fortunately able to leap the hedge by the road-side, and thus enabled them to escape observation. This circumstance was the more fortunate, as the ambassador (as was then usual) was travelling in one of the King's coaches; and their recognition by some of the royal servants would certainly have been the consequence of a personal encounter.

" But a more important incident had nearly arrested their progress. In crossing the river at Gravesend, for want of silver, they had given the ferryman a gold piece. The man was equally astonished and grateful for such liberality; and supposing that his benefactors were proceeding across the channel for the purpose of fighting a duel, he thought it the kindest step he could take to hint his suspicions to the authorities of the nearest town. Accordingly, information was instantly despatched to the Mayor of Canterbury; and just as the Prince and Buckingham were about to mount fresh horses, they were summoned to the presence of that important personage. The duke, finding concealment impracticable, divested himself of his beard, and privately informed the mayor who he really was : — he was going, he said, in his capacity of Lord High Admiral, to acquaint himself secretly with the condition and discipline of the fleet. His identity was easily proved, and the adventurers were allowed to depart. A boy, who rode post with their baggage, had also recognised their persons, but the silence of this individual was not very difficult to be bought."

Metropolitan visitors to this much-frequented resort, need hardly be informed of the fine view afforded from the eminence of Windmill Hill ; in which the Thames, now indeed a wide and exulting river, hastening to the embraces " of that salt and bitter sea, that swallows it up at last," is the most prominent and beautiful object, glowing blue as the skies above it, and dotted with an apparently innumerable multitude of snowy-sailed vessels, entering and departing from the great mart of the world.

In the neighbourhood of Gravesend is a spot sacred to every reader of Shakspeare— Gad's Hill—the scene of the " mad prince's"

world-renowned exploit with Sir John Falstaff. On sailing down the stream at high-water, the eminence is plainly visible, and scarcely fails, to the man who knows its name, to awaken a long train of pleasant recollections. Even the man of figures and accounts forgets them for awhile, and dwells with pleasure on the reminiscence; but the dreamer, the poet, the lover of romance, the man who loves to cherish these topographical pleasures which are the great charm of travelling, whether we travel twenty miles or two thousand;—what delight does he not find! Such a man disembarks immediately. He is not content with the

glimpse of the hill obtained from the deck of
a steam-boat, but trudges forward valiantly,
until his own feet tread the actual soil of which
he has so often heard, and which is associated
with so much romance and so much genuine
comedy. "Here," he says, traversing the
ground leisurely up and down, "here lay fat
Jack, with his ear to the ground, and dolefully
asked the prince whether he had any levers to
lift him up again; and swore that for all the
coin in Henry IVth's exchequer, he would not
trust his own flesh so far afoot again. Here,
perchance, is the spot, where he bullied the
travellers, finding they were afraid, and called
them gorbellied knaves, fat chuffs, and chew-
bacons. Here, too, may be the bush, where
the Prince said to Poins, that if they could
rob the thieves, and go merrily to London, it
would be argument for a week, laughter for a
month, and a good jest for ever (and lo, it has
turned out even as the Prince predicted). And
here, too, may be the very spot, where the
rogue, Falstaff, roared, and gave up his ill-
gotten spoils so easily to that very Prince and
Poins, of whom he was saying but a minute before, that they were both arrant cow-
ards, and that in Poins especially, there was
no more valour than in a wild duck. Yes—

here is the scene," continues he, with all the enthusiasm of a pilgrim at the shrine of a saint, forgetting that all was but a coinage of the great poet's brain, that the inimitable Jack never trod this earth at all—but that he still lives in the world of fiction, where he will live till the English language is forgotten. But no matter: these mirages, raised by the enchanting wand of the poet and painter, are among the most unalloyed delights of our existence. They gild with a halo of light many a dreary landscape; and warm a bleak and barren hill with the glow and animation of life. We who have visited this spot more than once or twice or thrice, indulge in the same dream every time we go, and would be sorry indeed to believe that even the hundredth visit to the spot, would find us insensible to its claims upon our heart, or undelighted with the charms of the Shakspeare who has enshrined it in his verse for ever.

But we have wandered from the banks of the Thames, where, opposite to Gravesend, stands an historical spot, requiring proper and honourable mention from our pen, Tilbury Fort, the scene of Elizabeth's bravery and animation, when her shores were threatened with invasion. The fort was built by Henry VIII. to protect

the towns on the river from the recurrence of
scenes such as that which took place at Gravesend in the reign of Richard II.   It was enlarged and strengthened by Charles II. when
the Dutch fleet sailed up the Medway in
1667, and burned three men-of-war opposite
Chatham.

The spot where the English army was encamped in 1588, is a short distance further
down the stream, at West Tilbury, where the
traces of the encampment are still visible.   The
country was in a state of the greatest alarm.
The naval forces of England at that time were
not very considerable; and had not the very
elements conspired against Spain, had not her
most experienced naval commanders been cut
off by death at the very moment they were
about to join the expedition, leaving the command to the unskilled and inefficient Duke of

Medina Sidonia, there is no saying what the
result might have been, or whether England
would have held the same rank among the
nations that she holds now.* Bale fires blazed

* The naval reader may be pleased to see a correct account, from a contemporary historian, of the various vessels
that composed the English fleet at that period. The list is
copied from Stowe's Annals, and will afford the sailor of the
present day some notion of the very small maritime strength
of England in the days of Queen Elizabeth, and that too in
a case of emergency, when every available ship was put into
requisition. "The navy set forth and arrived to the seas,"
says Stowe, "consisted partly of her Majesty's ships, partly
of the ships of her subjects, which were furnished out of
the port towns whereunto they belonged. Of this navy the
chiefest and greatest part was under the charge of the Lord
Charles Howard, Lord Admiral; the rest of the ships, in
great number, were assigned unto the Lord Henry Seymour,
Admiral of that fleet to guard the narrow seas. The States
also of the United Provinces in the Low Countries sent
about the same number of forty ships out of Holland and
Zealand, well appointed and furnished in warlike manner,
which joined with the English fleet under the charge of the
said Lord Henry Seymour, playing upon the coast of Dun-
kirk and Flanders.

" SHIPS UNDER THE LORD ADMIRAL'S CHARGE.

"Her Majesty's Ships from Queenborough towards Plymouth
in the month of January last past, under Sir Francis
Drake :—

The Revenge, The Swiftsure,
Hope, Aide.
Nonpareil,

upon every hill. Every man held himself ready for the fight; and in London it was deemed so important that the darkness of its streets by night should not afford cover for the de⸗

" From Queenborough towards Plymouth the 16th May, under the Lord Admiral.

The Bear,
  Triumph,
  Elizabeth,
  Victory,
  Ark,
  Bonaventure,
  Lion,
  Mary Rose,
  Dreadnought,
  Foresight,
  Swallow,
  White Lion.

Pinnaces.

The Charles,
  Moon.

Other Ships of the best sort.

The Leicester,
  Royal Merchant,
  Roe Buck (Sir Walter
    Raleigh's),
  Edward Bonaventure,
  Golden Noble,
  Hopewell of London.

By the Londoners of their charge. Ships 16.

The Hercules,
  Toby,
  Centurion,
  Minion,
  Margaret and John,
  Ascension,
  Mayflower,
  Primrose,
  Red Lion,
  Tiger,
  Gift of God,
  Burre,
  Royal Defence,
  Golden Lion,
  Brave,
  Thomas Bonaventure.

Pinnaces, four.

The Diana,
  Passport,
  Moonshine,
  Relief.

signs of traitors within, or aid the surprises of
enemies without, that every householder was
ordered to hang out a light before his door,
and see that it burned till dawn, under pain

Of Bristol.

The Minion,
    Unicorn,
    Handmaid,
A Pinnace.

Of Barnstaple.

The Dudley,
    God save her,
    Tiger.

Of Exeter.

The Bartholomew,
    Rose,
A Pinnace.

Of Plymouth.

The Elkora,
    Spark,
    Hope,
    Drake,
    Barke Bond,
    Barke Bonnar,
    Barke Talbot,
    Fly Boat,
    White Lion (the Lord
        Admiral's),
A Pinnace (the Lord Shef-
    field's),
    Pinnace (Sir Wm. Winter's),
And sundry others of the
        west parts.

" HER MAJESTY'S SHIPS UNDER THE LORD H. SEYMOUR'S
CHARGE.

The Rainbow,
    Vanguard,
    Antelope,
    Bull,
    Tiger,
    Scout,
    Tremontaine,
    Achates,

The Sun,
    Merlin,
    Signet,
    Spy,
    Fancy,
    Gally Bona,
    Brigandine,
    George (a hoy).

Other English ships there were from the ports of the north
part of the realm, besides Flemish ships of Holland and

of death. But needless severity of this kind was not wanting to arouse the spirit of the nation, and the Queen knew it. With the strength of mind of a man, and the tact of a woman, she thought that the spectacle of a queen leading her own armies to the struggle, would act upon the chivalrous feelings of the multitude; and she was right. She appeared among her soldiers at Tilbury, and having ridden through the lines with a cheerful and animated countenance, delivered the following speech—unlike the royal speeches of the present day—with a good deal of meaning in it.

" My loving People,

" We have been persuaded of some, that are careful of our safety, to take heed how we commit ourselves to armed multitudes, for

Zealand, in number forty. As also ten ships of war by the merchant adventurers of England, at their own proper costs and charges, set out of the City of London under the charge of Captain Henry Bullengham, (over and above the other sixteen ships and four pinnaces set out at the City's charge,) to wit—

The Pansy,	The Dolphin,
Rose-Lion,	Jewell,
Anthony,	Antelope,
Salamander,	Toby,
Providence,	George Noble."

fear of treachery; but, I assure you, I do not live to distrust my faithful and loving people. Let tyrants fear. I have always so behaved myself, that, under God, I have placed my chiefest strength and safeguard in the loyal hearts and goodwill of my subjects. And therefore I am come amongst you, as you see at this time, not for any recreation and disport, but being resolved in the midst and heat of the battle, to live or die among you all; to lay down for my God and for my kingdom and for my people, my honour and my blood even in the dust. I know I have the body but of a weak and feeble woman; but I have the heart and stomach of a king — ay, and of a King of England too; and think foul scorn that Parma or Spain, or any prince of Europe, should dare to invade the borders of my realm; to which rather than dishonour shall grow by me, I myself will take up arms; I myself will be your general, judge, and recorder of every one of your virtues in the field. I know already for your forwardness you have deserved crowns; and we do assure you, on the word of a Prince, they shall be duly paid you. In the mean time, my lieutenant-general shall be in my stead, than whom never Prince commanded more noble or worthy subject; not doubting, but by your obedience to my general, by your concord in the camp, and by your valour in the field, we shall shortly have a famous victory over these enemies of my God, my kingdom, and my people."

This valiant and indeed eloquent speech, had the anticipated effect. An attachment to her person, says Hume, became a kind of enthusiasm among the soldiery, and they swore never to abandon the glorious cause of their Queen and their country. But their valour, and that of their general, Dudley, Earl of Leicester, was destined never to be put to the test. Before the Armada could get out of Calais, where it had put in to await the reinforcements of the Duke of Parma, the storm and the English admiral committed sad havoc among its cumbrous vessels. The guns of Tilbury Fort were not called into use; and the Armada, sailing northward, to make the tour of the British Isles ere its return to Spain, was miserably wrecked on the barren shores of Orkney. England was freed from the most imminent danger that had threatened her shores for centuries; and the pride of Spain was more effectually humbled, and at much less cost, than if the arms of the English people had gained the victory.

Elizabeth remained two days among her soldiers at Tilbury, passing the night at the neighbouring village of Horndon-on-the-Hill, in the house of one Master Edward Rich, a justice of the peace for Essex. The camp was very shortly afterwards dissolved, all danger being over, and public thanksgivings were offered up in all the churches of the kingdom for the happy deliverance of the nation. The Earl of Leicester, so highly complimented for his abilities and zeal by the Queen, just lived long enough to witness the general joy, and died twenty-five days after his gallant appearance by the side of his sovereign at Tilbury. His death, as he had not contributed to the triumph, was scarcely noticed. Drake and Howard were the names in the people's mouths, and the fleets of England were justly more in honour than her armies. The flags taken from the Spaniards, were publicly exhibited by the clergy at Paul's Cross, and the next day were hoisted from the battlements on London Bridge, looking towards Southwark, among the traitors' heads that always frowned from that gate of death; and there being that day a great fair upon the bridge, the concourse of people to behold the flags was greater than had ever been known to assemble on that ancient structure.

The wide reach of the river from Gravesend and Tilbury seawards, is called the Hope; and arrived at the end of that, we first obtain a glimpse of the not far distant ocean, and see the Nore, and the mouth of the river, about six miles in breadth. The Essex shore for all the rest of our course, is low and uninteresting; and a few insignificant villages, alone point their spires to the blue, to betoken the dwelling-places of man. The Kentish shore offers more attractions, and in this place becomes a peninsula, formed by the Thames and the Medway, known by the name of the Hoo. In the time of Hollinshed, the Hoo was nearly an island, and there was a proverb current, not much to the credit of its inhabitants—

He that rideth in the hundred of Hoo,
Besides pilfering seamen shall find dirt enow.

The district was formerly supposed to be under the especial patronage of Saint Werburgh, a Saxon lady, who, during her life-time, had a mortal antipathy to geese; and who, in her sanctity after death, freed every place she delighted to honour, from the presence of those fowl, except the inhabitants chose to keep them tame for their own convenience.

The first important place that solicits attention on this coast, is Higham, about a mile inward, and just beyond the marshes. It is generally believed, that Plautius, the Roman general, under the Emperor Claudius, passed the river from Essex to this place with all his army, in pursuit of the flying Britons. The achievement, if ever performed, was a difficult one, as the river is not only wide, but deep and rapid. "The probability," says Hasted, in his History of Kent, "of this having been a ford in the time of the Romans, is strengthened by the visible remains of a causeway leading from the bank of the Thames through the marshes by Higham, southward; and it seems to have been continued across the London high road on Gad's Hill, to Shorne, Ridgeway (implying the way to the ford or passage, the word *Rhyd* in the ancient British language signifying a ford), about half a mile beyond which it joined the Roman Watling Street, near the entrance into Cobham Park. The charge of maintaining that part of the causeway which was in the parish of Higham, as also of a bridge, was found by the judges on their circuit to belong to the priories of Higham nunnery, an institution founded by King Stephen, who appointed his daughter Mary the first prioress.

Between Higham and Tilbury there was a ferry for many ages, and accounts of it are to be met with so late as the reign of Henry VIII, before which Higham was a place much used for the shipping and unshipping of corn and goods in large quantities. In the reign of Elizabeth, there seems to have been a fort or bulwark here for the defence of the river, the yearly expense of which to the state, for the pay of a captain and soldiers, was no more than twenty-eight pounds two shillings and sixpence.

Cliffe, the next place visible, is a village, which was called Bishop's Cliffe in the time of William the Conqueror. Before that period, all the bishops in the province of Canterbury, used to hold an annual meeting in this church on the first of August, to settle rules for the governance of the clergy. The incumbent of Cliffe was once believed to have Episcopal jurisdiction. The church is large, and bears evident marks of its former importance. It once was rich in the possession of monumental brasses; but the soldiers of the Commonwealth, who were quartered in it, made considerable gains by selling them to the founders, and very few of them are now remaining. In the chancel are six stalls, like those in cathedral churches, and the tradition of the place is, that they were formerly filled by a dean and five prebendaries.

About two miles beyond Cliffe, are the ruins of the ancient Castle of Cowling, built in the year 1381 by Lord Cobham, the father of Sir John Oldcastle, one of the earliest martyrs to the Protestant faith. It is a tradition reported in the old histories of Kent, that the castle was so large and strong, that its builder feared he might give offence at court and attract suspicion. To obviate this, he caused the following lines to be cut in a brazen scroll, with an appendant seal of his arms, in imitation of a deed or charter, and fixed it upon the easternmost tower of the chief entrance, that it might be visible to all comers.

> Knoweth that beth and shall be,
> That I am made in helpe of the contree,
> In knowing of whiche thinge
> This is ye chartre and witnessing.

Sir John Oldcastle, then owner of this superb fortress, was hanged in chains, and burned in St. Giles's Fields, London, in the year 1418, for the alleged crimes of heresy and treason, committed about three years previously. The character of Sir John has been drawn in the brightest colours by the martyrologists; but there is little doubt, leaving his religious opinions out of the question, that his political crimes were sufficiently heinous to have drawn upon him the punishment he suffered from any sovereign in Europe. He denied the power of the judges to try him, as having been appointed by an usurper—a character which history cannot fix upon Henry V. He appears also, like many other martyrs, to have been a dangerous fanatic; and he told Sir Thomas Erpingham, a few minutes before his execution, that he would rise from the grave on the third day, and procure peace and victory for the persecuted sect of the Lollards. An unsuccessful attempt to take this castle, was made by Sir Thomas Wyatt, in the Kentish insurrection of 1553, against Queen Mary.

On the opposite shore we pass the Island of Canvey, a low, swampy place, about five miles in length, behind which, on the mainland of Essex, are the ruins of Hadleigh Castle, and the town of Leigh. The former is in the village of the same name, and was built by the powerful Hubert de Burgh, in the reign of Henry III. who was also the original builder of York Place, afterwards called Whitehall, in Westminster. At his death, Hadleigh came into the possession of Thomas of Woodstock, Duke of Gloucester, murdered at Calais by order, it is supposed, of Richard II.; upon whose throne, and life, he had made an attempt, in conjunction with others. His widowed duchess quitted Hadleigh soon afterwards, and hid her sorrows from the world amid the recluses of the nunnery at Barking.

The remains of the castle stand on the brow of a steep hill, from whence there is a magnificent view over the wide mouth of the river into Kent. The ancient walls, overgrown with moss, and choked up with weeds and brambles, and every year yielding up a fragment to the insatiable hands of decay and time, present the traces of much former grandeur. They inclose an area of a somewhat oval form, and are strengthened by buttresses on the north and south. The entrance is at the north-west angle, between the remains of two towers; and close to it may be discovered the course of a deep ditch, that formerly extended along the north side. About the middle of the last century it was in the possession of Sir Francis St. John, Bart., in whose time part of it was demolished, and the remainder suffered to fall into decay.

Leigh is a small fishing-town, celebrated eight hundred years ago for its fine grapes, rivalling those of Hamburg. It has none to boast of now. Its church, upon a hill, commands an extensive view over the Thames.

About three miles further is the pretty watering place, Southend, pleasantly situated on a hill, and embowered in verdure. It is a town of comparatively modern origin, and the newest parts of it are built in a style of considerable elegance. It possesses the usual attractions of watering places,— a news-room, a theatre, and good bathing; but its views over the mouth of the Thames and the junction of the Medway, and the salubrity of the air, render it a favourite resort in the summer season.

On the Kentish side lies the low coast of the Hoo, and the Isle of Grain, with the insulet called Yantleet; none of them possessing any attractions to stay the progress of the traveller.

The Thames now mingles itself in the ocean. Its waters have long since lost their freshness; and the Nore light, stationed in the midst, gives notice to all that the course of the great stream is over. From the Essex to the Kentish shores the breadth of the *embouchure* is about six miles. From its source to the Nore the river has flowed for a space of two hundred and thirty miles, and been navigable for one hundred and eighty-eight. A mere brook in comparison with some of the mighty floods of the Old and New World ; a rivulet compared with the Volga, the Danube, the Don, and some other streams of Europe ; but richer and more glorious than them all. Over its placid bosom passes more wealth ; upon its banks resounds the hammer of more industry ; and in its ports are stationed more wonders of art and civilization, and more engines of power and conquest, than in all the streams of Europe put together. And though its history abounds in no wild legends or startling traditions, to please the lover of romance, yet its association with the names of the great, the good, and the learned, who have dwelt upon its banks, and loved it, recommends it to the friend of his country. At every step of our course some recollection has been excited, which was worthy of being noted ; and if we in the course of our rambles up and down, and on either side of it, and its tributaries, have brought little or nothing to light which was new, at least we shall be allowed the merit of having diligently culled from a thousand different and scattered sources all the memorabilia of the river, and put them into shape and form. We have striven to be

exact without being elaborately learned ; we
have endeavoured to be a chatty companion, and
not a prosing Dr. Dryasdust ; and have loved
to conduct the reader into green woods and
lanes, and lovely nooks, as well as into old
castles, and mouldy churches, possessing few
attractions but their age to recommend them.
If without parade of erudition we have informed the reader ; if without the exercise of
fancy or invention we have amused him, we
have done well, and are satisfied.   In pursu-
ance of our original plan, we proceed to trace,
with similar objects, the sister stream of the
Medway ; and inviting our readers to accompany us, bid farewell to the THAMES.

THE RIVER MEDWAY.

CHAPTER X.

Spenser's Bridal of the Thames and Medway.—The Mutiny at the Nore. — Sheerness and Queenborough. — The Legend of our Lady of Gillingham.

EDWAY, as Spenser sings, was by nature intended to pay tribute to Thames, but prefers rather to roll on its own course, an independent flood, only mingling with the mightier river in the embraces of the ocean, where the career of both is at an end, "like lovers, in their lives estranged, but in their death united."

> Long had the Thames, as we in records read
> Before that day, her wooéd to his bedde;
> But the proud nymph would for no worldly meed,
> Nor no entreatie to his love be ledde,
> Till now at last relenting, she to him was wedde.

What reader of that old bard does not remember his gorgeous description of the

bridal, the Thames attended by all his tributary streams, and the Medway by hers; the
Bridegroom,

> That full fresh and jolly was,
> All deckéd in a robe of watchet hue,
> On which the waves glittering like crystal glass,
> So cunningly enwoven were, that few
> Could weenen whether they were false or trew.
> And on his head, like to a coronet,
> He wore, that seemed strange to common view,
> In which were many towers and castles set,
> That it encompast round as with a golden fret.

And then the Bride, without the coronet of
a royal city on her bank—

> The lovely Medua came,
> Clad in a vesture of unknowen geare
> And uncouth fashion, yet her well became,
> That seemed like silver sprinkled here and there,
> With glittering spangs, that did like stars appeare,
> And waved upon like water chamelot,
> To hide the metal; which yet every where
> Bewrayed itself, to let men plainely wot
> It was no mortal work that seemed and yet was not.

> Her goodly locks adown her back did flow
> Unto her waist, with flowers bescattered;
> The which ambrosial odours forth did throw
> To all about, and all her shoulders spread
> As a new Spring; and likewise on her head
> A chaplet rare of sundry flowers she wore;
> From under which the dewy humour shed,
> Did trickle down her hair, like to the hoar
> Congealéd little drops that do the morn adore.

But the place of their bridal, as the poet
calls their confluence into the sea, has sterner
recollections than such as these; for here took
place, in 1797, that famous mutiny of the
fleet, which spread so much alarm throughout
the nation, occurring as it did, at a time when
Europe was convulsed by the struggle of con-
tending principles, and England was watched
by jealous and powerful enemies, eager to take
advantage of her weakness. The mutiny of
the Nore will always render the confluence of
the Thames and Medway a memorable spot
in the annals of England. Sheerness, whose

dock-yard walls and low roofs are now visible, and beside which the fleet was moored at the time, is also associated with that event; a short history of which will not be ill-timed, as we await the departure of the Chatham steam-boat, which is to take us up the Medway.

For many months before the outbreak of the mutiny the seamen of the British navy had complained of the smallness of their pay, alleging, with great reason, that it remained exactly the same as in the days of Charles II; whereas, provisions, and living in general, had almost doubled in price since that period. They had also high notions of the rights of man : — the ideas which had convulsed France were germinating all over Europe, and our sailors, in common with others, could not, at such a time, and with such notions of equality, brook the insolence of stripling and inexperienced officers, who showed their imagined superiority by harsh words, and tyranny, to better men than themselves. But this grievance, though felt, was never made the ostensible cause of complaint; the inefficiency of pay was alone insisted on, and that in the most respectful manner. The Government of Mr. Pitt took no notice of their demands, founded upon reason as they were, and were quite taken aback by surprise, when the first mutiny broke out in the channel fleet, under Lord Bridport on the 13th of April 1797.

On the return of the fleet into Portsmouth some days previously, a secret correspondence was settled between all the ships that composed it, which ended in an unanimous agreement that no ship should lift an anchor until the grievances of the seamen were redressed. On the 15th Lord Bridport, in total ignorance of the spirit of the men, ordered the signal to prepare for sea. Immediately the crew of the Queen Charlotte, a first-rate man-of-war, and his lordship's own vessel, raised three deafening cheers, as a signal to the rest of the fleet that they refused to weigh the anchor. The crews of the other vessels followed the example ; and notwithstanding all the exertions of their officers, refused to put to sea. Every ship's company then proceeded to the election of two delegates, and Lord Howe's cabin was fixed upon as the place where they were to hold their consultations. On the 17th an oath was administered to every man in the fleet, to support the cause in which they had engaged ; ropes were reared to the yard-arm in each ship, as a signal of the death-punishment that would be inflicted on every man who proved traitor to the cause; and several officers who had rendered themselves obnoxious, were put ashore. The crews treated the admiral with the greatest respect, and drew up two petitions, one to the Admiralty, and the other to the House of Commons, stating their grievances, in firm but respectful language, representing, that while their bravery and loyalty were equal to those of the army, the pensioners of Chelsea had received an increased allowance, while those of Greenwich remained at the old rate. They declared their readiness to continue true Englishmen, and brave defenders of their country, but insisted on an increase of pay and provisions, or the liberty of going ashore while in harbour, and on the continuance of their pay to all wounded seamen, until they were either cured or discharged. After some negotiations, their demands were acceded to; but not without a show of offended dignity on the part of the Government; and the men returned to their duty on the 23rd of April.

All alarm had subsided in the public mind, when, fourteen days afterwards, a fresh mutiny broke out. The seamen mistrusted the promises and the intentions of Government, and insisted upon some more positive pledges, that the stipulations would be kept; and that a

general pardon would be granted for all offences. In this emergency, Lord Howe, beloved by the navy for his kindness of heart,
and admired for his successes and his bravery,
was despatched to communicate with the mutineers. By his exhortations, and his assurances
of the fulfilment of all that the Government
had promised, order was restored, and the seamen of Portsmouth and Plymouth finally returned to their duty.

These occurrences it has been necessary to
repeat in order to explain those that afterwards took place in the Medway. They were
the subject of warm debates in Parliament, in
which the opposition, while it agreed to the
increase in the navy estimates which they occasioned, severely handled the conduct of the
ministry for not paying earlier attention to the
reasonable demands of the seamen, before they
were made by men who showed by their conduct that they would brook no refusal.

On the 22nd of May, in less than two weeks
afterwards, when the nation was beginning to
forget its alarm, and was congratulating itself
on the happy issue of an event that might have
been productive of such serious mischief, the
third mutiny broke out at the Nore, more me-
nacing and more alarming than its predeces-

sors. The crews took possession of their respective ships, elected Delegates, who afterwards elected a President, a Secretary, and
other officers, and drew up a statement of demands less reasonable, and in terms more insulting than those made by the mutineers of the
Channel Fleet. As the mutineers kept up no
communication with any men or body of men
but the Board of Admiralty, it was impossible
for many days to ascertain what were their real
intentions. The most alarming rumours were
spread and believed, each day's being more
painful than those of the day preceding; and,
when on the 6th of June, intelligence was
received in London, that four large vessels
had deserted from Admiral Duncan, who was
stationed off the coast of Holland, to join the
mutineers in the Medway, the consternation
knew no bounds: the shores of England appeared open to the first invader who chose to
approach, and men of all parties strove to heal
the unhappy breach, and prayed to the God
of nations for the restoration of order.

The vessels that deserted were the Agamemnon, the Leopard, and Isis, men-of-war,
with the Ranger sloop. The brave Duncan,
when he found himself deserted by part of his
fleet, called his own ship's crew together, and

made the following simple, manly, affecting, and eloquent address to them.

" My Lads, I once more call you together with a sorrowful heart from what I have lately seen, the disaffection. of the fleet: I call it disaffection, for the crews have no grievances. To be deserted by his fleet, in the face of an enemy, is a disgrace which, I believe, never before happened to a British admiral: nor could I have supposed it possible. My greatest comfort under God is, that I have been supported by the officers, seamen, and marines, of this ship, for which, with a heart overflowing with gratitude, I request you to accept my sincere thanks. I flatter myself much good may result from your example, by bringing those deluded people to a sense of their duty, which they owe not only to their King and country, but to themselves.

" The British navy has ever been the support of that liberty which has been handed down to us by our ancestors, and which I trust we shall maintain to our latest posterity; and that can only be done by unanimity and obedience. The ship's company and others who have distinguished themselves by their loyalty and good order, deserve to be, and doubtless will be, the favourites of a grateful country. They

will also have, from their own inward feelings,
a comfort which will be lasting; and not like
the fleeting and false confidence of those who
have swerved from their duty.

" It has often been my pride, with you, to
look into the Texel, and see a foe which dread-
ed coming out to meet us: my pride is now
humbled indeed: my feelings are not easily to
be expressed: our cup has overflowed and made
us wanton. The all-wise Providence has given
us this check as a warning, and I hope we shall
improve by it. On Him, then, let us trust,
where our only security can be found. I know
there are many good men among us; for my
own part I have had full confidence of all in
this ship: and once more beg to express my
approbation of your conduct.

" May God, who has thus far conducted you,
continue to do so; and may the British navy,
the glory and support of our country, be restored to its wonted splendour, and be not only
the bulwark of Britain but the terror of the
world. But this can only be effected by a
strict adherence to our duty and obedience,
and let us pray that Almighty God may keep
us in the right way of thinking. God bless
you all!"

The whole crew melted into tears as the

admiral spoke, there was not a dry eye among them; and collectively and individually they swore to abide by him in life or in death. The remaining vessels of the fleet caught the enthusiasm, though they did not hear the eloquence that excited it, and they all remained faithful to their duty. The admiral, though his force was thus weakened, took up his usual station off the Texel, to watch the motions of the Dutch fleet, and accept battle if it were offered.

At the Nore the accession of these ships increased the confidence and the demands of the mutineers. They insisted upon still further increase of pay and provisions, and other indulgences which had not been even hinted by those of the Channel fleet. They complained especially of the unequal distribution of prize-money, by which the officers received so much and the seamen so little, and blamed their pre-mutineers of Portsmouth and Plymouth for not stipulating for some new regulations in this respect. Richard Parker, their president or admiral, as he was called, was a young man of much natural ability, good education, and indomitable resolution, and presided at all the interviews with the agents sent down by the Admiralty or the Government to confer with them. Admiral Backner, the commanding officer at the Nore, was directed by the Lords of the Admiralty to inform the seamen that their demands were totally inconsistent with the good order and regulations necessary to be observed in the navy, and for that reason could not be complied with; but that if they would immediately return to their duty, each and all would receive the royal pardon, and oblivion cover their past offences. Parker replied to this by a firm declaration that the seamen had unanimously determined to keep possession of the fleet until the Lords of the Admiralty themselves had repaired to the Nore, and re-dressed the grievances of the navy.

This was a bold demand, but the Government deemed it right that some members of the Board of Admiralty should proceed to the Medway. The Earl Spencer, Lord Arden, and Admiral Young, proceeded thither accordingly, and had an interview with Parker and the delegates. The conference was but short. Parker was firm and would not abate one iota of his former demands; the Lords were equally firm, and the conference broke up abruptly, leaving matters in a worse state than before. A proclamation was immediately issued, offering pardon to all who returned to their duty; a message was sent to Parliament by his Ma-

jesty ; and a bill was introduced to the effect, that
persons who should endeavour to seduce either
soldiers or sailors from their duty, or instigate
them to mutinous practices, or form any mutinous assembly, should on conviction be deemed guilty of felony and suffer death. The bill
was passed through all its stages with unexam-
pled rapidity, and received the royal assent on
the third of June. Another motion was then
made by Mr. Pitt to prevent all communication with the ships that should be in a state of
mutiny, and to enact, that if after the King's
proclamation any person should voluntarily con-
tinne in any such ship, that person should be
declared guilty of mutiny and rebellion, and
should be liable to all the punishments of those
crimes accordingly. There was some opposition from the old Whig party to the severity of
the latter, but it passed the houses by a great
majority. As the mutineers had threatened to
stop all vessels entering the Thames, circular
letters were despatched to all the outports on
the third of June, forbidding all vessels clearing
out for the Thames or Medway to quit their
stations until further orders. An embargo was
also laid upon all vessels in the port of London,
forbidding them to proceed lest they should be
seized by the mutineers. As it was rumoured

that the mutineers intended to put out to sea,
all the buoys and beacons were removed from
the mouth of the river, in order should any
attempt be made to get away that the ships
might be run aground.   Additional troops were
thrown into Sheerness, the mutineers having
manifested a disposition to bombard that town;
and furnaces and hot balls were kept ready to
burn the fleet had such an attempt been made.

In order that their hostile intentions might
become apparent, the mutineers seized two
vessels laden with stores that attempted to pass
the Nore, and sent notice ashore that they intended to block up the Thames, and cut off
all communication between London and the
sea, until the government acceded to their
demands.   They acted upon this determination
by moving four of their largest men-of-war
across the river, and stopped several ships that
were proceeding to the metropolis.   But this
was going too far.   The men knew it,— some
began to waver, and even the most reckless to
lose confidence in one another.   To prevent too
much power from being lodged in the hands
of any one man, the office of president was en-
trusted to no one longer than a day, and ships
whose crews were suspected of any wavering
or lukewarmness, were stationed in the midst

of the other vessels, that they might be fired upon from every side, if they manifested the slightest disposition to escape. Notwithstanding these precautions, two vessels contrived to elude their vigilance, put out to sea, and sailed to Portsmouth, where they returned to their duty. The seamen at this port, and at Plymouth, the authors of the former mutinies, each addressed an admonition to those of the Nore, warning them that they had gone too far,—that their present proceedings were a disgrace to the British Navy,—that they should be content with the advantages already secured to them, and return at once to their allegiance. But the delegates, now so deeply implicated, were in such a condition that they were afraid to submit. They thought no clemency would be extended to them, and that their only hope was to render themselves still more formidable, and force the government into compliance, or an amnesty. Impressed with these notions, they resolved to persevere. The committee of delegates meeting on board the Sandwich, sent for Lord Northesk, the captain of the Mon tague, whom they had kept prisoner on board of his own vessel, and asked him to be the bearer of a message to the King. The message was couched in terms of great respect to-

wards his Majesty, but of much severity towards his ministers, requiring entire compliance
with the original demands, and threatening,
in case of refusal, to put out to sea immediately. They told Lord Northesk that they
considered him the seamen's friend, and asked
him to be the bearer of the message, and to
pledge his word of honour to return to them
within fifty-four hours. Lord Northesk readily
undertook the mission, but stated candidly that
their demands were so unreasonable that he had
not the slightest hope they would be complied
with.

In the mean time the acts of mutiny continued. Some officers, more than usually un-
popular, were ducked in the sea, and then
sent ashore, but in general the strictest discipline was maintained by the delegates in the
fleet. Nine rules for the guidance of the men
were agreed upon, and promulgated : first, that
every ship should diligently keep a quarter-
watch, and that every man found below, in
his watch, should be severely punished ; second,
that every ship should give three cheers morning and evening ; third, that no woman should
go on shore from any ship, but that as many
might come in as pleased ; fourth, that any
person attempting to bring liquor into a ship,

or any person found drunk, should be severely punished; fifth, that the greatest attention should be paid to the officers' orders; sixth, that every seaman and marine should take an oath of fidelity, not only to themselves, but to the fleet in general; seventh, that no ship should lift anchor to proceed from port until the desires of the fleet were satisfied; eighth, that no liberty should be given to pass from ship to ship till everything was settled; and ninth, that no private letters should be sent ashore.

Notwithstanding these regulations, a want of unanimity began to prevail. The King, of course, took no notice of the message sent by Lord Northesk, and this increased the distrust, and diminished the confidence of the men. On the 7th of June an extraordinary Gazette was published, warning all persons whatever to avoid communication with the following ships, whose crews were declared to be in a state of mutiny and rebellion; namely, the Sandwich, the Montague, the Director, the Inflexible, the Monmouth, the Belliquieux, the Standard, the Lion, the Nassau, the Repulse, the Grampus, the Proserpine, the Brilliant, the Iris, the Champion, the Comet, the Tysiphone, the Pylades, the

Swan, the Inspector, the Agamemnon, and
the Vestal. The proclamation at the same
time authorized the commissioners of the Board
of Admiralty to accept the submission of such
ships, or any one of them, or any of the men
belonging to them, who would immediately
on returning to their duty be forgiven for
all past offences.

In the mean time diligent preparation was
made at Sheerness to reduce them to submission by force. A large vessel called the
Warrior was fitted out at Chatham, manned
wholly by volunteers to act against them, and
everything showed the determination of the
Government to make no further concessions.
Every day the disunion of the mutineers increased, and on the 13th the Agamemnon,
the Standard, and the Nassau, each of sixty-
four guns, the Iris frigate of thirty-two, and
the Vestal of twenty-eight, slipped their cables
and got under the protection of the guns of
Sheerness. Two more line of battle ships got
away in the course of the night, and on the
following day Government offered a reward of
500l. for the apprehension of Parker. Four
of the delegates attempted to escape in an open
boat, but finding both shores lined with troops,
they went out to sea and turned the North

Foreland. Being pursued by a cutter, they ran into the Isle of Thanet, where they were taken by the volunteers. On the 14th, the Sandwich, Parker's ship, drifted to Sheerness, with the red flag of mutiny taken down, and the white flag hoisted in its stead. As the garrison were not certain of her intention they made ready their guns to defend the town, and sent out some officers in a boat to parley with the crew. All the sails of the Sandwich were furled, and it became quite manifest that her intentions were peaceable. The persons who seemed to command said they came to surrender, and to give up Parker and the rest of the delegates. Arrived within gun shot of the great battery, some boats' crews went on board, and brought out Parker, Davis, Higgins, Gregory, Denison, and about twenty other delegates, who were immediately conveyed to the black hole of Sheerness, and confined, heavily ironed, till the following morning, when they were sent under a strong escort to Maidstone gaol. One of the delegates of the Agamemnon shot himself through the head when the crew laid hold of him. Parker had been arrested by one Lieutenant Mott, with the concurrence of the crew; he made little or no resistance, and was merely confined to his cabin till the vessel was drifted ashore. Government immediately proceeded to the trial of the mutineers : a court-martial was held on board the Neptune at Greenhithe under the presidence of Admiral Sir Thomas Pasley. The trial lasted four days. Parker conducted himself with the most admirable composure, cross-examined the witnesses with great skill and tact, and made a calm, clear, and eloquent defence, denying nothing that had been proved, or even alleged against him, but urging in extenuation that he had saved the fleet. It was he who had established order among the mutineers ; he had presided but to control the evil passions of the men, who, but for his advice, and the authority that he acquired over them, would have broken out into acts of civil warfare, bombarded the towns of their native country, or sailed with the fleet to a foreign port. He was found guilty unanimously, and sentenced to death. The 30th of June, a week after the conclusion of the trial, was fixed upon for the day of execution. On that morning, at eight o'clock, the ships having been ranged in order opposite Sheerness, the Sandwich at the head, in such a position that it could be distinctly seen by all the fleet,

Parker was brought from his place of confinement. He had passed the night with great composure, and on being awakened in the morning, paid the most scrupulous attention to his personal cleanliness and appearance, and dressed himself in a new suit of mourning. To the chaplain who attended him he denied most solemnly that the mutineers ever held or intended to hold any correspondence with republicans, anarchists, or disaffected persons on shore. He asked Lieutenant Mott, who arrested him, and who commanded the marines by whom he was accompanied to the fatal scaffold, whether he might be allowed a glass of white wine His request being granted, he drank it off, saying that he drank it first to the salvation of his soul, and secondly as a pledge of forgiveness to his enemies. He then made a very short address to the ship's company, in which he acknowledged the justice of his sentence, and hoped that his death would be deemed a sufficient atonement, and that the lives of others might be spared. He then inquired whether the gun that was to deprive him of life was ready primed and loaded, and being answered in the affirmative, he mounted the scaffold with a stately and steady step;

the fatal bow-gun was fired, and the reeve-rope catching him, ran him up, though not with great velocity, to the yardarm, where he remained suspended for about an hour, in sight of the fleet, and of a great crowd of spectators who had assembled on the Isle of Grain. Thus perished a man who possessed talent and conduct which, under happier circumstances, might have earned him an honourable name. His courage in facing almost alone the wrath of a great nation, his general unsullied character, and the power once acquired, which he undoubtedly exercised to restrain and curb the violence of less sensible and more ferocious men, single him out, notwithstanding his one great crime, as a noble-minded and certainly very remarkable man. His dying prayer was not heard. His death was not atonement enough ; several of the mutineers were sentenced to very severe punishment, and no less than seven of them were hanged together opposite Sheerness, a few days afterwards, besides several who were executed at Portsmouth.

Sheerness, where these events occurred, is still one of the principal stations of the British fleet. Several ships of war are always moored in the Medway, under the command of a distinguished admiral. The town lies in a low, unhealthy swamp; and has always a considerable military force to aid the fleet in protecting the joint entrances of the Thames and Medway.

On the restoration of Charles II. Sheerness contained but one small fort with twelve guns, to defend the passage—a force miserably insufficient. After the Dutch, in the year 1667, had proved its insufficiency in a very painful manner to the English people, by forcing a fleet up the stream, and burning some vessels at Chatham, the place was immediately increased to a regular fortification. It has been several times augmented and improved since that period, and is now an important town. No enemy's ship can pass it without the hazard of being sunk or blown out of the water. Several smaller forts have also been constructed on the other side of the river. For many years the town was much more unwholesome than it is now; and it is far from being salubrious, owing to the scarcity of fresh water. Shortly after the famous mutiny, that evil was remedied : a well was sunk to the depth of three hundred and twenty-eight feet, which has ever since produced an unfailing supply.

The fine man-of-war, the Howe, bearing
the flag of a vice-admiral, is an object of
great curiosity to the people of London,
who come down thousands at a time by
the steam-boat, in the fine weather, to inspect
this wooden wall of England. Every arrange-
ment is made on board the vessel for the accommodation of the public, and a man appointed for the purpose goes round with each party,
and explains the wonders of the ship; from
the clean decks;—so clean, that, to use a common saying, we might eat a dinner off them
and not want a tablecloth;—to the tanks in the
hold, sufficiently capacious to contain water
enough for eight hundred or a thousand men
for a six months' voyage. The guns, each in
the nicest order—the large kitchen—the store-
room full of biscuit and flour—the armoury,
with its pikes, pistols, dirks, and other implements of war, arranged fantastically, but me-
thodically, in stars and circles, are successively
visited, and successively elicit the approbation of the crowd. The officers of the ship,
too, are always full of politeness to the stranger,
and of courtesy and hospitality combined, to
all who are fortunate enough to have a personal introduction to any one among them.
Those who have dined at their mess, and

passed a night on board, as we have, will not
easily forget their gentlemanly bearing, their
unaffected kindness, or their liberal hospitality. The Howe was built after the war, and
has, consequently, seen no service, or even
quitted the shores of old England ; but she
is ready to defend them, and behave as an
English ship ought, should ever the unfortunate necessity arise. The brave Marshal
Soult, on his departure from this country,
after his mission as ambassador extraordinary
at the coronation of our present most gra-
cions sovereign, delayed his homeward voyage
for a few hours to visit the Howe, where he
was received by his gallant friend Vice-Admiral Sir Robert Otway, and entertained with a
sumptuous *déjeûner à la fourchette.* The speeches
made upon the occasion by the English
sailor who gave, and the French soldier who
partook of, the feast, did honour to the hearts
of both. It is to be wished, for the sake of
Europe and the world, that the warriors of
both countries will ever cultivate the same
spirit, and only meet for the purposes of amity
and good fellowship. We, who pen these
pages, were invited to that feast, but by some
unlucky fate we only arrived within sight of
the Howe, when all was over, and could just

distinguish, through the thick falling rain, the
French steamer, with the Marshal on board,
at the verge of the horizon, ploughing the
waters towards France. Great was our sorrow
thereat, as the reader may imagine, — not for
the loss of our *déjeûner*, for on that score we
were not allowed to have reason to complain,
but for the loss of the interesting spectacle
of the ancient foe of England sitting in peace
and friendship at the table of entertainers who
had forgotten all enmity, and had no other
feeling towards him than those of generous
appreciation of his courage, respect for his
character, and friendship, devoid of all old
prejudices, for the people whom he represented.

At Minstèr, the spire of which is visible as
we sail up the river, there was formerly a
nunnery, or minster, which gave name to the
town, founded so early as the year 673 by
Sexburga, mother of King Egbert. But the
village is chiefly remarkable as the burial-place
of old Sir Robert de Shurland, renowned in
Kentish legends. He was created a knight
banneret by Edward I. for his gallant conduct
at the siege of Carlaverock in Scotland, and
possessed considerable lands in this neighbourhood. On his tomb in Minster church he was

represented lying cross legged beneath a Gothic arch, with a shield on his left arm, an armed page at his feet, and at his right side the head of a horse emerging from the sea. This horse's head became a sore puzzle to the country people, and various tales were invented to account for its being placed there. The legend that obtained most credit is given in Harris's History of Kent, to the effect that Sir Robert de Shurland having quarrelled with a priest, buried him alive. Fearful of the consequences, he swam on his horse two miles through the sea to the King, who was then on shipboard near the island, and obtained his pardon. He then swam back to the shore, where, being told by some one that his horse was a magician or he never could have performed such a feat, he dismounted immediately, and cut the animal's head off as unworthy to live. The legend adds, that the knight was out hunting about a year afterwards (another legend says exactly a year and a day afterwards), when the horse on which he rode stumbled, and threw him violently on the ground. His head came in contact with some hard substance, and he received so severe a fracture of the skull that he died in a few hours. The hard substance being examined, was found to be the skull of

the former steed, which he had destroyed for
being a magician !

Antiquaries and men of sense are not to be
put off with this foolish legend, and Phillipot,
in his account of Kent, explains that the figure
of the horse's head upon the knight's tomb may
possibly be typical of a grant of the wrecks
of the sea bestowed upon him by King Edward I. in the tenth year of his reign. The
privilege was always considered, he says, to comprise only such articles from a wreck as a man
upon a horse could ride into the sea at its
lowest ebb and touch with the point of his
lance. Samuel Ireland conjectures that the
horse's head may have been merely sculptured
on his monument as a mark of his affection
for some favourite animal. Hogarth once made
a tour to Minster to see this tomb, accompanied
by a Mr. Forrest of York Buildings, and some
other gentlemen, and Mr. Forrest, we are informed by Samuel Ireland, wrote some verses
embodying the legend, which we have not,
however, been able to discover.

At a short distance up the stream, on the
East Swale, a branch of the Medway, stands
the ancient town of Queenborough, formerly
called Cyningborough, or King Borough, from
its having been the residence of some of the

Kings of Kent during the Saxon Heptarchy. It bears no traces of antiquity, but consists chiefly of one wide street, principally
made up of modern buildings, and inhabited
by fishermen and oyster dredgers. It was formerly a free borough, and in the reign of
Elizabeth, although it consisted of but twenty-
three inhabited houses, sent two members to
Parliament. To Cromwell's Parliament it sent
one member. At the time the Reform Bill
was introduced, it was a place of much more
importance; but its privileges being rather too
great for its deserts, the borough was placed
in the annihilating schedule, and it now returns
no member to Parliament.

Proceeding up the stream, and passing between a great number of low swampy islands,
mere marshes, unfit for the habitation of man,
we arrive at the little village of Gillingham,
and the fortress of Upnor Castle, pleasantly
situated on a gentle eminence on the right
of the narrowing river. This place, with
Chatham, at which we shall presently arrive,
was celebrated before the Reformation, for
its wonder-working virgin, who was called
Our Lady, and sometimes the Rood of Gillingham

An old legend, repeated in Kent when

Lambarde wrote his Perambulation of that county, thus accounts for the cessation of the miracles at her shrine. The dead body of a man floating in the Medway, was cast ashore in the parish of Chatham, where it was buried, after due inquiry, by the Churchwardens. The parish clerk who officiated at the funeral, re-tired home to rest; but a sense of oppression was upon him, and his sleep was disturbed and broken. About midnight, however, he fell into a more refreshing slumber, from which he was awakened by a loud knocking at his window. Still more inclined to sleep than to get up, he turned on his side, after asking in his roughest voice, " who was there ?" The answer sent a cold shudder through his frame. Being a holy man, he knew the solemn voice of Our Lady of Chatham, who commanded him to arise and follow her. He arose immediately, and came down into the street, where she await-ed his coming, sitting on the steps of the door. A halo of glory was around her head, and he bent before her in reverential awe. " Follow me, O clerk," said she, " for this day ye have buried beside my grave the corpse of a sinful man. He so offends my eyes by his ghastly grinning, that unless he be removed, I can do no more miraculous workings in your town.

That so great a calamity should not befall the poor people, take thou mattocks and pike, and come with me, take up the body and cast it again into the river."

Though the night was cold and wet, and he was not accustomed to such labour, he procured mattocks and followed her in silence. That he might not doubt her divine power, he noticed that wherever she placed her foot, the grass immediately grew, and the flowers began to blossom, and at one place where she rested for awhile, a whole garden of verdure and beauty started up around her. At last they arrived at the churchyard, which was a good distance from the Clerk's house, where Our Lady pointed out the spot of her own sepulture, and then that of the drowned man, telling the clerk to set to work immediately and relieve her sainted ashes from the ghastly presence of that sinful neighbour. The big drops of perspiration stood on the brow of the clerk. He could not speak to the being of another world, but he did her bidding in solemn silence. He dug for many hours until he arrived at the coffin, our Lady looking on with a melancholy and dignified smile. She motioned him to open it, and take the body on his back, and cast it into the Med-

way. He did so. The corpse grinned horribly upon him, but he had no power to let
it fall, and he walked away to the river's brink.
He had the curiosity to look back, when he saw
the figure of our Lady melting gradually away
into the thin air, and seeming no more than the
light silver mist that floats upon the mountain.
With a violent effort he threw the corpse into
the river : the water bubbled furiously : a ray
of light danced cheerily above the grave of our
Lady, and the clerk feeling his mind relieved
from a load of sorrow, walked back to his own
home, and slept comfortably till the morning.
Anxious to know whether this occurrence were
not a dream, he arose early and walked forth
to the churchyard. He was convinced that it
was no night vision, that he had indeed seen
the virgin of Chatham, long before he arrived
at that place ; for, from his own door, all the
way they had passed, he noticed the track of
verdure where the unearthly feet had trodden,
and the little parterre of flowers that still grew
on the place where they had rested. From
that day forth he was a calmer and a better
man, and the towns-people long pointed with
reverence to the little tufts of grass, the earthly
witnesses of the miracle. But, alas ! for Gillingham, it suffered by the good fortune of Chat-

ham. The body of the drowned man was
wafted down by the stream, and found by a
fisherman of that village. He took it ashore,
and it was decently buried in the churchyard.
The Lady of Gillingham was wroth at the
pollution, but caring less for the good people
in whose parish she wrought miracles, or not
having the good sense of the Lady of Chatham
to apply for mortal aid in the removal of the
nuisance, she withdrew her favour from the
place for ever, her shrine lost its healing virtues, and the prayers of the faithful were of
no avail. It was observed at the same time
that the earth where the drowned man was
buried began immediately to sink, and so continued for many years, until the body was deposited in the great pit of perdition, when the
earth was heaved up again, by no mortal means,
and restored to its former smoothness. Lambarde says, this legend, though only known to
some very old people in his time, was not long
previously " both commonly reported and faith-
fully credited of the vulgar sort," having been
received by tradition from the elders of a former age.

When part of the church of Chatham was pulled down in 1788, several fragments of ancient
sculpture were discovered, and among others the

headless figure of a Virgin and Child, having a mantle fastened across the breast by a fibula set with glass in imitation of precious stones. This was generally supposed to be the figure of Our Lady of Chatham.

CHAPTER XI.

Chatham.—Rochester and Stroud.—Rochester Bridge and Castle.—Aylesford.—Birth-place of Sir Charles Sedley.— Hengist and Horsa. — Remarkable Cromlechs. — Kit's Cotty House.—The Rood of Grace, and Tricks of the Monks of Boxley.—Penenden Heath.

E now, having rounded a considerable bend in the river, arrive within sight of the three adjoining towns of Chatham, Rochester, and Stroud, or as the soldiers billeted upon the inhabitants call them, Cheat'em, Roh'em, and Starve'em. Chatham extends along the east bank of the Medway, and is a long, straggling ill-built town, which contains a large population, and has an air of considerable bustle and business. In the Domesday Book it is called Coeltham, and Ceteham, and is described as having a church, and six fisheries value twelve pence. It remained but an insignificant place until the time of Elizabeth, when the Dock was erected, and then was laid the foundation

of its present importance. Camden describes
it as "stored for the finest fleet the sun ever
beheld, and ready at a minute's warning, built
lately by our gracious sovereign Elizabeth, at
great expense, for the security of her subjects
and the terror of her enemies, with a fort on
the shore for its defence."

James I. and Charles I. increased the dock
and raised many additional buildings. In the
reign of Charles II. a first-rate ship of one
hundred guns called the Royal Sovereign was
built here, and the King visited the docks to
inspect the ship before she was launched.

Many large vessels have since been constructed here, including the ill-fated Royal George, in which the brave Kempenfeldt and his twice five hundred men were buried in the deep.

In the eighteenth century, during nearly the whole of which England was at war either with one nation or another, great additions were made to the town and docks of Chatham. In the year 1758 when the country was threatened with invasion, an Act of Parliament was passed for the purchase of additional lands, and the erection of such works as might be necessary to secure this important arsenal from the attempts of an enemy. The famous fortification called the Lines of Chatham were forthwith commenced, and were continued from the banks of the Medway above the Ordnance Wharf round an oblong plot of ground, measuring about half a mile in width and a mile in length to the extremity of the dock-yard, where they again join the Medway. Within this area, besides the naval establishment, are included the upper and lower barracks, which have been built for the garrison, the church of Chatham and the hamlet of Brompton, the latter of modern origin. Various additions have been made to the security of the place since 1758, and another act was passed in 1782 for the purchase of lands and the erection of buildings.

It was here that the British army was to have taken up its position if Buonaparte had effected a landing upon our shores, and the fate of himself and of England to have been decided. During the late war twenty large forges were continually at work, and some of the anchors made weighed as much as fourteen tons. The Rope House is nearly twelve hundred feet in length, where cables are made one hundred and twenty fathoms long, and twenty-two inches in circumference. There are altogether four docks for repairing, and six slips for building ships. Over the entrance the Lords of the Admiralty in the year 1806, ordered the shattered mainmast of Lord Nelson's ship the " Victory " to be placed as a memorial of the decisive battle of Trafalgar, and as a memento of great deeds, to be continually in the sight of our seamen.

The " Chest of Chatham," for the relief of aged and destitute sailors, was established in the reign of Elizabeth, each of the men in her fleet contributing a portion of his pay for the relief of the sufferers after the defeat of the Spanish Armada. It was much forwarded by the exertions of the Earl of Nottingham, then Admiral of the fleet, aided by the great Sir Francis Drake, and Sir John Hawkins. Shortly after the Mutiny at the Nore, the Chest of Chatham was removed to Greenwich Hospital, in consequence of sundry abuses which had crept into the distribution of the charity. The principal abuses on which the commissioners recommended the removal of the Chest and the placing it under the direction of the Lords of the Admiralty, and the Governor and other officers of Greenwich Hospital, arose from the system of agency, by which the pensioners were but too often deprived of a considerable portion of their allowance. The estates of the Chest were also let considerably under their value, and in some instances proved a loss to, instead of an augmentation of, the funds. The commissioners therefore recommended that they should be sold and the produce invested in the funds. The stock belonging to the Chest amounts to about 300,000*l.* of which 10,000*l.* was contributed early in the present century by some charitable individual who concealed his name, and also bequeathed the same munificent sum to Greenwich Hospital.

Chatham gives the title of Earl to the house of Pitt, so illustrious among the most illustrions, for the two great men it produced in the last century. The place formerly gave the title of Baron to the Duke of Argyle, but the title became extinct on the death of John, second Duke, in the year 1743, whose Scottish dignities alone passed to his brother Archibald, the third Duke.

Rochester bridge and the ruins of the old castle now rise majestically over the Medway, and impress even the most careless passenger with the conviction that he has arrived at an ancient and time-honoured place. This is the famous bridge that divides the men of Kent from the Kentish men, a distinction apparently without a difference, but much insisted upon by the former. The natives born east of the bridge are the men of Kent; those west, the Kentish men; the former being considered the best and boldest, a character they have given themselves, although not universally acknowledged by others, since their pretended set-to with William the Conqueror, at Swanscombe, when they obtained the confirmation of their privileges from that grim successful warrior.

Rochester was the Durobrivae of the Romans, and one of their stipendiary cities. Many Roman remains have been discovered in various parts of it, strengthening the conjecture that the present city occupies the actual site of the Roman one. Within the walls of the great tower or keep of the castle, and in the gardens, great quantities of coins have been at various times dug up, including some of the Emperors, Vespasian, Trajan, Adrian, Antoninus Pius, Marcus Aurelius, Constantius, and Constantine the Great. The cathedral is partly built with remains of Roman bricks. In the neighbouring fields, and at a place called Bally Hill, other remains of antiquity have been explored; remnants of mosaic pavements, urns, jugs and *paterae* of fine red earth.

Rochester was an important place during the Saxon dynasties in England; and from its wealth, and its position on the Medway, was continually exposed to the ravages of the Danes. It was more than once pillaged and destroyed by these greedy foes. In the year 676 Ethelred, King of Mercia, razed it to the ground. In 839, the Danes burned and pillaged it, and committed unheard-of cruelties. In 885, they made a second attempt upon it, but were repulsed by the inhabitants, under the command of Alfred the Great. In the tenth century it was twice burned down by the Danes, and the Medway became a common highway for that piratical people.

At the conquest, Rochester, along with many other possessions in various parts of England, was bestowed by the conqueror, on his half-brother, Odo, Bishop of Baieux, upon whose disgrace, in 1083, it reverted to the Crown. Rochester was made a bishop's see so early as the year 597, by Ethelbert, first christian King of Kent, and a church dedicated to St. Andrew, was built for Justus, the Bishop, in 604. The present cathedral was commenced by Gundulphus promoted to this diocese in 1077, and carried on by his successors until the year 1130, when it was solemnly dedicated by Corboyle, Archbishop of Canterbury, in the presence of Henry I. and his Queen Matilda. It contains many ancient tombs and statues, which the antiquary will be pleased to visit. Most visitors, however, will rather remember with melancholy interest, that within its walls, Ridley the martyr often preached to his flock; and that Sprat, Atterbury, Zachary Pearce, and other eminent prelates, were bishops of this diocese.

Next to the cathedral, the most remarkable objects at Rochester are the bridge and the picturesque ruins of the castle. There seems to have been a wooden bridge at the conquest. It became at last so dangerous, and

cost so much to keep it in repair, that the inhabitants petitioned Parliament, at the end of the fourteenth century, to aid them in building a bridge of stone. Sir Robert Knolles, a great warrior of that day, took the matter in hand, and by his exertions among his friends, a sufficient sum was subscribed to build a stone-bridge, the finest then in England, with the single exception of that at London. Of this Knight, Stowe preserves these laudatory verses:

O Robert Knolles, most worthy of fame,
By thy prowess France was made tame,
Thy manhood made the Frenchmen yield,
By dint of sword in town and field.

Sir Robert also erected a chapel and a chantry, in the former of which a tablet hung for two hundred years or more, inscribed with the names of all the subscribers. Among many others of less note, were those of Knolles and Constance his wife, Sir John Cobham and Margaret his wife, Cardinal Bourchier, Archbishops Morton and Chicheley, and Richard Whittington Lord Mayor of London, more famous, perhaps, than all the rest, from the well-known tale of his cat, the delight of all the nurseries of England. The bridge is five hundred and sixty feet long, and fifteen broad, and is formed with eleven arches of which the largest is about forty feet. The Medway is here very deep and rapid, and it was long supposed that the piles of the bridge were built upon the rock. Such, however, is not the case. Rochester Bridge was long the handsomest though not the largest bridge in England. It was never blocked up by houses and made a common market of, like that of London, but always open as it is now. In this respect it was undoubtedly the first to set an example, which has since been universally followed. The chantry called All Soul's Chapel, now a private house, was intended by Knolles and Cobham, its founders, for the performance of mass three times a day, that all travellers passing over the bridge might have an opportunity of attending these offices and praying for the souls of the departed who had raised so fine a structure for their accommodation. This custom seems to have prevailed at one time over all Christendom. The popular superstition, so well known from its pleasant application by Burns, in his " Tam o' Shanter," that neither devil, witch, nor evil spirit dared to cross a bridge or a running stream, seems to have had its origin in this custom of consecrating bridges. In Ireland, even now, it is said to be the custom in some parts, for people who pass a bridge, to pull off their hats, and mutter a prayer for the soul of the founder.

Rochester Castle, in the opinion of Lambarde, the learned perambulator of Kent, was erected by William the Conqueror. The frequent discovery of Roman coins in that part more than in any other, would justify the supposition that, even in the time of the Romans, some fortress existed here, and that William, as in the case of the Tower of London, erected another upon the ruins of the old castle. It stands on an eminence near the river, and looks grand and imposing when viewed from the bridge, or from a boat on the stream. Like Melrose Abbey, of which the poet so sweetly sings, Rochester Castle looks well "by the pale moonlight."

"The sun but flouts its ruins grey;"

but when a fair full moon rises behind it, and the observer is on the opposite shore of the Medway, it seems a ruin most grand, and venerable, and melancholy. The architect was Gundulphus, Bishop of the diocese, who surrounded it, on the three sides removed from the Medway, by a very deep moat. The walls are twenty feet high, and about seven thick, and form a quadrangle of about three hundred feet. But the great square tower is the most prominent. Its sides are parallel with the walls of the castle, about seventy feet square at the base, and twelve feet thick, and so lofty as to be visible from a distance of twenty miles. During the sanguinary disputes between Henry III, and his insurgent nobles, it underwent several sieges, and the city suffered considerably from its adherence to the Royal cause.

In the High-street of Rochester, near the Custom-house, is a house appointed for the reception of poor travellers, bearing an inscription that the charity was founded by Richard Watts, Esq. by his will, dated 22nd of August, 1579, for six poor travellers, who, not being rogues or proctors, may receive gratis, for one night, lodging, food, and fourpence each. The inscription has often caused a smile among the members of the respectable body, excluded from the benefits of the charity; and a tradition of the town, states that the antipathy of the worthy testator to proctors, arose from the fact, that being once on the point of death, he employed one to draw up his will; but recovering shortly afterwards, he found that contrary to his intentions, the proctor had conveyed a considerable portion of the estates to himself. He immediately cancelled the will, and hated proctors ever after. This tradition has arisen apparently from a misunderstanding of the word. Proctors, in those days, were not the same body as now, but the term was applied to a set of fellows, sham attorneys, who travelled about the country, compounding felonies, and very often acting as receivers of stolen goods, and who were not improperly classed with rogues and vagabonds in the mind and will of good Mr. Watts. Strype, in his "Annals of the Reformation," has the following passage which may serve to elucidate the point. " If some like course [committal to a house of correction] were taken with the wandering people, they would easily be brought to their places of abode. Being abroad, they all in general are receivers of all stolen things that are portable; as, namely, the tinker in his budget, the pedlar in his hamper, the glass man in his basket, and the *lewd proctors which carry the broad seal and the green seal in their bags, and cover infinite number of felonies, in such sort that the tenth felony cometh not to light; for he hath his receiver at hand in every ale-house and in every bush. And these last rabble are the very nurseries of rogues.*" For the support of this charity, Mr. Watts left an estate, valued at that time at thirty-six pounds per annum, but now producing between five and six hundred pounds.

Passing the bridge we arrive in Stroud, formerly a suburb of Rochester, but since the passing of the Reform Bill an independent Borough. About half-a-mile from the town, on the banks of the river, are the remains of a building formerly called the Temple, and which belonged to the Knights Templars, and where they lived in grim state at the time that order flourished in England. There are considerable fisheries at Stroud, especially for oysters, by the trade in which a great portion of the population is chiefly supported, and with which the London markets are in great measure supplied.

Ascending the Medway from Rochester to Aylesford, we pass through a succession of beautiful rural scenery, and the pleasant villages of Cuxton, the ancient Coclestone, or, as some say, Cuckoldstone, Woldham, and Snodland, none of which, however, claim the attention of the passenger, after they have once excited his admiration for their simple loveliness.

The village of Luddesdon, at a short distance from the river and on the road to Cobham Park, is connected with an old legend of the Medway, and the ruins of the Temple already mentioned. When the Knights Templars flourished in all their glory, one of their members, Sir Reginald Braybrooke, had been to visit the Lord Cobham, and was returning to the Temple by a lonely path on the river's brink, when he was pierced to the heart by an arrow from a hand unseen. Next morning he was found weltering in his blood, quite dead, with the fatal arrow still sticking in his side. The Templars used every means to discover the assassin, but in vain: and in commemoration of the deed, and to solicit the prayers of all faithful passengers for the soul of their brother, they erected a triangular monument on the spot where the corpse was found, with a cross on each side, fronting the three roads that united at this place. The spot ever afterwards obtained the name of the Three Crosses. The murderer was not discovered during his own lifetime, but the secret was brought to light in a singular manner.—In one bitterly cold winter night, some years afterwards, one of the brethren, who had been to administer the last consolations of religion to an expiring sinner, arrived at Luddesdon in a woeful plight from cold and exhaustion. He saw but one light, from the window of a poor hovel in the village, and, knocking at the door, he entered to solicit shelter and a seat by the fire. He found the place inhabited but by one poor old woman, who was sick in bed. She was almost in the last extremities, and the instant the ecclesiastic entered, he remarked that the coverlet of her bed was no other than the cloak of the murdered Sir Reginald Braybrooke, whose confessor he had been. He immediately conjured her, ere she hastened into the presence of her God, to tell whether she knew anything of the murder. She then confessed that her husband, an old soldier, who fancied that he had been wronged and insulted by Sir Reginald, had shot the fatal arrow to his heart:

that after the commission of the deed he never enjoyed one moment's repose or happiness, and that one morning, a few months afterwards, he was found at the bottom of a chalk-pit dashed to pieces. She did not know whether this catastrophe was accidental, or whether in a fit of remorse he had put an end to his miserable life. Having made this confession she expired, and the priest, taking away the cloak, conveyed it to the Temple, where it was long preserved by the knights as a sad relic of their brother. The precise spot where the monument stood is not now known, all traces of it having long since disappeared. A small public house in the neighbourhood afterwards borrowed a name from it, with a most whimsical perversion. From Three Crosses, the original name of the monument, it was corrupted in the course of time to the Three Crouches; and a modern landlord, seeing no meaning in these words, improved it and made it more intelligible to his customers, by giving his house the sign of the "Three Crutches!" Close to this house, on a rising ground overshadowed by one of the largest walnut-trees in England, is the spring that formerly supplied the pilgrims to this spot with water.

Returning, after this little digression, to the
stream from which we have wandered, we arrive at Aylesford, with its old-fashioned bridge,
built in the reign of Charles II. The domain
was granted by Henry III. to Richard Lord
Grey, of Codnor. One Frisburn, the squire of
this valiant noble, and who had accompanied
him to the Holy Land, founded in 1240, under
his patronage in Aylesford Wood, the first
priory of Carmelites ever established in England. Various others were established in other
parts of the country during the next five years,
and in 1246, a general chapter of the order was
held at Aylesford, and one John Stock, a fanatic, who had lived for thirty years in a hol-
low tree, and lived upon herbs and water, was
chosen superior of the fraternity. The manor
passed through various families into that of
Wyatt. After the execution of the head of
that house for his rebellion against Queen
Mary, it was granted to Sir Robert Southwell,
and from him it passed to the family of Sedley.
Here, at Aylesford Priory, in the year 1639,
was born the witty and profligate Sir Charles
Sedley, the poet and dramatist. He was the
posthumous son of Sir John Sedley, of Aylesford, sheriff of Kent in the reign of James
I. His wit was brilliant, but his morals im-

pure, and Charles II, of a mind so congenial to his own, said of him, that " Nature had given him a patent to be Apollo's viceroy." Sir Charles was a noted Mohock in his time; a disturber of the public peace at night, and a frequenter of rude and dissolute company. His poems have nearly all an immoral tendeney. He contributed his part to the corruption of the manners of that age, for which he was afterwards punished in the sorest part, by the seduction of his only child, the beautiful Catharine Sedley, created Countess of Dorchester by her seducer James II. It is possible that Sir Charles, in the bitterness of his grief at the disgrace that fell upon him, may have reflected within himself that a man who had, perhaps, corrupted by his own lascivious and impure wit the morals of many, once perchance as innocent as his own daughter, was rightly punished, and that Heaven had made his pleasant vices a whip to scourge him. He never forgave the injury James inflicted upon him; and though he had asked and received various favours from him, took a very active part in forwarding the revolution that drove him from the throne. Being accused of ingratitude by some friend of James', he replied : " his Majesty has made *my* daughter a countess, and I

am only doing all I can to make *his* daughter
a queen." He died at the commencement of the
seventeenth century. His works were collected and published in two volumes in 1719.

Aylesford Priory was sold during his mino-
rity to Sir Peter Rycaut, whose son, Sir Paul
Rycaut, the eastern traveller, and author of a
work on the "State of the Ottoman Empire,"
died and was buried here. Before the death
of Sedley, its original proprietor, the estate
again changed hands, and came into the possession of Heneage Finch, afterwards Baron
of Guernsey and Earl of Aylesford, in which
family it still remains.

Aylesford was the scene of the great battle
fought in the year 445, between the Britons
under Vortigern, and the Saxons under Hengist and Horsa, in which the Britons obtained
the victory after considerable loss, and the
death of Catigern, the brother of their king.
Horsa, the Saxon leader, was also among the
slain; and both the savage chiefs were buried
on this fiercely contested field. Their *cromlechs*
remain to this day, and are among the most
interesting antiquities of the county of Kent.
Lambarde, Phillipot, Pegge, Lysons, Hasted,
and other writers, have devoted a considerable
space to the description of these remains, and

from these, but principally from the latter, the following particulars with regard to them are collected. They are well worthy of a visit not merely from the professed antiquary, but from the rambler in search of the picturesque. The principal cromlech, called Kit's Cotty House, stands on the downs, about a mile north-east from Aylesford church. It is composed of four immense stones, unwrought, three of them standing on end, but inclining inwards, and supporting the fourth, which lies transversely over them, so as to leave an open space beneath. The dimensions and weight of these stones are nearly as follow. The height of that on the south side, is eight feet, its breadth seven and a half, its thickness two, and it is supposed to weigh about eight tons. The northern stone is seven feet high, seven and a half broad, two thick, and weighs about seven tons. The middle stone is very irregular: its medium length, as well as breadth, may be about five feet, its thickness fourteen inches, and it weighs about two tons. The upper stone or impost, which is the largest of all, is also very irregular: its greatest length being twelve feet, its breadth nine and a quarter, its thickness two, and its weight near eleven tons. The width of the recess at bottom is nine feet, at top seven and a half, and the height from the ground to the upper side of the covering stone is nine feet. This is supposed to be the burial place of Catigern, the brother of the British chief. About seventy yards towards the north-west, there was formerly another stone of a similar kind and dimensions; but it was broken to pieces and removed by some Vandal of the eighteenth century.

At the distance of about five hundred yards south by east from Kit's Cotty House, are the remains of another cromlech, consisting of eight or ten immense stones, now lying in a confused heap, it having been thrown down at the beginning of the eighteenth century, by the then proprietor of the estate, who intended to have the stones broken to pieces, to pave the court-yard of the barracks at Sheerness. The stone was however found of such extreme hardness, that the design was abandoned as too expensive. Still nearer to Aylesford, is another single stone, called by Dr. Stukeley, the coffin. It is upwards of fourteen feet long, six broad, and two thick.

That these cromlechs are the burial places of the savage chieftains of ancient Britain, has never been disputed. Antiquaries (the Doctors Dry-as-dust of the profession, we were going

to say, and must say for want of a better word,)
have differed however, as was to be expected,
about the bones buried beneath, and have carried on a violent paper war as to whether Kit's
Cotty House was the burial place of a British
or a Saxon chief—whether Catigern or Horsa
were mouldering beneath. The current opinion
that has prevailed for many ages is, that Kit's
Cotty House is the cromlech of the British
warrior, and that Horsa was buried at Horsted,
about two miles further towards Rochester.
The etymology of both names would seem to
support this opinion. The spot of Horsa's
burial is now in a wood, with nothing to point
it out to the notice of the curious. Phillipot
says, that in the memory of the grandfathers
of his day, there were the remains of several
huge stones, resembling those at Kit's Cotty
House, but they had been all broken up and
removed at the time he wrote. Several pieces
of old brass, remains of swords and spurs, have
been dug up from time to time at the place.

On proceeding up the course of a little rivulet, that discharges itself into the Medway on
its western bank, the antiquary will find the
remains of another cromlech, which, in connection with those already mentioned, may
afford ground for further speculation. These

remains are in the neighbourhood of Adding-
ton, and are thought to mark the burial place
of some other chieftain who fell in the same
great battle.

On the east bank of the Medway, after passing Aylesford, stands Boxley Hill, commanding an extensive view over a beautiful country,
watered by this clear, but now narrow, river.
The village of the same name, or more properly speaking, the Cistercian Abbey, whose
ruins still remain, is famous for a monkish
fraud which was practised here just before the
dissolution of the religious houses, and known
by the name of the Rood of Grace. It was
a small image of Saint Rumwald, which, by
the ingenious mechanism of the priests, was
made to roll its eyes, move its lips, and raise
its hands, when the faithful brought their offerings to the shrine. The Rood or Image of
the Virgin, in connection with this of Saint
Rumwald, was supposed to work miracles,
and cure all diseases; and great crowds of de-
votees daily thronged to Boxley Abbey, bringing their rich gifts to the cunning monks.
Lambarde, who wrote from personal knowledge, describes in his Perambulation, the
mode in which the imposition was carried on.
Those who wished to benefit by the Rood of

Grace, first confessed themselves to one of the monks, and having done so, they were ordered to lift in their arms the image of Saint Rumwald, who, by its motions, would discover whether they were of pure life, and worthy to be favoured by the Rood of Grace or Holy Virgin. This image was so light, that a child of seven years of age might have lifted it with ease; and any person who gave a sufficient offering, was allowed to lift it. If, however, the offering were too small, the priests, by a cunning contrivance of a screw, fastened it to the wall in such a manner, that no strength, however great, could stir it. Great laughter was often caused by the sturdy efforts of Herculean fellows to move it; and many a maiden of pure life, and matron of hitherto good fame, went away with ruined reputation, merely because they had not made the screw-driver of Saint Rumwald their friend, by a liberal offering. Those, however, who had contributed sufficient, were allowed to proceed to the higher mysteries of the Rood, where there was a further demand upon their purse, ere the eyes of the figure rolled benignantly upon them, and ere it lifted its hands to bless them, and cure their infirmities. "Chaste virgins and honest married matrons," says Lambarde, "went

oftentimes away with blushing faces, leaving
without cause, in the minds of the lookers-on,
suspicion of unclean life and wanton behaviour;
for fear of which note and villany, women of
all others stretched their purse strings, and
sought by liberal offering to make Saint Rumwald's mane their good friend and master. But
mark here, I beseech you, their pretty policy,
in picking plain folks purses. The matter
was so handled, that without treble oblation,
that is to say, first to the confessor, then to
Saint Rumwald, and lastly to the gracious
Rood, the poor pilgrims could not assure themselves of any good gained by all their labour, no
more than such as go to Paris Garden, the Belle
Sauvage, or some such other common place, to
behold bear-baiting, interlude, or fence play,
can see the pleasant spectacle, unless they first
pay one penny at the gate, another at the entry
to the scaffold, and a third for a quiet standing." The deception was discovered in 1538,
by an agent of Cromwell, Earl of Essex, and
the images were brought to London, and publicly showed to the assembled populace in front
of Paul's Cross. All the springs of the mechanism were successively exhibited, amid the
laughter of the crowd; and the images being
broken to pieces, were thrown into a fire, en-

kindled in the open street for the purpose, and burned by Dr. Hilsey, the Bishop of Rochester, in whose diocese the fraud had been practised.

Penenden Heath is partly in this parish and partly in that of Maidstone. It has been a place for public meetings for many centuries. It was here that Archbishop Lanfranc exhibited his complaint against Odo Bishop of Baieux, half brother of William the Conqueror, for extortion; and which led to the downfal of that prelate. Here also are held county-meetings, and elections for members of parliament. The last great meeting held here was shortly before the passing of the act for Catholic emancipation, in 1829.

CHAPTER XII.

Allington Castle. — Reminiscences of Sir Thomas Wyatt the poet, and his Son.—Maidstone.—Tunbridge.—Penshurst, the seat of the Sidneys. — Hever Castle. — Eden Bridge. — Conclusion.

E next, about two miles further up the Medway, arrive at the ruins of Allington Castle, sacred to the memory of one of the fathers of English poetry, and claiming from us a notice of love and homage. A castle is supposed to have existed here in the Saxon times. It was granted to Sir Henry Wyatt by King Henry VII, as a reward for his services in the cause of the House of Lancaster, and a slight repayment of his losses in the long disastrous wars of the rival houses. Sir Henry was made a Knight of the Bath by Henry VIII, and at the battle of Spurs was made a Knight Banneret. He was treasurer of the King's chamber in 1525, and filled many other important offices. He chiefly resided at Allington Castle, where, in the year 1503, his accomplished son Thomas was born.

Thomas early manifested a love for poetry, and formed an intimate friendship with the Earl of Surrey — imbued with the same tastes, and like himself, burning with the love of the divine art. Since the then distant age of Chaucer, no poet worthy of the name had appeared, to raise the dignity of English verse. The groves of the Muses were silent and deserted, until these two song-birds appeared to reawaken the voice of music in the land, and incite others by their example, to lend their aid to swell the harmony, that was so soon afterwards to burst in full and joyous chorus, in the song of Spenser and his immediate successors.

Sir Thomas Wyatt, the *Incomparabilis,* as Leland calls him, and "the delight of the Muses and of mankind," as he is called by Wood, was likely to attract the notice of King Henry VIII, from the position occupied by his father at court; and we find, that after his father's death he was employed by that monarch on several occasions of great importance. He and Surrey were the greatest ornaments of the court; both distinguished as soldiers; both handsome and noble in person; and both renowned as the sweetest, and almost the only poets of the day.

We are told of Sir Thomas that he was a man of great wit and readiness, and that his sparkling conversation was the delight of the court: that, in fact, he combined the wit of Sir Thomas More with the wisdom of Cromwell, Earl of Essex. It is said of him that he helped to bring about the Reformation by a *bon mot,* and precipitated the fall of Wolsey by a jest; but this is, perhaps, saying too much. His jest about Wolsey does not merit repetition, and that which is said to have aided the Reformation, if it were the one that has been handed down to us, is not so much a jest as a very pertinent remark. When Henry was perplexed respecting his divorce from Catherine of Arragon, and had qualms of conscience as to the sinfulness of setting the Pope at defiance, Sir Thomas is reported to have exclaimed, " Lord, is it not strange that a man cannot even repent of his sins without the Pope's leave ! " Henry was inclined to this opinion himself, and was of course well pleased to have it strengthened by the pithy exclamation of his courtier. Sir Thomas had at this time a more numerous acquaintance among men of merit and ambition than any gentleman in the kingdom. He had great discernment in finding out the peculiar talent of those who sought his friendship, and the most generous appreciation of merit in others, and the utmost readiness to advance it where he found it. So great, too, was his influence at court, that it became a proverb, when any man received preferment, " that he had been in Sir Thomas Wyatt's closet."

The accomplishments and gallant bearing of Sir Thomas are supposed to have made some impression upon the heart of Queen Ann Boleyn; but it is too much to say, that because she may have admired the poet and the gentleman, or been fond of his conversation, that she encouraged a guilty passion for him, or he for her. This, however, has been said, but upon no sufficient authority; and Sir Thomas Wyatt was at the same time a married man, living most affectionately with his family. The chief ground for this calumny upon two amiable persons, seems to be, that Wyatt, in one of his sonnets, speaking of the mistress of his heart as being named Anna, and in another deplores the miseries that had befallen him in May, a month so pleasant to all men, but so sad to him. It will be remembered, that that unhappy lady was executed in the month of May. A suspicion, however, was enter-

tained˜ of him by his contemporaries, and 'on
the trial it was attempted to implicate him in
the fate of Norreys, Smeeton, and the others,
who suffered in that sad story, but the suspicion against him soon passed away. He was
imprisoned in the Tower in 1536, not from
any participation in this affair, but on account
of some quarrel he had had with the Duke
of Suffolk, the particulars of which are not
known. He was soon released; and in the
following year was knighted, and made Sheriff
of Kent. He was also chosen by the King, to
show the especial confidence he had in him,
to fill the honourable post of his ambassador to
the Emperor of Germany; in which office,
after some months, he was joined by the noto-
rions Bishop Bonner.

Wyatt acquitted himself to the satisfaction
of the King; but as the dignity he was obliged
to keep up impoverished him considerably,
and he received no adequate allowance from
the King, he solicited his recall. His letters to
Cromwell Earl of Essex, at this time, drew
forth replies from that able and amiable man,
which reflect great credit upon his memory.
They are filled with kind and gentlemanly
advice upon the profuse expenditure which,
both in his public and private career, was the

great failing of Sir Thomas; a failing, by the
by, which he shares with many other poets.
Cromwell acted the part of a disinterested,
thoughtful, and affectionate friend; and being
pressed by Wyatt, fearful that Bonner, who
had preceded him to England, and who was
known to entertain an animosity against him,
would prejudice the King's mind against him,
he procured his recall in 1539.   Henry expressed great satisfaction with his exertions to
fulfil duly the difficult objects of his mission,
and Wyatt repaired to Allington Castle, to
arrange his pecuniary affairs, which had fallen
into some confusion.

He was not allowed to remain long in seclusion.   The Emperor proceeded, towards the
end of the same year, through France into
the Low Countries; and it was thought ad-
visable to despatch an ambassador to watch his
motions.   Wyatt was again selected to fill the
office, and remained abroad for about a year.
On his return he met the same honourable
reception he had experienced before, and seemed to all eyes to be high in the King's favour.

Within a few weeks after his return, his
friend Cromwell, one of Nature's own noblemen though the son of a blacksmith, fell into
disgrace, was tried, found guilty, and executed

for high treason. Bonner, who was now in power, justified Wyatt's preconceived distrust of him. By his means Wyatt was accused of having spoken disrespectfully of his royal master to the Emperor of Germany, and of having held treasonable correspondence with Cardinal Pole. He was forthwith thrown into the Tower, where it is believed he was treated with much rigour. In a short poem, addressed from his place of captivity, to his friend Sir Francis Brian, he makes it appear that he was fettered, kept in a dungeon, where the close air wore away his life, and where he could judge of the " rain, wind, or weather, by his ears," but not by his sight. The disrespectful words, which it was alleged he had used of the Majesty of England to the Emperor, were, " that he feared the King should be cast out of a cart's tail, and that, by God's blood! if he were so, he were well served, and he would that he were so."

Wyatt, on his trial, gained all hearts in his favour by his firmness and his modesty. When called upon for his defence, he made the malice of his accusers so apparent, and refuted seriatim, so successfully each charge against him, that he was triumphantly acquitted. But his narrow escape disgusted him with courtly

life; he obtained permission to retire to Al-
lingtou Castle, and Henry bestowed upon him
some lands in Lambeth, and made him High
Steward of the manor of Maidstone. He now
devoted himself to the cultivation of poetry,
and the improvement of his estates. It was
at Allington, amid his own woods, and on the
banks of the sweet stream that ran through
them, that he penned his satires addressed to
John Poyntz, on the vices of courts and the
quiet pleasures of the country.

> Mine own John Poyntz, since ye delight to know
> The causes why that homeward I me draw,
> And fly the press of Courts whereso they go;
> Rather than to live thrall under the awe
> Of lordly looks, wrapped within my cloak;
> To will and lust, learning to set a law,
> It is not that because I scorn or mock
> The power of them, whom Fortune here hath lent
> Charge over us, of right to strike the stroke;

But true it is that I have always meant
Less to esteem them than the common sort,
Of outward things that judge in their intent,
Without regard what inward doth resort.
I grant, sometime of glory that the fire
Doth touch my heart.   Me list not to report
Blame by honour, and honour to desire.
But how may I this honour now attain,
That cannot dye the colour black a liar ?
My Poyntz, I cannot frame my tongue to feign,
To cloak the truth, for praise without desert
Of them that list all vice for to retain.
I cannot honour them that set their part
With Venus and with Bacchus all life long,
Nor hold my peace of them, although I smart :
I cannot crouch nor kneel to such a wrong ;
To worship them like God on earth alone,
That are as wolves these sely lambs among.
I cannot with my words complain and moan,
Yet suffer nought ; nor smart without complaint :
Nor turn the word that from my mouth is gone.
I cannot speak and look like as a saint ;
Use wiles for wit, and make deceit a pleasure ;
Call craft council,—for lucre still to pant :
I cannot wrest the law to fill the coffer,
With innocent blood to feed myself to fat,
And do most hurt where that most help I offer.

This is the cause that I could never yet
Hang on their sleeves that weigh, as thou mayst see,
A chip of chance more than a pound of wit :
This maketh me at home to hunt and hawk ;
And in foul weather at my book to sit ;
In frost and snow then with my bow to stalk ;

Noman doth mark whereso I ride or go.
In lusty leas at liberty I walk,
And of these news I feel nor weal nor woe,
So I am here in Kent and Christendom,*
Among the muses where I read and rhyme,
Where, if thou list, mine own John Poyntz to come
Thou shalt be judge how I do spend my time.

---

* The following explanation of this strange phrase " neither in Kent nor Christendom," which is still in use, is
given by Fuller, the author of the " Worthies." " This
seems a very insolent expression, and as unequal a division.
Surely the first author thereof had small skill in even
distribution, to measure an inch against an ell; yea, to
weigh a grain against a pound. But know, reader, that
this home proverb is English Christendom, whereof Kent
was first converted to the faith. So then Kent and Christendom (parallel to Rome and Italy) is as much as the first
cut and all the loaf besides. I know there passes a report,
that Henry IV, King of France, mustering his soldiers at
the siege of a city, found more Kentish men therein than
foreigners of all Christendom besides, which (being but
seventy years since) is by some made the original of this
proverb, which was more ancient in use, and therefore I
adhere to the former interpretation." Grose quoting this
explanation in his Provincial Glossary, says, " the proverb
rather seems intended as an ironical reproof to the good people of Kent for overrating the importance of their county;
the Kentish men formerly claiming the right of marching in
the van of the English army." A more obvious interpretation seems, as the words imply, that Kent by the satirist,
who invented the saying, was considered so rude and barbarous as not to be included in Christendom. Wyatt, who
was a Kentish man, did not like this distinction, and takes
care to say that he lived both in Kent and Christendom.

In another satire addressed about the same time to the same gentleman, the poet tells the fable of the town mouse and the country mouse, and expresses his own determination not to imitate the latter, and be swallowed by a cat for his pains; an allusion apparently to his royal master. He concludes, speaking of the Court and its inmates:

> Henceforth, my Pointz, this shall be all and sum,
>   These wretched fools shall have no more of me;
> But to the great God, and unto his doom,
>   None other pain pray I for them to be:
> But when the rage doth lead them from the right,
>   That looking backward, Virtue they may see,
> Even as she is, so goodly fair and bright;
>   And whilst they clasp their lust in arms across,
> Grant them, good Lord, as Thou mayst of thy might,
>   To fret inward for losing such a loss.

Notwithstanding his love of the country, and his ardent hope that he might have no more to do with courts, he was not allowed to remain in his darling privacy. On the arrival of ambassadors from the Emperor of Germany in the autumn of 1542, the King commanded Wyatt to meet them at Falmouth, and escort them to London. He was certainly, from his previous employment, the fittest person for the duty, and as he could not disobey the mandate, he set out immediately. But he never reached his destination. The weather was extremely unfavourable for travelling; he overheated himself too, by hard riding, and on his arrival at Sherborne, near Basingstoke, in Hampshire, he was seized with a fever, from which he never recovered. He had some friends in the town who paid the utmost attention to him, and especially Mr. Horsey, who was unremitting in his kindness. But all aid was unavailing; his constitution gave way, and he expired after a few days' illness, in the thirty-ninth year of his age. He was interred at Sherborne, in the family vault of the Horseys; but no inscription marks the spot where he sleeps.

Of all the mourners that he left behind him, none mourned so sincerely as his friend the Earl of Surrey,—himself destined, at no distant period, to join his heart's co-mate in an untimely death. He has left in the following lines, an eloquent description of the character and acquirements of his friend.

Wyatt resteth here that quick could never rest
  Whose heavenly gifts increased by disdain,
And virtue sank the deeper in his breast;
  Such profit he by envy could obtain.
A head where wisdom mysteries did frame;
Whose hammers beat still in that lively brain,
As on a forge, where that some work of fame
Was ever wrought to turn to Britain's gain.

A visage, stern but mild, where both did grow
Vice to contemn, in virtue to rejoice:
Amid great storms, whom grace assured so,
To live upright, and smile at fortune's choice.
A hand that taught what might be said in rhyme;
That reft Chaucer the glory of his wit;
A mark, the which (unperfected for time)
Some may approach, but never more shall hit.
A tongue that served in foreign realms his king;
Whose courteous talk to virtue did inflame
Each noble heart; a worthy guide to bring
Our English youth by travail unto fame.
An eye whose judgment none effect could blind,
Friends to allure and foes to reconcile:
Whose piercing look did represent a mind
With virtue fraught, reposed, devoid of guile.
A heart where dread was never so imprest
To hide the thought that might the truth advance;
In neither fortune, lost nor yet represt,
To swell in wealth, or yield unto mischance.
A valiant frame, where force and beauty met;
Happy, alas! too happy, but for foes,
He lived, and ran the race that nature set,
Of manhood's shape ere she the mould did lose.
But to the heavens that simple soul is fled,
Which left, with such as covet Christ to know,
Witness of faith, that never shall be dead:
Sent for our health, but not received so.
Thus for our guilt this jewel we have lost,
The earth his bones—the heavens possess his ghost.

The poet left an only son of the same name, called, to distinguish him from his father, Sir Thomas Wyatt the younger. His mother was the Lady Elizabeth Brooke, third daughter of

Lord Cobham. He it was who made the famous insurrection against Queen Mary, which cost him his life, and brought many others to the scaffold. He was a man of great consequence, not only in his own county, but throughout England, wherever the Protestant party had adherents. When the persecutions carried on by the Roman Catholics, under the authority of Mary, had alarmed the people, and when her projected marriage with Philip of Spain had rendered them ripe for rebellion, Sir Thomas was looked up to by his party to head a grand national movement, to drive her from the throne. He undertook to raise the county of Kent; Sir Peter Croft, Sir Peter Carew, and others, undertaking to effect a simultaneous rising in Devonshire, Cornwall, Wales, and the Midland Counties.

This formidable outbreak failed for want of proper concert among its leaders, and many hundreds of persons perished miserably on the scaffold. The Princess Elizabeth, who was suspected of being privy to it, was, as is well known, confined for a short time in the Tower on the charge of treason against her sister, resulting from her correspondence with Wyatt, who, however, exculpated her with his dying breath from all knowledge of his proceedings.

No previous insurrection since the time of Jack Cade had excited such alarm in London as this of Sir Thomas Wyatt. As soon as it was made known to the Lord Mayor that Sir Thomas was up in Kent, additional guards of substantial citizens were placed at the city gates, and the aldermen, common councilmen, and others, patrolled the streets in armour all night long, to guard against surprise. Five hundred men were equipped at the cost of the city, and sent by water to Gravesend, and thence across the country towards Allington Castle, to keep him in awe. They found that he had proceeded to Rochester Castle, of which he had taken possession. The Duke of Norfolk, who commanded the Queen's forces, had possession of the bridge, on which he had stationed four pieces of ordnance to besiege the castle. Brett, the captain of the Londoners, on his arrival at the bridge, suddenly turned upon his company and addressed them in an eloquent speech in favour of Wyatt; urging them what a shame it would be if they drew their swords against their countrymen, who had been driven by tyranny to take up arms; whose cause was righteous, and who only wanted to deliver the land from proud Spaniards and strangers. The Londoners immediately raised a loud shout of "*a Wyatt, a Wyatt,*" and seizing upon the cannon turned them against the Queen's forces. Wyatt, see-ing the movement in his favour from the battlements of the castle, sprang upon his horse, and with a score of his stoutest fel-lows behind him, galloped in among the Lon-doners; and the Queen's forces, panic-struck with the suddenness of the movement, and the loss of their artillery, took to flight. Wyatt, with this reinforcement, proceeded towards Deptford, and thence to Southwark, intending to assault the city, but failing, he marched up the Surrey shore of the Thames to Kingston, where he crossed and endeavoured to enter London from the west. All the city were up in arms, the Tower guns were in readiness, and every thing prepared for a decisive strug-gle. " All the Court," says Stowe, " were wonderfully afraid, and drums went through London at four o'clock in the morning, com-manding all soldiers to arms, and to meet at Charing Cross." Wyatt, hearing that the Earl of Pembroke had taken up arms against him, stayed at Knightsbridge until the morning, that his men, who were weary with their long march, might refresh and strengthen themselves by sleep and a supply of rations. Wyatt planted his artillery upon the spot now known as Hay Hill, Berkeley Square, and here a skirmish took place.   Wyatt gained the advantage, and pushed on towards Charing Cross, apparently carrying all before him, and making people suspect that the Earl of Pembroke had turned traitor, and was aiding instead of repulsing him. " Then there was," says the quaint old historian, " a running and crying out of ladies and gentlewomen, shutting of doors and windows, and such a shrieking and noise as was wonderful to hear."   Wyatt forced his way through Temple Bar to Ludgate, where being met with a superior force, he returned again through Fleet Street to Temple Bar, his adherents dropping off one by one as they saw the reinforcements that were arriving from every side to crush them.   Wyatt, at length, saw his gallant band reduced to less than a score of combatants, and, giving up the struggle, thought only of securing his safety by flight.   He set spurs to his steed, but was met in the Strand by a party of the Queen's troops and taken prisoner.   He was immediately conveyed along with Brett, and some other leaders, to the Tower.   On his arrival at Traitor's Gate, Sir John Bridges, the Lieutenant, took him fiercely by the collar, saying, " O thou villain and unhappy traitor! how couldst thou find in thy heart to work such detestable treason against the Queen's Majesty? If it were not that the law must pass against thee, I would stick thee through with my dagger!" Wyatt crossed his arms on his breast, and looking at the Lieutenant with a stern face, merely replied, "We are not struggling for mastery now," and passed on to his dungeon.

The life of Lady Jane Grey, who had been long a prisoner in the Tower under sentence of death, might have been spared had it not been for this unfortunate rebellion. Five days after the capture of Wyatt she was executed; the Queen thinking, after these events, that there could be no safety for her while her rival was alive. On the third day after she and her husband had suffered, twenty gibbets were erected in different parts of London, and fifty of Wyatt's followers were hanged, drawn, and quartered, and their limbs exposed on the city gates. Four hundred more of inferior note were led to the Queen at Westminster, in couples, with halters about their necks; and her Majesty, looking from the windows of the palace to the Tiltyard, where they were drawn up in this miserable array, thought it best to pardon them, lest the spectacle of so much blood should prove too revolting to her subjects. The Duke of Suffolk, father of Lady Jane Grey, was next beheaded; and, lastly, Wyatt, after he had been confined in the Tower from the 12th of March to the 11th of April. As he was brought out to the Green to suffer execution, he addressed himself to one Bourne, the Queen's secretary, and implored him to speak favourably of him to the Queen, and beg her countenance for his unhappy wife and children; adding, that if it had pleased her Majesty to have given him his life, he would have done her such good service as would have gone far towards making reparation for the great treason he had committed. But since she would not spare him, he could only trust that God would show him that mercy which was denied him by his fellow-creatures. When he came upon the scaffold he desired all men to pray for him, and commenced the awful preparations for death. We quote his dying speech from Stowe :—" ' Good people,' said he, ' I come here presently to die, being thereto lawfully and worthily condemned, for I have sorely offended against God and the Queen's Majesty. I trust God will forgive me, and will take mercy upon me. I beseech the Queen also of forgiveness.' —

'She hath forgiven you,' said Doctor War-
ton, the chaplain who attended. 'Then,' continued Sir Thomas, 'let every man beware
how he taketh anything in hand against the
higher powers ; unless God be prosperable
to his purpose it will never take good effect
or success, whereof you may now learn of
me, and I pray God I may be the last exam
ple in this place for that or any other like.
And whereas it is said and noised abroad that
I should accuse the Lady Elizabeth and the
Lord Courtney,—it is not so, good people, for
I assure you neither they nor any other now
yonder in hold was privy to my rising before
I began, as I have declared no less to the
Queen's Council, and that is most true.' And
so without any more talk Sir Thomas put off
his gown, untrussed his points, then taking
the Earl of Huntingdon, the Lord Hastings,
Sir T. Strangwish, and many others by the hand,
he plucked off his doublet and waistcoat, and
then kneeling down laid his head on the block ;
and raising himself again to his knees, after a
few words spoken with his eyes lifted up towards heaven, he knit the kerchief over his
eyes, and holding up his hands, suddenly laid
down his head, which the executioner took
from him at one stroke."

Thus perished, in the flower of his manhood, Sir Thomas Wyatt the younger, whose name had success rewarded him, would have shone among the brightest in the page of English history : Elizabeth would have reigned a few years earlier, and Lady Jane Grey, Cranmer, Ridley, Latimer, and a thousand illustrious victims would have been saved from the scaffold and the stake.   But he failed, and he ranks among traitors and rebels.   Posterity, however, has done his memory some injustice, and he does not rank so high as the Russells and the Sidneys, because he flourished at an earlier period, and because his motives, though as noble, are not so well known.   If he sought his end by civil war, it should be remembered that in his day there was no Parliament worthy of the name, in which the great change he was desirous of making for the benefit of his country, could be constitutionally effected.   He was a brave soldier, and a true patriot in heart, and not the common rebel that some have represented him.

After his execution, the estates of Allington as belonging to a traitor, reverted to the Crown, and remained untenanted during the reign of Mary. Queen Elizabeth granted them on lease to John Astley, her master of the jewels, to whose son, Sir John Astley, they were afterwards granted by letters patent at the annual rent of 100*l*. 2*s*. 6*d*. They have since come into the possession of the Earls of Romney.

The castle of Allington had been long in ruins before Hasted published his " History of Kent." A very small remnant of it is now in existence, and forms a part of the adjoining farm-house, " which itself," says Hasted, " seems to have been built out of the ruins of Sir Thomas Wyatt's house." There was formerly a park belonging to the castle, as we learn from the poems of Sir Thomas Wyatt the elder, but it was cleared away soon after the forfeiture of the domain.

The parish of Allington is very small, and in the year 1808, consisted but of one house besides the castle and the parsonage. Some parts of the castle were lately inhabited, and some few additional houses have been built. The church is small and mean, and contains some monuments of the seventeenth century, but none of them are remarkable.

The next place on the Medway is the ancient town of Maidstone; so named, it is thought, from Medway-stone. Its Roman name was Madaviacis, thought to have been derived from the British. In this town, as already stated in our account of Dartford, Wat Tyler and his rebels had their head-

quarters, before they marched to Blackheath
to attack London. Here, also, Sir Thomas
Wyatt, the poet's son, began his insurrection.
Being joined by many of the principal inhabitants, over whom his influence from his own
character, as well as his father's, was considerable, the whole town fell under the displea-
sure of Queen Mary. It lost, in consequence,
all the privileges of self-government which it
had enjoyed from a very early age, and remained disfranchised until the second year of
Elizabeth, when the Queen, by letters patent,
restored their rights, and granted some additional privileges, among which was a confirmation of their ancient prescriptive right of send-
ing two burgesses to parliament, the granting
to the mayor the authority of a justice of
the peace, and the exemption of the townsmen from foreign sessions. Several other charters have been granted to the town by James
I, Charles I, and George II. The manor belongs to the Earls of Romney, who have a
seat in the neighbourhood of the town called
the *Mote.*

Maidstone is a small, quiet, simple, and plea-
sant-looking town. The chief trade is in hops.
It is considered the county town of Kent, and
here the assizes are held, and on some, now
happily rare, occasions criminals are executed.

There is a small bridge over the Medway. The river is navigable for barges of fifty or sixty tons, and the tide flows up to the town, although the river is so narrow. Close by, the Lenn, one of the streams mentioned by old Michael Drayton as " bearing the limber train of the Medway," falls into the parent river.

There are several antiquities at Maidstone which are worth notice. On the eastern bank of the river, at a short distance from the parish church, are the remains of St. Mary and All Saints' College, built by Courtenay, Archbishop of Canterbury, at the close of the fourteenth century. The gate is the only part that gives any idea of the beauty or grandeur of the original building, which is now converted into a farm-house. Near the High Street are the remains of another ancient foundation, called the Friary, supposed to have been part of a convent of Franciscans founded by Edward III. and the Earl of Cornwall in 1331.

"The church," says Hughson, "is spacious and handsome, and consists of a nave, aisle, and chancel, with an embattled tower, in which are eight bells. On the tower formerly stood a spire that was destroyed by lightning in 1730. The walls are also embattled and supported by buttresses. The whole is enlightened by large windows, divided by mullions, with rich tracery above; the east window is particularly handsome. The chancel was rebuilt by Archbishop Courtenay in 1395, who then altered the dedication of the church to All Saints, it having been previously dedicated to the Blessed Virgin." The Archbishop was buried in the middle of the chancel, in a grave between five and six feet deep, where his skeleton was found in the year 1794, in consequence of a search made for it by the Rev. Mr. Denne, who was one of the Dry-as-dusts who had carried on a long controversy about these very bones. The one party contended that they lay in Maidstone, and the other that they were buried in Canterbury. Mr. Denne made search accordingly, and gained the victory.

Maidstone was the birth-place of Thomas Trapham, surgeon to Fairfax and Oliver Cromwell, and the man employed to prepare the body of Charles I. for interment. He it was who used the coarse and infamous expression relating to that office, " *I have sewed on the head of a goose.*" Maidstone also gave birth to Andrew Broughton, secretary to the High Court of Justice, and employed in that capacity to read to the unfortunate Charles the charge preferred against him, and the sentence of the Court. He was one of those excepted at the restoration from the Act of Indemnity. He fled to Switzerland, and died at Vevay at an advanced age.

From Maidstone to Tunbridge, a distance as the crow flies of about twelve miles, but by the windings of the Medway of eighteen or twenty, the river takes its course through a beautiful country, abounding with small villages, and almost covered with luxuriant hop grounds. The Medway receives at Yalding, about half way between the two towns, the waters of the " clear Beule," or Beult, a little trout stream, which runs for about fifteen miles. This district is one of the finest in the fine county of Kent, and towards the end of May, when its abundant cherry and apple trees are in bloom, scenting the breeze with their odorous treasures, appears redolent of peace and plenty. But to the gossiping traveller it offers nothing to stay him long;—men cannot always prattle of waving woods, enamelled meads, or hedge-rows green; so, having pointed out the district to the lover of seclusion and rural scenery, we pass on our way to the busier haunts of men, in search of the places where the great and good have been born or have died, where philosophers have preached and poets sung, or remarkable men have strutted away their little hour ere the grave engulphed them.

Among the pleasant villages in the ride from Maidstone to Tonbridge are Baring, Teston, Farleigh, Nettlestead, Yalding, Lillyhoe, and Wateringbury; and among the country seats which arise on every commanding knoll, amid every green refreshing coppice, are Hailes Place, Barham Court, and Mereworth Castle, surrounded by very extensive woods, and affording a most delightful prospect over the Medway and its rural banks. This place formerly gave name to an ancient family who held the manor

for about two centuries, and after whose ex-
tinction it passed to the Malmains, Bohuns,
and Bambres. The latter built a spacious castle which was possessed in succession by the
Earls of Arundel and the Lords of Aberga-
venny. From them it came to the Le De-
spencers, whose heiress Lady Mary Fane was
created Baroness Le Despencer by King James
I. The son of this lady was made Earl of
Westmoreland by the same monarch, and his
grandson erected the present castle. Smart,
now an almost forgotten versifier, wrote a poem
upon the hops of Kent, in which he mentions
this castle.

> Nor shalt thou Mereworth remain unsung,
> Where noble Westmoreland, his country's friend,
> Bids British greatness love the silent shade ;
> Where piles superb, in classic elegance
> Arise, and all is Roman like his heart.

The famous Palladio of Italy, so often taken
as a model by our English architects in their
designs for the country-houses of our nobility
and gentry, is the structure that was imitated
by Mr. Colin Campbell, when he built this
under the direction of Lord Westmoreland.
It formerly contained, and perhaps does still
contain, a valuable collection of pictures.

Tonbridge, or the town of bridges, is seated

upon the Medway, and four nameless streams, which here pour their waters into that river. From the bridges over these waters the town obtained its name. Here the Medway ceases to be navigable, and up to the year 1740, it was not navigable further than Maidstone, but an act was then passed by which the improvement was carried into effect at a considerable expense.

Tonbridge Castle, now in ruins, was built about forty years after the Conquest, by Richard de Clare, Earl of Brionne in Normandy. His own castle of Brionne had been destroyed by the famous Robert the Devil, familiarized by name, at least, to the public of late years, by the opera bearing his unenviable soubriquet; and Rufus, in compensation for that loss, gave him a square league of land at Tonbridge, upon which he erected a new castle more magnificent than the old one. The possessor of this estate in the reign of Henry VIII. was Edward De Bohun, Duke of Buckingham, who having been executed for treason, his estates were forfeited to the crown. Since that time the castle has been suffered to fall to decay. Tonbridge, though small, is a flourishing town. Its church is a handsome and spacious edifice, dedicated to St. Peter and St. Paul, and contains several monuments of the neighbouring families, but none of them remarkable.- The Grammar School, in the patronage of the Skinner's Company of London, was founded in the reign of Queen Elizabeth by Sir Andrew Judde, a native of the town, and Lord Mayor of London. In this school was educated Sir Sidney Smith, the gallant hero of Acre, buried in a strange land, and as yet without a monument to his memory in England.

We are now approaching the source of the Medway; the stream has become a mere brook; an active man might, without much difficulty, jump over it: and it soon loses its name in that of the many small streams which unite together to form it. But 'ere we bid it farewell, upon one part of its banks we must linger with a fond delay : the groves of Penshurst, where Sidney, the darling of his age, was born,—where that other Sidney, the stern republican, lived and wrote,— where Sacharissa lived, and where Waller sung. Penshurst Place is an extensive pile, disposed in the form of a quadrangle, enclosing a spacious court, and comprehending a great hall, chapel, gallery, and numerous suites of apartments. The state rooms are furnished and decorated with much magnificence ; and the place contains a valuable collection of old portraits, including all the illustrious members of an illustrious house. The park includes more than four hundred acres, gently diversified with hill and dale, from which may occasionally be seen the two small confluent streams of the Medway and the Eden. Near a fine sheet of water called Lancup Well, stands the noble oak, about twenty-two feet in circumference, which is said to have been planted at the birth of the gallant Sir Philip.

Penshurst was granted by King Edward VI. to Sir William Sidney, the Lord Chamberlain of his household. Philip was the son of Sir Henry Sidney, Lord Deputy of Ireland, and

was born on the 26th of November 1544. Before he had attained his twenty-ninth year,
when he returned to England after his continental travels, he had acquired a reputation all
over Europe as the most gallant gentleman and
most accomplished scholar of his age. The King
of France, Henry III. appointed him one of
the gentlemen of the royal chamber.   The
Poles put him in nomination for the throne of
that country, and Queen Elizabeth delighted
to honour him. The Prince Palatine of the
Rhine having been offered the high honour
of the Garter, gave Sidney his procuration to
receive his stall, and take possession of it in

his name, upon which occasion Mr. Sidney received the honour of knighthood.

Who does not remember the many fond stories of Sidney's bravery, his generosity, and his learning, which his admiring contemporaries have handed down concerning him? He was the Mæcenas of the age—the man to whom hundreds of poetasters and many poets looked up as their patron. The author of "The Defence of Poesy" and the "Arcadia," was the critic whose approbation was sufficient to ensure success; and who, of all the eminent men of that day, was selected by the then unknown and unbefriended Spenser, as the patron of his "Faery Queen." While the work was yet in manuscript, the poet sent it to Sir Philip, who was so transported with delight, if we may believe the old tradition, that he rose up in an ecstacy, and ordered his steward to give the author fifty pounds. Cooled a little, he began to read again, but coming to another beautiful passage, he started up again in rapture, and ordered the poet to have a hundred pounds. Still as he read, his rapture grew; and he finally raised his gratuity to two hundred pounds, and shut up the book for that day, lest, as he said, he should be tempted to give away his whole estate. A pretty story, which we devoutly believe, and which we hope no arithmetical man of precision, no too curious inquirer into dates and other ugly matters of the like sort, will ever interfere with and destroy.

> We have a vision of our own,
> And why should he undo it?

The "Arcadia" was not written at Penshurst, but at Wilton, the seat of the Earl of Pembroke; but that nobler work, "The Defence of Poesy," was planned and composed amid the groves of his paternal seat, and while he was Knight of the shire for the county of Kent. Every reader will remember that work, and its affectionate dedication to his sister—that sister, upon whose death Ben Jonson wrote the beautiful epigram — it can scarcely be called an epitaph.

> Underneath this sable hearse,
> Lies the subject of all verse,
> Sidney's sister, Pembroke's mother:
> Death! ere thou hast slain another
> Learned, and fair and good as she,
> Time shall throw a dart at thee.

The grass upon which we tread — the trees that wave over us—everything we behold in the face of nature at Penshurst acquires additional interest as we reflect upon these things. We can almost fancy we behold the gallant Sir Philip walking arm-in-arm with his beloved

sister through the glades, and hear him discoursing to her of romance, and chivalry, and poetry.
Or we can fancy him at the still hour of midnight, strolling alone amid his " paternal acres "
and their venerable trees, enditing that sweet
sonnet,

> " With how sad steps, O moon, thou climbst the sky,
>   How silently, and with how wan a face."

We must not forget, however, while dwelling
upon the popular reminiscences of one Sidney, that the next century produced another
whose name was to be enshrined among the
great and good of English history—the honest
and stern republican, Algernon. Through a
long and busy life, he steadily adhered to his
early principles, and supported, with no inconsiderable influence, the cause of popular freedom—showing, in his own person, what many
others of its supporters at that time did not,
that he was a worthy apostle of the freedom
he preached. Cromwell found in him a powerful friend, until Sidney discovered that he also
was a despot, and he then withdrew his support,
and retired to private life, to the family seat of
Penshurst, where it is generally believed that
he composed his well known " Discourses on
Government." After the Restoration, he lived
abroad till 1677, when he returned, made his

submission, and was pardoned. The manner in which he was implicated in the conspiracy against Charles II. is well known, and has been alluded to in our account of the Rye House; and not less known is the manner in which the evidence was strained against him to ensure his condemnation. Bishop Burnet, who knew him well, describes him as "a man of most extraordinary courage: a steady man, even to obstinacy; sincere, but of a rough and bois-terous temper, that could not bear contradic-tion. He seemed to be a Christian; but in a particular form of his own. He thought it was to be like a divine philosophy in the mind: but he was against all public worship, and everything that looked like a church. He was stiff to all republican principles; and such an enemy to everything that looked like monarchy, that he set himself in high oppo-sition against Cromwell when he was made Protector. He had studied the history of government in all its branches, beyond any man I ever knew." And as he lived, he died. His name has become a household word; and the great statesmen of our day receive the praise of their countrymen in proportion as they

" —Serve well the sacred cause
That he and Hampden died for."

Waller, the poet, in his youth was a frequent visitor to Lord Leicester, the then representative of the house of Sidney, and occupier of Penshurst. His well known Sacharissa, to whom he addressed so many of his poems, was the Lady Dorothea Sidney, the daughter of that nobleman. She, however, heeded not the voice of song, or the accomplishments of the poet, but gave her hand to the Earl of Sunderland, who had, besides a title, a longer rent-roll than Waller. The latter, as far as worldly wealth was concerned, would have been no bad match for the lady; but she was too proud to form a connexion with a commoner. Waller did not grieve very much; and it is related of them, that they met again when they were both considerably past sixty, when the lady asked her former admirer when he would again write such verses upon her as he had written in his youth. "When you are as young, madam, and as handsome, as you were then," was the gallant, and yet ungallant, reply of the poet, who turned upon his heel, and left her.

The Lady Dorothea was the eldest of eight daughters. Her sister, the Lady Lucy, was also honoured by the encomiastic verses of this courtly rhymer. She was, it appears, very

young when he wrote them; but they are superior to those (filled with poor conceits and
rhodomontade, instead of passion) which he
addressed to the elder. In his poem to the
Earl of Leicester, then absent in France, he
can find no more natural compliment than to
say, that the trees of Penshurst groan and
make moan that their lord is abroad; and that
his deer repine and think themselves unjustly
slain by other hands than his, and long for the
day when their blood shall stain his arrows!
In the same park, thinking of the charms of
the haughty Sacharissa, he launches out in the
following strain,

> While in this park I sing, the listening deer
> Attend my passion, and forget to fear;
> When to the beeches I report my flame,
> They bow their heads, as if they felt the same.
> To gods appealing when I reach'd their bowers,
> With loud complaints they answer me in showers;
> To thee a wild and cruel soul is given,
> More deaf than trees, and prouder than the heaven.

It appears in no degree wonderful that the
lady was not caught by such verses as these,
and as little wonderful that the severe, but
just critic, Samuel Johnson, should have said
of Waller, that it was not easy to look without
contempt upon his love verses.

The present age will not confirm the opinion
of the past as expressed by a poetical admirer,

Yet what he sung in his immortal strain,
Tho' unsuccessful, was not sung in vain ;
All, but the nymph that should redress his wrong,
Attend his passion, and approve his song.

Leaving this ancient seat of the Sidneys,
the Medway is lost; four streams, two of
which rise in Sussex, one in Surrey, and the
other in Kent, claim the honourable name,
but to neither of them can it in strict justice
be applied. The honour must be divided
among them ; neither is the Medway, but each
contributes to produce it. In most maps the
name is given to the Surrey branch, that rises
near Bletchingley, and flows past Eaton bridge
to Hever Castle, Chiddington, and Penshurst.
The Sussex branch rises near East Grinstead, and
flows to Hartfield, Groombridge, and Ashurst,
and joins the former at a short distance south-
east of Penshurst. Obliged to make a selec-
tion, we shall pursue the windings of the Surrey stream, and leaving Penshurst and its pa-
triotic and literary reminiscences behind us,
tramp along the by-roads to Hever Castle.
This venerable ruin was built by William de
Hever, in the reign of Edward III, and is
chiefly remarkable for being associated with the

names of two of the queens of Henry VIII.
It was purchased from the family of Hever by
Sir Geoffrey Boleyn, from whom it descended
to his grandson, Sir Thomas Boleyn, the father
of the luckless Queen Anne Boleyn. Upon
his death, it was claimed by Henry VIII. in
right of his wife, and afterwards granted by
him to his repudiated consort Anne of Cleves.
That quiet and amiable person lived here in
seclusion for some months after her divorce,
and some authorities say that here she ended
her days. This, however, is not true. De
Thou, in his History, is also in error when he
says that she retired to the Court of her brother, the Duke of Cleves, and that there she
died. By the provision of an act, whereby
estates in several counties of England were
granted her for life, she was forbidden to leave
this country, and she died at her house in Chelsea, and was buried in Westminster Abbey.

From this place we follow the river to Eden,
or Eaton bridge, remarking by the way, that by
some this branch of the Medway is called the
Eden. This village is small, but pretty and
rural, and is remarkable as one of the very many
places in England that were affected by the
great earthquake at Lisbon in the year 1755.
A pond of about an acre in extent, was ob-

served to be agitated in a very peculiar manner, on the day in question; but no further
mention was made of the matter, until the
news arrived in England of the calamity in
Portugal, when it was brought again to the
recollection of the neighbours, and public notice taken of the fact.

The Medway, which we have thus tracked
from its junction with the ocean, where it is
a broad, rapid, and deep river, to the neighbourhood of its source, where it is but a few
feet in width, and so shallow that sometimes
it may be traversed dry-shod, flows altogether
about eighty miles, for about sixty of which
it is navigable. It is spanned by twenty-
three bridges, and its navigation is aided by
fifteen locks. It flows through a delightful
country, and is remarkable as the deepest river
in England.

END OF THE MEDWAY.

FROST FAIRS ON THE THAMES.

FROST FAIRS ON THE THAMES.

A CHAPTER FOR ANTIQUARIES.

THE task would have detained us too long in one spot if we had stayed in the course of our voyage down the Thames, to note the memorabilia of Frost Fair, as it has several times been held upon its bosom opposite London. Many curious pictures of the manners and customs of former generations may be gathered from such accounts of these festivals as have reached our times; and in this chapter we propose to collect them for the amusement of the general reader, as well as for the antiquary, for whom it is more especially designed. The latter will not be displeased to find, at the beginning of our chapter, a chronology of frost as regards the Thames; and we hereby present it without further observation, than the mere remark, that no detailed accounts have reached us of

2 A 2

any of the fairs held upon the Thames prior to the year 1683-4, when our information, both in prose and verse, becomes tolerably extensive.

In the year 250 the Thames was frozen over for nine weeks; in 291 for six weeks; in 401 for two months; in 558 for six weeks; in 695 also for six weeks, when booths were built, and a market held upon the ice; in 827 for nine weeks; in 908 for two months; in 923 for thirteen weeks; in 998 for five weeks; in 1063 for fourteen weeks; in 1114 for four weeks; in 1207 for eleven weeks. In 1434-5 the frost lasted from November 24th to February 10th, the Thames being passable on foot from London to within a mile of Gravesend; in 1565 the frost lasted six weeks; in 1683 thirteen weeks. In 1716 a fair was held on the Thames for several days; again in 1739; then in 1778; and lastly, in 1814.

Holinshed informs us, that in 1565, " the 21st of December, began a frost, which continued so extremely that on new year's eve people went over and along the Thames on the ice from London Bridge to Westminster. Some played at the foot-ball as boldly there as if it had been on the dry land; diverse of the court shot daily at pricks set up on the

Thames; and the people, both men and women, went on the Thames in greater numbers
than in any street of the city of London. On
the 31st day of January, at night, it began to
thaw, and on the fifth day was no ice to be
seen between London Bridge and Lambeth,
which sudden thaw caused great floods and
high waters, that bare down bridges and houses,
and drowned many people."

There being no further records of any earlier
frosts, we shall proceed with that of 1683,
when the cold was so intense that the trunks
of oak, ash, walnut, and other trees, were cleft
asunder, so that they might be seen through;
and the cracks were often attended with noises
as loud as the firing of musketry. A full
account of the severe weather of this year is
given in a sheet, not, however, of the choicest
English, preserved in the British Museum,
printed for J. How, at the Coach and Horses,
without Bishopsgate Street, 1684; and entitled,

"A STRANGE AND WONDERFUL

"RELATION

"OF MANY REMARKABLE DAMAGES, SUSTAINED BOTH AT
SEA AND LAND, BY THE PRESENT UNPARALLELED FROST.

" This island and age wherein we live," says
the author, (whose orthography we have cor-

rected, but whose language, with all its imper-
fections in other respects we have left unal-
tered,) "have experienced as many strange and
prodigious observations of nature's effects, together with as many and various kinds of
afflicting judgments from the correcting hand
of an offended God, as any nation in preceding
times can demonstrate, and rather seems the
total sum of all, than a parallel of any ; as,
sword, plague, fire, &c.   But whether the
present unparalleled frost may be attributed
to the effects of natural causes, or not rather
to the scourging hand of an offended God, I
shall not determine, though the .consequences
following seem to proclaim the latter, and
loudly call for humility and amendment of
life, lest a worse judgment fall upon us.   But
leaving this general caution and instruction, I
shall present your view with such remarkable
passages as certain knowledge, credible report,
and spreading fame have brought to light.

" From Deal, it has been observed that a
vessel belonging to Lubeck (which her colours
signify), riding in the Downs for several days,
has been in great distress ; which by their signs
and weffs (the language of seamen in such
cases) is understood by them as well as if they
discoursed face to face ; whereupon several

yachts and other vessels have attempted to relieve them, but all industry ineffectual; the vessel being congealed and environed with a massy
substance of ice; so that it is altogether inac-
cessible, and now no further attempts can be
made for their relief, because the sea for above
a mile from the shore is so hard frozen beyond
our apprehensions to imagine or chronologies
to parallel. From Liverpool, in Lancashire, we
have advice, that two vessels lying at anchor
had their cables one night severed asunder
by the sharpness of the ice, notwithstanding
the industry of the distressed mariners, who
are now drove from hope of succour. Though
attempts have been made by some, beyond probability of their own safety, to relieve them,
but in vain, whose fear is not so much for their
want of provision as the danger of being bilged,
(a sea term for breaking holes in the vessel),
with the ponderous strokes of such bulky congealed cakes of ice, as the impetuousness of the
unruly surges cast against them.

" It has been also observed, that the ice has
cut away most of the buoys or sea-marks, as
well in the south as north channel, so that
such as have weathered the distresses in har-
bours, and escaped dangers at home, by the
frost, are, notwithstanding, incident to those

dangerous wrecks of rocks and sands, and shun-
ning Scylla may fall upon Charybdis.

" It is also credibly attested that vast solid
cakes of ice, of some miles in circuit, breaking
away from the eastern countries of Flanders
and Holland, &c. have been by the east and
north-east winds driven upon the marine borders of Essex, Suffolk, and Norfolk, to their
no small damage.

" And it is also reported, that some skait-
sliders upon one of those large icy plains, were
unawares driven to sea, and arrived living
(though almost perished with cold and hunger)
upon the sea coast of Essex; but as to the certainty of this report I refer to the credit of
succeeding intelligence, as also those wonderful damages upon the coast of Scotland relating of the loss of some shipping, and the
lives of many ingenious and industrious navi-
gators; nor may those prodigious and lamen-
table damages seem strange, when in our own
harbour, the river of Thames, several ships,
both inward and outward bound, as well at
Redrif as other adjacent places, have been
broken to pieces, and sunk by the effects of
this so unparalleled a frost.

" It is needless to inform London (for whom
principally this intelligence is collected), what

unheard of rendezvous is daily kept upon the
face of her navigable river; what long and spa-
cions streets of booths and tents are builded ;
what throngs of passengers, both horse and
foot, do travel; what pyramids of provisions,
baked, boiled, and roast ; what deluges of wine,
coffee, beer, ale, and brandy, for sale ; what fleets
of vessels sailing upon sledges; what troops
of coaches, caravans, and waggons; what games
and new invented sports and pastimes, bull-
baiting, bear-baiting, &c.; together with shops
for the vending of most sorts of manufactures
and for working artificers, the account of which
alone would require a volume to describe; and
therefore omitting its description in particular,
I must leave it with amazement and admiration
in general.

" But to speak of the land, where the damage
is no less considerable than at sea, there being
such an overwhelming snow in Scotland, that
man and beast, though not equally, are too
sensible of the affliction. Also in England, in
several places, through the extraordinary violence of the present frost, no water can be had
for cattle in many miles, which general com-
plaints will need no other confirmation than
from the tongues of the cattle themselves, who
with pity have been observed to lick the ice

to abate their thirst, for want of their fill of refreshing water.

" From a credible person in France to a gentleman of worth in London by letter, before the sea was blocked up by this extreme frost, mention is made of the severe effects produced by the extremity of cold as well of weather as of charity, attesting by modest computation that no less than sixty persons have lately died upon the road between Paris and Calais; and doubtless many in the city of London, through the same extremes, have perished in the same calamity, of which a weaver in the parish of St. Giles's Cripplegate was one, and though I take no notice of others whose wants call upon the Diveses of this age to consider the condition of the Lazaruses in the streets."

The following, in relation to this frost, was communicated to the Gentleman's Magazine, for February 1814, by a respectable friend from a memorandum left by his great grandfather. " 20th December 1683, a very violent frost began, which lasted till the 6th of February in soe great extremitie that the pooles were frozen eighteen inches thick, at least; and the Thames was so frozen that a great street from the Temple to Southwark was built into shops and all manner of things sold.   Hackney coaches plyed there as in the streets. There were also bull-baiting and a great many shows and tricks to be seen. This day the frost broke. In the morning I saw a coach and six horses driven from Whitehall almost to the bridge, yet by three o'clock this day, next to Southwark, the ice was gone so as boats did row to and fro, and the day after, all the frost was gone. On Candlemass-day (2nd February) I went to Croydon market and led my horse over the ice at the ferry at Lambeth. As I came back I led him from Lambeth upon the middle of the Thames to Whitefriars stairs, and soe led him up them; and this day an ox was roasted whole over against Whitehall, and King Charles II, with the Queen, did eate a part of it."

There is a curious little duodecimo volume in the British Museum, published for " D. Brown at the Black Swan and Bible without Temple Bar, and J. Waltho at the Black Lyon in Chancery Lane over against Lincoln's Inn, 1684." It is entitled " An historical account of the late great frost, in which are discovered in several comical relations the various humours, loves, cheats, and intrigues of the town as the same were managed upon the river of Thames during that season."

" This frost," says the author, " began about
the 16th of December last, and so sharply set
in, that in a fortnight's time, or thereabouts,
the river of Thames, who, one might think, by
the daily flux and reflux of her twice-returning
tides in the space of twenty-four hours, and the
native course of her own rapid streams, was secured against the force of the hardest weather ;
yet this river, beyond the bridge of London
upwards, was all frozen over ; and people began
to walk thereon ; and booths were built in
many places, where the poor watermen, whose
boats were locked up, and could not work
them for their usual livelihood, made a virtue
of necessity, and therein retailed wine, brandy,
beer, ale, and other liquors, which, for the
novelty of the same, very few but were in a
short time their customers ; and their trades increasing, their booths began to be increased
and enlarged for the reception of multitudes of
people, who daily resorted thereunto, insomuch
that in a short time road-ways were made from
place to place, and without any fear or apprehension the same was trod by men, women,
and children. Nor were the same only footpaths, but soon after, hackney-coaches began
to ply upon the river, and found better custom
than if they had continued in the streets, which

were never, in the midst of business, half so crowded, so that the same became the only scene of pleasure in and about London. The fields were deserted, and the river full ; and in Hillary term, which soon after ensued, it was as usual for the lawyers to take coach by water to Westminster as through the Strand ; and so public was the same, that in a short time it obtained the name of Frost Fair.

" A whole street of booths, contiguous to each other, was built from the Temple Stairs to the barge-house in Southwark, which were inhabited by traders of all sorts, which usually frequent fairs and markets, as those who deal in earthenwares, brass, copper, tin, and iron, toys and trifles ; and besides these, printers, bakers, cooks, butchers, barbers, coffee-men, and others, who were so frequented by the innumerable concourse of all degrees and qualities, that, by their own confession, they never met elsewhere the same advantages, every one being willing to say they did lay out such and such money on the river of Thames.

" Nor was the trade only amongst such who were fixt in booths, but also all sorts of cries which usually are heard in London streets, were there ; the hawkers with their news, the costermonger with his fruit, the wives with

their oysters, pyes, and gingerbread, and such
like. Nor was there any recreation in season
which could not be found there, with more
advantage than on land; such as foot-ball play,
nine-pins, cudgells, bull and bear-baiting, and
others which on the occasion was more ordinary, as sliding in skates, chairs, and other
devices, such as were made of sailing-boats,
chariots, and carrow-whimbles; so that at one
view you might behold the thriving trader at
his shop, the sportive at their recreations, the
laborious with their burthens at their backs,
and every one, with as little concern or fear as
if they had trod the surface of the more cen-
tred element. And in all places smoking fires
on the solid waters, roasting, boiling, and pre-
paring food for the hungry and liquors for the
thirsty; eating, drinking, and rejoicing, in as
great crowds as Smithfield during Bartholomew
Fair could ever boast.

" But, as thus far my relation only extends
to the general, which I doubt not but most of
those who were in London, and in health, can
join with me in the truth of, and to whom I
speak of no novelty, their own eyes having
been witnesses of this and much more; so that
I shall leave the same, and proceed to what
may more deserve their attention, whilst I relate

the several amours, intrigues, cheats, and humours, carried on and managed upon the said river during this season. That so by these as so many items to the memory of the peruser they may put him in mind of a season so memorable, and the which his eyes, or perhaps those of his posterity, may never see the like again."

The author then goes on to relate at great length the humours, loves, cheats, and intrigues above alluded to, of how country squires, who had come from afar to behold the sports, were fleeced of their superfluous cash and jewellery, by the too fair and most frail ladies of London. How honest men were deceived; and how rogues of every degree profited.

We will let the author speak for himself, and relate one of his stories in his own way. He first of all states, that two country gentlemen, who had come to London to see Frost Fair, were separated accidentally from each other by the great crowd on the ice. One of them, being smitten by the charms of a pretty lass, was by her inveigled and hocussed, as we would call it in the present day, robbed of all his money, and conveyed, fast asleep, to a solitary booth on the Thames, and there left to

his fate. " His friend, in the meantime," says
our author, " fruitlessly endeavoured to find
him ; and at last, being about to give up the
search and go to his lodgings, as he was very
cold, he was resolved to strike into a booth and
take a glass of wine, and advantage of the
fire ; making enquiry of the master of the same
whether he had seen such a gentleman as he
described our other squire to be, pass that
way ? To which a person standing by, much
like a gentleman in his garb, told him : ' Sir, I
believe I saw such a gentleman as you speak of
about a quarter of an hour ago walk by this
booth with a lady in his hand, and I believe
they may be landed on Lambeth side, to which
I saw them incline.' ' A lady !' says our present Squire, ' it cannot then be the same, for I
am certain he is not acquainted with any hereabouts.'—' How know you, sir,' says the landlord, ' but he may have met with some kind
lady that obliges him with her company ; for, if
I am not mistaken, I remember whom this
gentleman means. If so, he was in a fair peri-
wig, a broad gold-laced cloak, and a waist-belt,
embroidered.'—' The very same,' replied the
squire. ' Oh, rogue ! has he these tricks ?
Would I could catch him, I would make sport
with him in this adventure.'—' Sir,' says the

gentleman, 'I believe they must return this way, and it may not be very difficult as he comes back to surprise them.'

" Whether this discourse was of design or not I cannot learn, though I suppose it might; and the squire sat down, expecting his friend and lady, and began to drink with the gentleman. Some persons near them being at play at cards, the gentleman proposed a game for a bottle. 'With all my heart,' says the squire; 'I like the diversion.' Whereupon the cards were brought, and they went to it for a bottle, which the squire won. They then renewed the sport, and began to play for money, which, in short, our squire had such good luck in, that he won most of the gentleman's stock, to the value of ten or fifteen guineas.

" At this time the evening approached, and there was no sight of his friend. The gentleman being very desirous to win back his money that he had lost, persuaded the squire, if he would go ashore at Lambeth, he could obtain money there of some relations he had, and he would pay it off; adding, that he might, perhaps, meet the party he was in search of, and surprise him with his lady at some tavern thereabouts. The squire consented, paid the reckoning, and went with him. But in vain were all inquiries for his friend : no such person could be heard of. The other gentleman having recruited his pockets, with much persuasion got the squire to play again, which he was the more unwilling to do that it grew late, and there was danger in passing the Thames. But the gentleman told him, the moon would shine, and all was safe. He therefore sat him down to his sport, where success still attended him, and in three or four hours, which passed the more merrily away, he broke the gentleman a second time of twenty guineas, which were all he had.

" About this time, and after a passing bottle, he took his way over towards Westminster Stairs. He went all alone to this place just as the clock struck twelve, and was got half way over, when he perceived from behind a booth two red-coats start up and make towards him. Being thereat a little surprised, he made his speed the greater toward the shore ; but they having soon overtaken him, presented their pistols at his breast, and bade him stand and deliver ! The squire, in great fear, began to tell them he had no money, and many such excuses, which were no answers to them. They pursuing their work, got him down, and robbed him of near a hundred and fifty guineas,

and stripped off all his upper garments, binding
him with his hands behind him ; and in this
miserable condition, exposed to the season, did
they unrelentingly leave him, telling him, if
he made the least noise, they would certainly
return and cut his throat. Not knowing in
this extremity what to do ; fearing their
threats on the one hand, and on the other, that
he must perish with cold if not quickly relieved, he saw them make away with all the
haste they could. Believing them to be out
of hearing, he cried out for help, and the shore
not being far off, he was heard by a person that
kept a public-house, who came and unbound
him at such time as he was ready to starve
with cold, and thorough wet with the snow,
which had melted under him.

" The good man conveyed him to his house,
and by a good fire brought him to himself,
where he related the whole circumstances of
the robbery. The host desired him to go to
bed, and told him he would make a diligent
inquiry about the same the next morning.
When the morning dawned the landlord came
to his bed-side, and bade him be of good cheer,
for that he had taken a rogue, whom he verily
believed was one of those that had robbed him.
The squire was glad at the news, and inquired

into the particulars. ' Sir,' says he, ' about six this morning I got up, and went by the light of the moon to a booth, which I have on the Thames, and where, in the straw, I found a man, habited as you describe the robbers. He was fast asleep; and after I had waked him he called for his wife and companions, which was all I could get out of him for a great while, till, looking about him, after some time, he began with fear (I suppose being sensible of his guilt) to pretend himself to be trepanned, and cheated; and at other times, madman-like, to cry out about his misfortunes, and a thousand other extravagant discourses, which I could make nothing of; so I have brought him hither, where he is below, in the hands of an officer, to see if you can identify him.'

" ' This must be one of the rascals,' says the squire; ' be sure you don't let the vagabond escape, and I 'll be with you presently, and make an example of the rogue.'

" In the mean time, as he was dressing himself to come down, the landlord was upbraiding the man, (who was no other than the squire who had gone off with the lady, and who also had been robbed, stupefied with drugs, and left all night in a booth,) and threatening him that he would most assuredly be hanged.

"'Do I dream?' said this disconsolate squire. 'Where am I! Oh, tell me! am I awake, or is this all a delusion?'—'Delusion!' cries the landlord, 'pretty delusion, indeed! you rascal! to rob a man, and leave him for dead! 'Tis such delusion as shall delude you with a halter!'—'I am quite innocent,' replied the squire: 'I understand no more of this crime than the child unborn; and how I came where you found me I can give no other account than that I was found there.'—'A pretty excuse indeed!' said the constable; "rob men of their moneys, sirrah, get drunk, and ramble; and when you fall asleep you know not how you came thither! See whether this answer will serve the justice, and be enough at the assizes to save your cragg.'—'No, you rogue!' interposed the landlord, 'here's a gentleman, the honest gentleman, that will find you out. Answer him, if you can.'

"At which time the other squire had got up and come down. No sooner had he seen the woful metamorphosis of his friend, whom he recognized immediately, but he stood amazed at the same, and for some time, between shame and surprise, could not utter a word himself. 'And is it you, my friend, that I am accused of robbing?' said the other. 'Yes, you vaga-

bond,' interposed the landlord; 'and how dare
you be so impudently bold with a person of
quality whom you have abused?'—and thereupon he gave him a good hunch   'Hold!'
says the other squire, 'I know this gentleman,
however he became thus disguised, and will
answer for him that he is not the person you
take him for.'   And with that he embraced
him, and discharged the constable and his officers, to the great joy of our accused squire,
who longed to get in private, and discourse
with his friend touching the circumstances
they were both under; which they soon did,
telling each other the stories of their misfortunes.   They agreed, in conclusion, to be silent
as to the particulars, and to send for clothes,
and a supply of money, whereby they might
take leave of their friends, and repair into the
country, though with heavy hearts for their
misadventures in Frost Fair."

There are several contemporary prints of the
sports at the fair, with poetical descriptions,
some of which are preserved in the Museum,
in a collection of ballads, chiefly relating to
London, which were formerly in the possession
of George IV.   Of one of them, a large
broadside, with rude wood-cut, containing
Arundel House, Essex Buildings, and the

Temple, with a complete view of the river, with its booths, and various places set apart for bear-baiting, we shall quote the whole description, as containing several particulars not mentioned in the prose accounts. It is entitled,

"GREAT BRITAN'S WONDER, OR LONDON'S AD-MIRATION, being a true representation of a prodigious frost, which began about the beginning of December 1683, and continued till the fourth day of February following, and held on with such violence that men, and beasts, coaches, and carts went as frequently thereon as boats were wont to pass before.

" There was also a street of booths built from the Temple to Southwark, where were sold all sorts of goods imaginable, namely, cloaths, plate, earthenware, meat, drink, brandy, tobacco, and a hundred sorts of other commodities not here inserted. It being the wonder of this present age, and a great consternation to all the spectators.

> Behold the wonder of this present age,
> A famous river now become a stage :
> Question not what I now declare to you,
> The Thames is now both fair and market too ;
> And many thousands daily do resort
> There to behold the pastimes and the sport,
> Early and late, used by young and old,
> And valued not the fierceness of the cold;

And did not think of that Almighty hand
Who made the waters bear like to the land:
Thousands and thousands to the river flocks,
Where mighty flakes of ice do lye like rocks:
There may you see the coaches swiftly run,
As if beneath the ice were waters none ;
And sholes of people every where there be,
Just like to herrings in the brackish sea ;
And there the quaking water-men will stand ye,
" Kind master, drink you beer, or ale, or brandy ?
Walk in, kind sir, this booth it is the chief,
We 'll entertain you with a slice of beef,
And what you please to eat or drink, 'tis here,
No booth like mine affords such dainty cheer."
Another cries, " Here, master, they but scoff ye,
Here is a dish of famous new-made coffee."
And some do say, a giddy senseless ass,
May, on the Thames, be furnish'd with a lass.
But, to be short, such wonders there are seen,
That in this age before hath never been :
Before the Temple, there a street is made,
And there is one almost of every trade ;
There you may also this hard frosty winter,
See on the rocky ice a working printer,
Who hopes by his own art to reap some gain,
Which he perchance does think he may obtain ;
Here is also a lottery, and music too,
Yea, a cheating, drunken, lewd, and debauch'd crew;
Hot codlins, pancakes, duck, goose, and burnt sack,
Rabit, capon, hen, turkey, and a wooden jack.
In this same street before the Temple made,
There seems to be a brisk and lively trade,
Where ev'ry booth hath such a cunning sign,
As seldome hath been seen in former time,
The " Flying P— Pot," is one of the same ;
The " Whip and Egg-shell," and the " Broom" by name;

And there, if you have money for to spend,
Each cunning snap will seem to be your friend;
There you may see small vessels under sail,
All 's one to them, with or against the gale;
And as they pass, their little guns do fire,
Which feedeth some, and puffs them with desire
To sail therein, and when their money 's gone,
'Tis right, they cry, the Thames to come upon;
There on a sign, you may most plainly see 't,
Here 's the first tavern built in Freezland-street;
There is bull-baiting, and bear-baiting too,
That no man living yet e'er found so true;
And foot-ball play is there so common grown,
That on the Thames before was never known:
Coals being dear, are carried on men's backs,
And some on sledges there, are drawn in sacks:
Men do on horseback ride from shore to shore,
Which formerly in boats were wafted o'er.
Poor people hard shifts make for livelihoods,
And happy are if they can sell their goods;
What you can buy for threepence on the shore,
Will cost you fourpence on the Thames, or more.
Now let me come to things more strange yet true,
And question not what I declare to you:
There roasted was, a great and well-fed oxe,
And there, with dogs, hunted the cunning fox;
Dancing o' th' ropes, and puppit plays likewise,
The like before ne'er seen beneath the skies.
All stand admired; and very well they may,
To see such pastimes, and such sorts of play!
Besides the things I named to you before,
There other toys and baubles are great store:
There you may feast your wand'ring eyes enough;
There you may buy a box to hold your snuff;
No fair nor market underneath the skies,
That can afford you more varieties.

There you may see some hundreds slide in skeets,
And beaten paths like to the city streets;
There were Dutch whimsies turned swiftly round,
Faster than horses run on level ground.
The like to this I now to you do tell
No former age could ever parallel;
There's all that can supply most curious minds
With such varieties of cunning signs,
That I do think no man doth understand,
Such merry fancies ne'er were on the land:
There is such whimsies on the frozen ice
Makes some believe the Thames a paradise.
And though these sights be to our admiration,
Yet do our sins call for loud lamentation.
Though such unusual frosts to us are strange,
Perhaps it may predict some greater change:
And some do fear may a fore-runner be
To an approaching sad mortality.
But why should we to such belief incline,
There's none that knows but the blest Power divine:
And whatsoe'r is from Jehovah sent,
Poor sinners ought therewith to be content;
If dreadful, then to fall upon the knee
And beg remission of the Deity.
But if beyond our thoughts he sends us store,
With all our hearts let's thankful be therefore;
Now let us all in great Jehovah trust,
Who doth preserve the righteous and the just.
And eke conclude, sin is the cause of all
The heavy judgements that on us do fall;
And call to mind, fond man, thy time misspent,
Fall on thy knees and heartily repent:
Then will thy Saviour pity take on thee,
And thou shalt live to all eternity.

Printed by M. Haly and J. Millet, and sold by Robert
Walton at the Globe on the north side of St. Paul's Church-

Yard, near that end towards Ludgate. Where you may have all sorts and sizes of maps, coppy-books, and prints, aot only English, but Italian, French, Dutch. And by John Seller, on the west side of the Royal Exchange, 1684."

There is another broadside in the same collection, entitled " The Thames uncased, or the Waterman's Song upon the Thaw: to the tune of *Hey boys, up go we*. London, printed for the author, and sold by J. Norris, at the King's Arms without Temple Bar, 1684." As this doggerel ballad is very rare, and has never been reprinted, the antiquarian reader will not be displeased at the reproduction in this place of some of the stanzas. As a whole, except for its allusion to the time, it is but little worth.

THE THAMES UNCAS'D,

OR,

THE WATERMAN'S SONG UPON THE THAW.

Come, ye merry men all
Of Waterman's Hall,
Let's hoist out our boats and careen;
The Thames it does melt
And the cold is scarce felt,
Not an icicle's now to be seen.
Let's pull down each skull
That hung up in hall,
Like weapon so rusty, and row;
Let's cheerly fall to't;
If we have not forgot;
For the frost is over now.

Let's set up our masts
    That stood like posts,
As props to our tents on the Thames;
    Or signe-posts made
    With an ancient display'd,
While our oars were the great cross-beams.
    Let's hoist up our sail
    That was a side vail,
To hide Doll when with brandy she'd glow,
    Or a roof compos'd
    You might else have been froz'd,
Though the frost be over now.

We'll no longer stand
    With a tapster's hand,
With the spigot for an oar,
    Crying out our trade is cold,
    Here's four gallons in hold,
I have drawn out but half my store:
    Prithee, lads, stand to 't,
    And help pump it out,
That the vessel once more may flow;
    Then come again
    With a thirsty train;
But the frost is over now.

Let's tune our throats
    To our usual notes,
Of Twitnam, Richmond, hey!
    Sir, skuller, sir?   Oars, sir?
    Loudly roar, sir;
Here's Dick, sir, you won't pass him by.
    Instead of good ale,
    And brandy wine stale,
Let's cry out, Westward, hoe!
    Shall we Mortlack make,
    Or for Brandford tack?
For the frost is over now.

The town too 's gone
That they waited on,
And the people flock'd to see,
It fled in one night
Quite out of our sight,
As the castles enchanted that be;
While country squire,
Whom journey might tire,
With wat'ry eyes cannot view
The street, a long way
That he came to survey;
For the frost is over now.

Not a horn can he buy,
Nor an earthenware toy,
His wife or his children to cheer;
Since Isis does turn
Her watery urn,
All the pitchers are march'd off here;
Nay, on the Thames wide,
There remains not a slide
On which he may whisk to and fro;
He returns as he came,
To his country dame;
For the frost is over now.

Meantime, if ought
Of honour you 've got,
Let the printers have their due,
Who printed your names
On the river Thames,
While their hands with the cold look'd blue;
There 's mine, there 's thine,
Will for ages shine,
Now the Thames aloft does flow;
Then let 's gang hence,
To our boats commence,
For the frost is over now.

Another broadside, the literary portion of which is somewhat superior to the last, but not much, is entitled,

"True description of Blanket Fair upon the River Thames, in the time of the great Frost in the year of our Lord 1683.

> How am I fill'd with wonder for to see
> A flooding river now a road to be ;
> Where ships and barges used to frequent,
> Now may you see a booth of sutling tent ;
> And those that us'd to ask " Where shall I land ye ?"
> Now cry, " What lack ye, sir,—beer, ale, or brandy ?
> Here, here, walk in and you shall surely find,
> Your entertainment good, my usage kind."
> Booths they increased dayly more and more,
> People by thousands flocking from the shore,
> And in such heaps they thither did repair,
> As if they had been hasting to a fair,
> And such a fair I never yet came near,
> Where shop rents were so cheap and goods so dear ·
> There might you have all kind of earthenware,
> You can scarce name a thing but what was there ;
> There was to sell both French and Spanish wine,
> And yet, perhaps, a dishclout for a signe ;
> In short, the like was never seen before,
> Where coaches run as if upon the shore.
> And men on horseback to and fro did ride
> Not minding either current or the tide.
> It was exceeding strange at first to see
> Both men and women so advent'rous be ;
> And yet at last it grew so very common,
> 'Twas not admired, it seemed strange to no man.
> Then from the Temple there was built a street,
> Made old and young and all admire that see 't,

Which street to Southwark reach'd; there you might see
Wonders, if you did love variety.
There was roast-beef and gammon to be sold,
But at so dear a rate I dare be bold
To say 'twas n'er sold so on the shore,
Nor on the Thames in haste be any more.
There were Dutch whimsies turning swiftly round,
By which the owners cleared many a pound.
And coal and corn was there in sledges draw'd,
As if the Thames would never have been thaw'd.
All kind of trades did to this market come,
Hoping to get more profit than at home.
And some, whose purses were a little swell'd,
Would not have cared how long the frost had held.
In several places there was nine pins play'd,
And pidgeon-holes for to beget a trade.
Dancing and fidling too, there was great store,
As if they had not been from off the shore.
The art of printing there was to be seen,
Which in no former age had ever been.
And goldsmiths' shops well furnished with plate,
But they must dearly pay for't that would ha't.
And coffee-houses in great numbers were
Scattered about in this cold freezing fair:
There might you sit down by a charcoal fire,
And for your money have your heart's desire.
No, no, if you the world should wander through,
No fair like this could pleasant seem to you.
There was the baiting of the ugly bear,
Which sport to witness hundreds did repair.
And I believe, since the world's first creation,
The like was never seen in this our nation.
And foot-ball playing there was day by day;
Some broke their legs, and some their arms, they say;
All striving to get credit, but some paid
Most dearly for it, I am half afraid.

Bull-baiting, likewise, there was known to be,
Which on the Thames before none ever see.
And never were poor dogs more bravely tost
Than they were in this strange prodigious frost.
Th' enraged bull perceiv'd his enemies,
And how to guard himself could not devise ;
But with his horns did toss them to and fro,
As if their angry meaning he did know.
Besides all this, a thing more strange and rare
Than all the things were seen in Freezland fair :
An ox was roasted whole, which thousands saw ;
For 'twas not many days before the thaw.
The like by no man in this present age,
Was ever seen upon this icy stage.
And this hard frost it did so long endure
It pinch'd, and almost famish'd many poor.
But one thing more I needs to you must tell
The truth of which thousands do know full well,
There was fox-hunting on this frozen river,
Which may a memorandum be for ever.
For I do think, since Adam drew his breath,
No Fox was hunted on the ice to death.

Thus have you heard what wonders there were seen,
How heaven and earth the people walk'd between.
And since the world at first had its creation,
The like was never seen in this our nation.
Yet was it hard and grievous to the poor,
Who many hungry bellies did endure.
Sad spectacles enough you might behold,
Who felt the effect of this prodigious cold.
But God who is most righteous, good, and just,
Will them preserve who in him put their trust ;
And when their dangers greatest seem to be,
Blest be his name, he then doth set them free.

Then let us all, while we have time and breath,
Be still prepared to meet with pale-faced Death.
That when he comes we need not be afraid,
Nor at his dart be frighted or dismay'd.
If we on Jesus Christ wholly depend,
He 'll prove to us an everlasting friend.

London: Printed by H. Brugis, in Green Arbor, Little Old
Bayly, 1684.

Besides these, several ballads, copper-plates, and wood-cuts, were published at the time. The following list of engravings, — many of them, if they exist at all, being only to be found in private collections, — was made by the late Mr. J. T. Smith, of the British Museum, whose general taste and antiquarian research were well-known. The list, most probably, is not complete, but imperfect as it may be, it will be found of value by the collector and antiquary.

" 1. A large broadside, entitled ' Wonders of the Deep, or the most exact Description of the frozen River of Thames; also, of what was remarkably observed thereon in the last great frost, which began about the middle of December 1683, and ended on the 28th of February following. Together with a brief Chronology of all the memorable (strong) frosts for almost six hundred years, and what happened in them to the northern kingdoms.' A very rude woodcut, with an explanation of the piece in figures, containing thirty-nine references, ending—

‘ The Hoop, the Rose, the Three Tuns, and the Bellows,
The Whip and Eggshell, entertains good fellows.’

" Then follow fifty-nine verses, and the chronology of memorable frosts ‘ London, printed by M. J. and J. M. for P. Brooksby, at the sign of the Golden Ball in West Smithfield, and at his shop at the Golden Harp and Ball, near the Bear Tavern in Pye Corner.’

" 2. ‘ Wonderful news from the River of Thames, to a pleasant new tune. Printed on the frozen Thames, by the loyal young printers, viz. E. and A. Milbourn, S. Hinch, J. Mason, 1683.’ Eight verses with the music.

" 3. ‘ An exact and lively Mapp, or representation of Booths and all the varieties of Shows and Humours upon the Ice on the river of Thames of London, during that memorable frost in the thirty-fifth year of the reign of his sacred Majesty King Charles II. A. D. 1683, with an alphabetical representation of the most remarkable figures. Printed and sold by William Warten, stationer, at the signe of the Talbott, under the Mitre Tavern in Fleete Street, London.’

" 4. ‘ A true description of Blanket Fair

upon the river Thames, in the time of the great Frost, in the year of our Lord 1683. London, printed by H. Brugis, in Green Arbour, Little Old Bayly, 1683.' A broadside sheet with a woodcut, and three columns of verses underneath.

" 5. 'Erra Pater's Prophecy, or Frost Faire, 1683. Printed for James Norris, at the King's Armes without Temple Barr.' This contains a whole length portrait of a man in a turban, with a view of the Thames and London in the back ground, and twelve verses underneath.

" 6. ' A Prospect of the frozen river Thames,' and below, ' Printed on the frozen Thames, Feb. 1683-4.' The booths are inscribed as follows : ' Tavern, Printing Booth, Oxford Booth, Loyal Coffee-house, Wiltshire Booth.' And the passage along them is inscribed ' Frezland Street, *alias* Blanket Faire.' The word ' Foot Ball' is the only other writing upon this plate.

" 7. The same copper-plate as the above with alterations, and with twenty-two numbers for reference, printed upon a broadside of letter-press, headed thus : ' The true and exact Representation of the Wonders upon the Water, during the last unparallel'd Frost upon the River of Thames, 1683-4.' The references are

printed below in fifty verses, in rhyme, beginning —

    ' The various sports behold here in this piece,'

And ending —

    ' But in six hours this great and rary-show,
      Of booths and pass-times all away did go.'

' London: printed by G. Croom, at the Blew
Ball'. . . . (here it is torn) . . . . . ' street, over
against Baynard's-Castle, 1684.' The additions
to this state of the copper-plate are the ' Tinker.'
marked 11 ; ' the Man fallen into a Hole,'
marked 16 ; the figure marked 2, and other
figures introduced ; and the booth next to the
' Loyal Coffee-house,' is marked ' Weavers,'
22.

    " 8. The copper-plate, commonly ascribed to
Faithorne. The Title in a Cartouche above,
and the reference by letters of the alphabet,
beginning ' the Temple Staires, with People
goeing upon the Ice to Temple Street,' A, ending London Bridge, Z. Printed for and sold
by William Warten, stationer, at the sign of
the Talbott, over against Fetter Lane end in
Fleet Street.' This is the first address. The
view is looking down to London Bridge.

    " 9. The same plate, with the address of War-
ten altered thus: ' at the signe of the Talbott

vnder the Mitre Tavern in Fleet Street, London.'

" 10. An impression of the last, ruled in squares, with letter-press numbers stamped on each; probably, for some lottery or game.

" 11. An original Drawing, by Wyck ; a View on the Frozen Thames, with a Booth in the foreground, bearing the sign of a pair of horns, hanging out under a wreath, and a flag with the Union Jack hoisted. The distant bank of the river is too indistinct to fix the precise point of view. At the top is written with a pen, in an old hand ' London Thaems, January the 15 Ao 1683-4.'

" Ten verses in letter-press with a border printed on the Thames.

' Behold the liquid Thames now frozen o'er
  That lately ships of mighty burthen bore ;
  The watermen, for want of rowing boats,
  Make use of booths to get their pence and groats.
  Here you may see beef roasted on the spit,
  And for your money you may taste a bit ;
   There may you print your name, tho' cannot write
  'Cause numb'd with cold,—'tis done with great delight,
  And lay it by, that ages yet to come
  May see what things upon the ice were done.' "

Frost of 1716.

The next celebrated frost upon the Thames was in the year 1715-16, thus mentioned by Gay in the second book of his entertaining poem of Trivia.

O roving Muse, recall that wondrous year
When Winter reign'd in bleak Britannia's air,
When hoary Thames, with frosted osiers crown'd,
Was three long moons in icy fetters bound;
The waterman, forlorn along the shore,
Pensive reclines upon his useless oar,
Sees harness'd steeds desert the stony town
And wander roads unstable, not their own;
Wheels o'er the hardened waters smoothly glide
And raise with whiten'd tracks the slipp'ry tide.
Here the fat cook piles high the blazing fire,
And scarce the spit can turn the steer entire.
Booths sudden hide the Thames, long streets appear,
And numerous games proclaim the crowded fair.
So when a general bids the martial train
Spread their encampment o'er the spacious plain,
Thick rising tents a canvass city build
And the loud dice resound through all the field.

In the public papers of the 12th of January 1715-16 appeared this advertisement · "This is to give notice to gentlemen and others, that pass upon the Thames during this frost, that over against Whitehall stairs they may have their names printed, fit to paste in any book, to hand down the memory of the season to future ages.

> You that walk there and do design to tell
> Your children's children what this year befell,
> Go print your names, and take a dram within,
> For such a year as this has seldom been."

Dawkes' News Letter of the 14th of January says, "The Thames seems now a solid rock of ice; and booths for sale of brandy, wine, ale, and other exhilarating liquors, have been for some time fixed thereon; but now it is in a manner like a town; thousands of people cross it, and with wonder view the mountainous heaps of water that now lie congealed into ice. On Thursday a great cook's-shop was erected, and gentlemen went as frequently to dine there as at any ordinary. Over against Westminster, Whitehall, and Whitefriars, printing presses are kept on the ice."

The London Post of January 21st 1716 contains the following :—

" Tuesday last four men, in a bravado, bound themselves not to leave one another whatever should happen, and to travel on the ice up the middle of the Thames as far as they could for four days together, and to avoid all the tracks that any had gone in before them. On this adventure they went from the Old Swan near the bridge over all the roughest of the ice, with long poles in their hands, till they came over against Somerset House, where one of them found it for his present occasion to fall in, but by the help of his pole recovered, having only cooled his posteriors; so they went on, and right against Lambeth another also had occasion to slip in up to his arm-pits, but he was helped out; but they still boldly went on, and none of them have ever since been heard of."

The Weekly Journal, or British Gazetteer, of January 21st says,

" Last Tuesday the Prince of Wales and the Duke of Marlborough, with several other noblemen, went on the Thames on the ice from Old Palace-yard to Lambeth, and back again, through the loud huzzas and acclamations of the people, who showed a general satisfaction at the sight of his Royal Highness."

A set of doggerel verses thus described the fair; and as we cannot get any better prose description of it, we must take one in rhyme.

> There miles together, for the common good,
> The slippery substance offers dainty food:
> Here healing port-wine, and there Rhenish flows;
> Here Bohea tea, and there tobacco grows !

In one place you may meet good Cheshire cheese;
Another proffers whitest Brentford peas!
Here is King George's picture; there Queen Anne's;
Now nut-brown ale in cups, and then in cans.
One sells an Oxford dram as good as can be,
Another offers General Pepper's brandy!
See, there's the Mall! and in that little hut
The best geneva's sold, and love to boot!
See, there a sleek Venetian envoy walks;
See, here an alderman more proudly stalks.
Behold the French Ambassador—that's *he!*
And this the honest sire and Captain Leigh!
Here is St. James's Street, yonder the Strand;
In this place Bowyer plies; that's Lintot's stand.

The News Letter of the 15th of February announced the commencement of the thaw, and in two days the river was entirely free of ice.

For the following list of the various prints of this fair we are also indebted to the late Mr. J. T. Smith.

" 1. ' Frost Fayre, being a true prospect of the great variety of shops and booths for tradesmen, with other curiosities and humours, on the frozen river of Thames, as it appeared before the city of London on that memorable frost in y² second year of our Sovereign Lord King George, anno Domini 1716. Printed and sold by John Bowles and Son, at the Black Horse in Corn Hill.'

" 2. Faithorne's copper-plate of 1683, altered

to the year **1716**.   The references different,
and engraved afresh.   'London : sold by John
Lenthall, stationer, at the Talbot, against St.
Dunstan's Church, in Fleet Street, London.
Price sixpence.'

" **3.** A copper-plate, ten inches two eighths
high (including the margin), fourteen inches
one eighth wide, inscribed, ' A Prospect of the
Fair kept upon the River of Thames (during
the time it was frozen, beginning on December
y° 3rd, and ended on the 28th of January
1715-16.   Drawn by C. Woodfield, as it appeared upon a View at the Temple Stairs, London.'
Below are twenty-eight references, beginning
' A. The Water-house at London Bridge,' and
ending, ' 4, New Cheapside.   Sold by J. Nut-
ting, at y° Crown in Fleet Street, near Water
Lane end.'

" **4.** A rude woodcut view of the sports on the
river, looking down towards London Bridge,
the Monument, Tower, &c.   Size, seven inches
high, including margin, eleven inches four-
eighths wide.   Below are eight verses — ' Behold the liquid Thames,' &c.   ' From the Print-
ing-house in Bow Church-yard.'   Thirteen references : some curious ; viz. 'B—Cripple Atkins
roasting an Ox.   F—A Shoulder of Mutton
roasting in a String at the Sign of the Rat in a

Cage. M—Huffing Jack. N—Will. Ellis, the Poet, and his Wife Bess rhyming on the hard Frost' Believed to be the only portrait of that poet. In a bordure in the centre is printed the name of 'Mr. David Hannott. Printed on the ice, at the Maidenhead at Old Swan Stairs, Jan. 25, 1715-16.'"

FROST OF 1740.

The frost of 1739-40 commenced on Christmas-day, and lasted till the 17th of the following February, when it began to break up; but the river was not clear of ice till the end of the month. The usual sports of a fair were made upon the ice; booths and drinking-tents erected; and also printing-presses, which in all these fairs upon the Thames seem to have been considered the greatest wonder of all. The verses beginning " Amid the arts which on the Thames appear," and " You that walk here, and do design to tell," were revived, and indeed appear to have been popular, till 1814, when we meet with them again.

The author of a little work, called " Frostiana," printed in 1814, and which gives a slight account of all the great frosts, with the exception of that of 1683-4, which is not even alluded to, thus describes, from some contemporary account, to which he has forgotten to give the reference, the severity of the season.

" The watermen and fishermen, with a peterboat in mourning, and the carpenters, bricklayers, &c., with their tools and utensils, in mourning, walked through the streets in large bodies, imploring relief for the necessity of their families. A few days after the frost had set in, great damage was done among the shipping by a high wind, which broke many vessels from their moorings, and drove them foul of each other, while the large flakes of ice there floated on the stream, overwhelmed various boats and lighters, and sunk several coal and corn vessels.

" By these accidents many lives were lost, and many others were also destroyed by the intensity of the cold, both on land and water. Above bridge the Thames was completely frozen over, and tents, and numerous booths were erected on it for selling liquors, &c. to the multitudes that daily flocked thither for curiosity or diversion. The scene here displayed was very irregular, and had more the appearance of a fair on land than a frail exhibition, the only basis of which was water. Various shops were opened for the sale of toys, cutlery, and other light articles. A printing-press was established, and all the common sports of the populace in a wintry season were carried on with augmented spirit, in spite or forgetfulness of the distress that reigned on shore. Many of the houses on the bridge, as well as the bridge itself, received considerable damage when the thaw commenced, by the driving of the ice."

The following is Mr. Smith's catalogue of the prints relating to this fair.

" 1. An engraving fifteen inches five-eighths high and one inch one-eighth margin below, width nineteen inches six-eighths. The title is ' An exact draught of Frost Fair, on the River Thames, as it appeared from White-hall Stairs, in the year 1740. Printed for, and sold by George Foster, print-seller, in St. Paul's Church-yard, London.' There are twelve verses, beginning, ' Old Thames, &c,' ending ' to us again.' There are two of the piers of Westminster Bridge on the right, and people mounting on one of them by a ladder, coarsely engraved. There is another engraving of this, apparently retouched all over, with the addition of a booth with a flag at the right-hand edge of the plate, and a little above it, a man up to his middle in the ice ; also a woman next to the man, who lifts both his arms up, on the same side of the plate.

" 2. A coarse engraving, nine inches high without the margin, twelve inches wide. In the margin above is ' The View of Frost Fair.' In the margin below are twelve verses beginning ' Scythians of old, &c.' and ending,

' This view to future times shall show
The medley scene you visit now.'

York Buildings tower is seen on the left. Though there is no date on the print, it evidently belongs to the frost of this year, as the two piers of the new Westminster Bridge are indicated on the right.

" 3. An engraving eight inches six-eighths high exclusive of margin, thirteen inches four-eighths wide : the title below is ' Frost and Ice Fair, shewing the diversions upon the river Thames, begun the 26th of December, 1739-40, ended February the 17th.' Sixteen verses, ' The bleak north-east' &c, and ending, ' Cheering streams.' To the left, are seen York Buildings waterworks, and St. Paul's ; to the right, are the two piers of the new bridge There are numbers on the plate, intended for as many as fifteen references, the same, apparently, as those to G. Beckham's Frost Fair, with a few exceptions. It is printed in red.

" 4. An engraving six inches six-eighths high,

twelve inches three-eighths wide, at the left-hand side close to the plate line, is 'G. B. inven. fc. according to Act of Parliament, January 18, 1739-40.' This is the first state of the plate; Mr. Smith's impression had the following name and date in letter-press, 'T. Beauford, printed on the river of Thames, when frozen over, January 21, 1739-40.'

"5. The same plate, as retouched and published the next day, as appears by Lord Orford's name in letter-press, thus 'The Right Hon. the Earl of Orford, printed on the river of Thames, when frozen over, January 22, 1739-40.' In this state the sky is darkened in places, and in the margin below is this title: 'Frost Fair. This transient scene,' &c. four verses. 'Printed on the river Thames in ye month of January, 1740;' also fifteen references and corresponding numbers inserted on the view.

"6. Another impression in the first state. In letter-press are the words 'Frost Fair,' the same references as were engraved afterwards, but without any numbers to them, and also the words, 'Printed on the river Thames in the month of January, MDCCXL. It is curious to observe the rapid sale of this plate, brought out January 18, and the references not engraved till January 22. It is one of the commonest frost prints of this date.

" 7. Another engraving by Beckham, six inches six-eighths high, twelve inches wide. The view taken from near a tobacco chimney, on the Surrey side. The title is below, ' Ice Fair, Amidst ye arts y^t on ye Thames appear,' &c. four verses. Printed on ye river Thames, now frozen over January 31, 1739-40.' Fifteen references, of which, No. 1, is ' Westminster Bridge, Sword and Spur, shown. 2—Westminster Abbey, Whitehall, and ye stairs.' On the right under the plate line is ' G. B. invent. fc. according to Act of Parliament, January 1739-40.' This is more curious and uncommon than the last.

" 8. An engraving apparently by C. Mosley, eight inches four-eighths high, twelve inches three-eighths wide. The title in the margin below Frost Fair, eight verses, ' The bleak north-east,' &c. ending, ' From shore to shore.' At the left, under the plate line, ' C. M. invent. fc. according to Act of Parliament.' The view shows the neighbourhood of York Buildings. At the top, in the margin, is, ' Printed upon the river Thames, when frozen, January the 28th, 1739-40.'

" 9. Another impression, differing only in a

trifling retouch of the shading to the printing booth, which is darkened. Below is this name in letter-press, in a square bordure, containing an inscription relative to the invention of 'The noble art and mystery of printing. Dorothy Jones, aged 74. Printed upon the Thames when frozen, February 6, 1740.'

" 10. An engraving seven inches high, eight inches wide. In the margin below is this title, ' Frost Fair, printed upon the ice on the river Thames, January 23, 1739-40.' Eight verses revived from 1683, and already quoted in our account of the frost of that year, ' Behold the liquid Thames, now frozen o'er, &c.' Boats and booths in the front, a church tower, and another high building among the houses on the bank : a very rude engraving. This impression has in letter-press below this name, ' James Theobalds, jun. Whitehall : printed upon the ice on the river Thames, February the 14th, 1739-40, and the verses as above.'

" 11. A broadside of letter-press, entitled, ' The English Chronicle, or Frosty Kalendar, with four columns of accounts of frosts for many years past; ' particularly the severe one this present year, in the months of December, January, and February, 1739-40. In the middle is a copper-plate five inches six-eighths high,

seven inches four-eighths wide, with twelve
references below, of which A—goldsmiths; B—
turners; C—y* rowling press printers; L—an
ox roasted.   Printed on the Thames, January,
1739-40.'   The view is a general one of the city,
with St. Paul's, the Monument, London bridge,
and numerous city churches.   In the foreground is a man sitting with a bottle and
glass, and saying, ' Bung your eye,' probably
a slang phrase of the day; another crying, ' but-
tons or buckles.'   It is inscribed ' London.'

  " 12. A drawing in India ink, said to be by
B. Lens, seven inches four-eighths high, thirteen inches wide, looking towards Lambeth Palace in the distance ; the two piers of the new
bridge fix it to the frost of 1740.   Booths, one
of which has a rolling press in it ; men playing at bowls ; and a sledge going round.   The
view is taken from near Whitehall.

  " 13. A frontispiece engraved by Bickham,
representing London Bridge, and the houses on
it, and booths on the ice, one inscribed ' Nobell
art of Printing,' another, ' old gold,' another
has a rolling press, in a bordure of icicles, and
a head of Winter, with expanded wings below,
under which is, ' G. Bickham, fecit.'   It belongs to an 8vo. tract, entitled, ' An account
of all the principal frosts for above an hun-

dred years past: with political remarks, and poetical descriptions. To which are added, a Philosophical Theory of Freezing; and a Frigid Essay upon Frost Fair. By Icedore Frostiface, of Freesland, Astrologer,

No longer Thames, the shores of London laves,
But chains of ice constrain his rising waves;
A rugged prospect the wide surface crowns,
Rocks, ruins, boats infix'd, and men and towns.

'Printed and sold at the Golden King's-Head, Printing booth, in Frost Fair; and by C. Corbett publisher, over against St Dunstan's Church, Fleet Street, 1740; price sixpence.'

Frost of 1788-9.

The Thames was again frozen in 1767-8, but the cold was not so intense as it had been on previous occasions; and the sports on the river, owing to the comparative insecurity of the ice, were not so well attended, nor did they last so long as on previous occasions. In the year 1788, however, the citizens of London had a complete revival of the ancient sports on the river. The frost set in on the 25th of November, 1788, and lasted with great severity for several weeks.

The following notices appear in a diary in

the " Gentleman's Magazine," " Monday, Jan.
12th—A young bear was baited on the ice opposite Redriff, which drew multitudes together,
and fortunately no accident happened to inter-
rupt their sport. Saturday, 17th—The captain
of a vessel lying off Rotherhithe, the better to
secure the ship's cables, made an agreement
with a publican for fastening a cable to his
premises. In consequence, a small anchor was
carried on shore, and deposited in the cellar,
while another cable was fastened round a beam
in another part of the house. In the night the
ship veered about, and the cables holding fast,
carried away the beam, and levelled the house
with the ground, by which accident five persons asleep in their beds were killed."

Another contemporary account in the " Gentleman's Magazine," says, " The river Thames,
which at this season usually exhibits a dreary
scene of languor and indolence, was this year
the stage on which there were all kinds of
diversions, bear-baiting, festivals, pigs and sheep
roasted, booths, turnabouts, and all the various amusements of Bartholomew Fair multi-
plied and improved. From Putney Bridge in
Middlesex, down to Rotherhithe, was one continued scene of merriment and jollity; not a
gloomy face to be seen, but all cheerfulness,

arising apparently from business and bustle. From this description the reader, however, is not to conclude that all was as it seemed. The miserable inhabitants that dwell in houses on both sides of the river during these thoughtless exhibitions, were many of them experiencing the extreme of misery; destitute of employment, though industrious, they were with families of helpless children pining for want of bread; and though in no country in the world are the rich more extensively benevolent than in England, yet their benefactions could bear no proportion to the wants of the numerous poor, who could not all partake of the common bounty. It may, however, be truly said, that in no great city or country on the continent of Europe, the poor suffered less from the rigour of the season than the inhabitants of Great Britain and London; yet, even in London, the distress was very great, and though liberal subscriptions were raised, many perished through want and cold. On this occasion the City of London subscribed £1500 towards supporting such persons as were not in the habit of receiving alms."

The following account of the same frost, is from "The Annual Register," under date of the 12th of February. "The Thames at Iron-gate to the opposite shore is frozen over, numbers of persons having walked across yesterday. At Shadwell the Thames is likewise frozen over, several booths are fixed on the ice; and yesterday an ox was roasted whole, and sold to the people who were skaiting and sliding. The scene on the river is very entertaining. From Putney Bridge upwards, the river is completely frozen over, and people walk to and from the different villages on the face of the deep. Opposite to Windsor street, booths have been erected since Friday last, and a fair is kept on the river. Multitudes of people are continually passing and repassing; puppet-shows, roundabouts, and all the various amusements of Bartholomew Fair are exhibited. In short, Putney and Fulham, from the morning dawn till the dusk of returning evening, is a scene of festivity and gaiety."

FROST OF 1814.

The next great frost upon the Thames was in 1814. The following contemporary accounts of " The Annual Register," and some others from Hone's " Every Day Book," will be read with interest.

" January 21st. In London the great accumulation of snow already heaped on the ground, and condensed by three or four weeks of continued frost, was on Wednesday increased by a fresh fall, to a height hardly known in the memory of the oldest inhabitants. The cold has been intensely severe, the snow during the last fall being accompanied with a sharp wind and a little moisture. In many places, where the houses are old, it became necessary to relieve the roofs, by throwing off the load collected upon them, and by these means the carriage-way in the middle of the streets is made of a depth hardly passable for pedestrians, while carriages with difficulty plough their way through the mass. The water pipes being generally frozen, it has become necessary for several days to afford supplies by opening the plugs in the streets, and the streams thus constantly flowing, add to the general mass of ice. An enormous increase has taken place in the price of coals, in consequence of the river navigation and other means of conveyance being so greatly impeded."

[The roads throughout the country were impassable. The mails from London to Oxford did not arrive for three days, and from Dover and Canterbury for the same period; and a circular was issued by Lord Sidmouth

on the 29th of January, to the Lords Lieutenant of the various counties, directing them
to take immediate steps for providing all practical means to remove from the highways and
principal roads of communication within their
respective counties, the obstructions which had
been caused by the snow. 'This object,' said
the circular, 'would afford employment to various classes of individuals, who were tempo-
rarily deprived of their usual earnings by the
inclemency of the season;' and their Lordships
were accordingly requested to communicate
without delay to the magistracy, and through
them with the trustees of turnpike roads, the
overseers of the poor, the surveyors of the
highways, and other subordinate officers of the
various districts and parishes, in such manner
as to insure the most speedy and effectual
means of carrying the intentions of the Government into effect.]

"January 27th.—Yesterday the wind having
veered round to the south-west, the effects of
thaw were speedily discernible.

" The fall of the river at London Bridge has
for several days past presented a scene both
novel and interesting. At the ebbing of the
tide huge fragments of ice were precipitated
down the stream with great violence, accom-

panied by a noise equal to the report of a small piece of artillery. On the return of the tide they were forced back again; but the obstacles opposed to their passage through the arches were so great as apparently to threaten a total stoppage to the navigation of the river.

"February 1st.—The Thames between Blackfriars and London Bridges continued to present the novel scene of persons moving on the ice in all directions and in greatly increased numbers. The ice, however, from its roughness and inequalities is totally unfit for amusement, although we observed several booths erected upon it for the sale of small wares, but the publicans and spirit-dealers were most in the receipt of custom. The whole of the river opposite Queenhithe was frozen over, and in some parts the ice was several feet thick, while in others it was dangerous to venture upon, notwithstanding which, crowds of foot passengers crossed backwards and forwards throughout the whole of the day. We did not hear of any lives being lost, but many who ventured too far towards Blackfriars Bridge were partially immersed in the water by the ice giving way. Two coopers were with difficulty saved.

"February 2nd.—The Thames this day presented a complete frost fair. The grand mall or walk extended from Blackfriars to London Bridge. This was named the city road, and was lined on each side by persons of all descriptions. Eight or ten printing-presses were erected, and numerous pieces commemorative of the 'great frost' were printed on the ice. At one of the presses an orange-coloured standard was hoisted with the watch-word '*Orange Boven*' in large characters. This was an allusion to the recent restoration of the Stadtholder. One of the printers issued a circular to the following effect: — 'Friends, now is your time to support the freedom of the press. Can the press have greater liberty? Here you find it working in the middle of the Thames, and if you encourage us by buying our impressions, we will keep it going in the true spirit of liberty during the frost.'

"February 3rd.—The number of adventurers increased. Swings, book-stalls, dancing in a barge, suttling-booths, playing at skittles, and almost every appendage of a fair on land appeared on the Thames. Thousands flocked to the spectacle. The ice presented a most picturesque appearance. The view of St. Paul's and of the city, with the white foreground, had a very singular effect; in many parts mountains of ice upheaved, resembled the rude interior of a stone quarry.

" February 4th.—Each day brought a fresh accession of pedlars to sell their wares, and the greatest rubbish of all sorts was raked up and sold at double and treble the original cost. The watermen profited exceedingly, for each person paid a toll of twopence or threepence before he was admitted to the fair; and something also was expected for permission to return. Some of them were said to have taken as much as six pounds in a day. Many persons remained on the ice till late at night, and the effect by moonlight was singularly novel and beautiful. The bosom of the Thames seemed to rival the frozen climes of the north.

" February 7th.—The ice between London Bridge and Blackfriars gave way yesterday, in consequence of the high tides. On Saturday, thousands of people walked on the ice from one bridge to the other notwithstanding there were evident signs of its speedy breaking up, and even early yesterday morning some foolhardy persons passed over from Bankside to Queenhithe. About an hour after this the whole mass gave way, and swept with a tremendous range through the noble arches of Blackfriars Bridge, carrying along with it all within its course, including about forty barges. The new erections for the Strand bridge impeded its progress and a vast quantity of the ice was there collected, but the strong current on the Somerset House side carried everything before it, and the passage of the river became at last free. Numbers of boats were then busily employed, saving rafts of timber and towing the drifted barges to the shore. We have heard that some persons who had the folly to remain on the ice to a very late hour on Saturday night either lost their lives or were in great jeopardy. They had remained carousing in the tents till midnight, and were suddenly alarmed by the parting of the apparently solid mass on which they stood. Being unable to reach the shore they contrived to get into two barges which had been stationary, but which were now borne upward by the tide, and which of course were quite unmanageable. One of these barges safely cleared Blackfriars Bridge; the other struck against a pier where it remained fast : luckily, however, there were some spectators of the dismal situation of the persons on board, who, having procured ropes, contrived to haul them up in safety."

THE END.

LONDON: PRINTED BY SAMUEL BENTLEY
Bangor House, Shoe Lane.

AND OTHER POEMS,

BY CHARLES MACKAY,

AUTHOR OF " THE THAMES AND ITS TRIBUTARIES," &c.

OPINIONS OF THE PRESS.

THE TIMES.

" The great merit of this poem is the pure spirit of religion with which every part of it is imbued ; a merit the more to be admired on account of its rarity in the productions of most modern bards. It has of late become a habit with poets, or rather with people who assume that name, to substitute a sickly sentimentality in the place of morals, and covertly to sneer at Christianity, and those wholesome truths which do not accord with the wretched laxity of their own conceptions of good and evil. Mr. Mackay is not a writer of this class. He is more original, though less extravagant than his contemporaries : his imagination is tempered by his judgment : neither his thoughts nor his words are on stilts, nor does he stalk and caper with awkward gesticulations for the gratification of fools, and the annoyance of the well-conducted. He has written a very excellent volume of poetry, which may be put into the hands of all readers, and from which few or none will not derive instruction or pleasure."

THE SPECTATOR.

" Mr. Mackay has kept clear of the excitement school, and (in his own words), ' has ventured to return to the ancient simplicity, with the little-con- soling hope, that, when quite palled with high feeding, and the unsubstantial fritter of mere words the public may, at some near, or at some remote period, look with a slight degree of favour upon a humble follower in that simple, na- tural, and enduring school of poetry, which has produced such writers as Goldsmith, Rogers, and Campbell.' Such poetry, we verily believe, is that which at present would be the most acceptable. It would have the zest of novelty, after the pomp and pageantry of Feudalism, the German horrors, and Oriental attrocities, to which the public have been so long inured, while the toil-worn, and care-worn spirit would be refreshed with its sweetness and beauty. But while the poetry chosen by Mr. Mackay for his model, is, pro- bably, the most pleasing, so is it also the most difficult ; every vulgar mode of excitement—everything coarse, garish, or exaggerated, is excluded. Purity of taste, strong, but natural feeling, sound and vigorous thought, a vivid, but re- gulated imagination, and the *curiosa felicitas* in language and versification, are all requisite, even for moderate success, in following the footsteps of the older English poets, and it is but doing Mr. Mackay justice to say that to this ex- tent he possesses those qualities.

" ' The Hope of the World' is in two cantos, and its object is to show the effect of Christianity in diffusing civilization, virtue, knowledge, and happiness, throughout the world. The topics which present themselves for this purpose are numerous and obvious. The best of them have been selected and illus- trated, some of them with much strength of thought and beauty of expression. The whole poem is marked by just views, liberal principles, and a spirit of true and natural piety, undebased by the bigotry and fanaticism of the day. There are beautiful things among the miscellaneous poems ; some of the lyrical pieces, especially, have much of the spirit of Beranger."

THE ATLAS.

" We cordially assent to Mr. Mackay's assertion of faith in the enduring interest of poetry. The love of poetry is not dead, and it never can die.

" ' It is not in nature,' says Mr. Mackay, ' that it should ;' and he says truly. Mr. Mackay's volume is worthy of the just enthusiasm he entertains for the muse he courts. His first and principal poem, 'The Hope of the World,' takes a rapid review, in two cantos, of the progress and condition of man, tracing him through the frauds, and cruelties, and evil passions of his early annals, and showing finally the benignant effects that followed the introduction of Christianity, by which the human heart was softened, the intellect cultivated, and the world freed from the thraldom of superstition and crime.

" In the conduct of this noble argument, he displays considerable poetical power, a wide reach of information, and strong reliance upon the greatness and beauty of his theme. The measure is always fluent and simple. There are no attempts at intricate melody, and consequently little variety in the flow of the verse. The poem is remarkably regular in its versification, always musical, and rarely distinguished by any bold deviations, or striking modulations of the rhythm. Uniform and graceful throughout, it will be read with pleasure, and leave a grateful and agreeable impression behind.

" The other poems in the collection are much above the average of modern verse. The lyrics are numerous, and marked by great freedom and breadth of expression. A few ballads and miscellaneous pieces enhance the interest of the volume, which is highly creditable to the good taste and genius of the author."

THE MORNING CHRONICLE.

" The author of the volume now before us, has aimed at a higher standard of 'poesie' than is usual among the modern aspirants to Parnassus' hill. He claims to be placed side by side with the poets of the old and simple, and yet withal vigorous school, which boasts of Goldsmith, and Rogers, and Campbell. This volume is full of chaste and well-turned sentiments, of earnest and sound feeling, with touches here and there of that force which awakens our best sympathies, and carries us along with the writer. The first poem is well conceived, and is treated in a manner that shows great taste and judgment. Among the minor poems are songs, not at all inferior to the productions of those most successful of all song writers, Burns, and Moore, and Lover. The volume is dedicated to Rogers, and is worthy of the fostering care of the author of ' The Pleasures of Memory.' "

THE LITERARY GAZETTE.

" 'The Hope of the World' is a poem in a style rarely attempted now-a-days ; and when attempted, still more rarely do we meet with the harmonious flow of numbers which Mr. Mackay presents to us. He is a daring man who calls himself even an humble follower of that ' simple, natural, and enduring school of poetry, which has produced such writers as Goldsmith, Rogers, and Campbell ;' and such our author declares himself to be. But without daring, there can be no success, and we find many beautiful passages in ' The Hope of the World,' doing honour to the school to which that poem belongs. Mr. Mackay is far from an unknown writer, and seldom have we met with anything, either in prose or verse, from his pen, which does not bespeak a purity of sentiment, and a facility of composition, making us well-pleased to renew our acquaintance.

THE BRITANNIA.

" The public is familiar with the name of this poet, and will be prepared to receive favourably any productions of his pen. His works already published, although they consist chiefly of ' Fugitive pieces,' evidence much taste and true feeling, and many of them have long been favourites in a thousand home-circles. He has here essayed a bolder effort. He will agree with us in considering it almost a vain attempt to make the most eloquent appeal of poetry to the heart in this matter-of-fact age ; nevertheless, wherever his volume may win its way, he will be admired and esteemed for the strength of his mind, the delicacy of his thoughts, and the fine harmonious verse in which he expresses them.

sive fame. There is a , y, generous tone, t g ne poem , much eloquent and impressive reasoning, and a pure and holy strain, which does honour to his heart, no less than to his head."

" From Mr. Mackay's ' Hope of the World ' much hope of the poet's future progress may be drawn. The poem is distinguished throughout by a fine sympathy for his fellow men, a practical tone of Christianity, and a clear comprehension of the true interests of humanity. The general characteristics of the numerous pieces in his volume, are the liberality and benevolence of the sentiments, and the correctness of the versification."

" The present volume will earn for its author no mean place among the aspirants for poetic fame. The principal poem, ' The Hope of the World,' in smooth, but nervous verse, describes the manifold blessings bestowed by a beneficent Creator, on man ; and the withering influence cast over them in the first ages of the world, by the unrestrained indulgence of the evil passions that lurk in the human bosom. From this black page of history the second canto turns to the dawning of a brighter day, in the introduction of Christianity, and traces, in a historical sketch of great power and beauty, its humanizing influence on mankind, and finally exults in the ultimate and glorious hope it brings to light. The other portion of the volume is composed of Sacred Melodies, Reveries, Songs for Music, and Ballads. The rhythmical cadence, and vigorous versification of many of these, remind us forcibly of Campbell's beauteous pieces. The fine flow of feeling and fancy, too, that runs through them all, charmed us much."

" In his Preface to this elegant volume of poems, the author observes that ' he has ventured to return to the ancient simplicity, with the little consoling hope, that when quite palled with high feeding, and the unsubstantial fritter of mere words, the public may, at some near, or at some remote period, look with a slight degree of favour upon a humble follower in that simple, natural, and enduring school of poetry, which has produced such writers as Goldsmith, Rogers, and Campbell." The period to which the author here looks forward for being appreciated as he deserves, is nearer at hand than he supposes. The public is already tired of ' the unsubstantial fritter of mere words ' in poetry ; it requires thought and feeling, instead of mere felicitous expression ; and this is precisely the volume that is calculated to gratify its improved taste. Nothing can well be chaster than Mr. Mackay's language, or healthier and more elevated than his general tone of feeling. His manner indicates a calm self-possession that is far more closely allied to real, unaffected sensibility, than those hysterical outbursts with which modern poetry has been so long deformed. His songs are particularly happy — spirited, graceful, and so remarkable for the melody of their rhythm, that we are surprised the majority of them have not yet been set to music. We shall be glad to see the author again in print, for, if we mistake not, he possesses the poetic faculty in no ordinary degree.

" The author of this highly meritorious work fairly sets forth in his preface his aim and object, and the basis upon which he proceeds.

" Mr. Mackay has chosen admirable models, and he has done them justice by his fancy, taste, and elegance of execution. The first and principal poem is that from which this elegant volume, or tribute to the muse, takes its name ; ' The Hope of the World,' a poem of two cantos, and of fifty-seven pages. The author, in very fluent and harmonious verse, sketches man as he might have been, and as nature intended he should be, and in a vein of piety, and a spirit of poetry, pursues this subject, tracing how the prejudices and illusions of our race have marred human happiness, and opposed the infinite benevolence of the Creator.

" Mr. Mackay is peculiarly happy in running through the various supersti-
tions that have afflicted our species, but he is afraid to come too near home.
But we must not philosophise too strictly in poetry, and, in this instance, we
must in justice acknowledge that the author has produced an elegant and very
pleasing poem. The minor poems are extremely beautiful. In these Mr.
Mackay is simple and perfectly natural, and without losing vigour or strong
imagination."

THE HERALD OF PEACE.

" Here is a poet devoting his talents to the cause of Peace, a very uncommon thing. He writes well, and is, we would say, very likely to find a per-
manent place among ' The English bards.' We expect that this volume will
be followed, some time to come, by another, which will raise the standard of
the author's poetical powers. In the first, and the principal poem, we have a
short history of the world, in which its misery, in consequence of intolerance
and ambition, is graphically delineated. Here the evil and folly of war is
very powerfully represented. Christianity, the author shows to be ' The
Hope of the World,' and he gives due prominency to its pacific character.
We wish Mr. Mackay success, and hail him as a coadjutor in the sacred
cause of peace."

THE NEW COURT GAZETTE.

" ' The Hope of the World' is the title of a didactic poem, the writer of
which, following in the classic track of Goldsmith, Rogers, and Campbell, seeks
to allure the reader from the two extremes of lawless and exciting passions
and of sickly sentimentality, into which poetry has of late years run, to ' the
ancient simplicity.' The exordium of the poem shows that man is capable of
happiness. The poet then traces the causes, as war, lust of empire, and religious differences, which have perverted the original intent of Providence, in
the creation of man. And proceeding from his errors to the mode of their
correction, he then proves that Christianity affords the hope, the certainty,
and the means of attaining to a ' reign of peace.' The poem is well constructed, the versification smooth, and the imagery correct. It always pleases
but never startles. Among the minor poems are many very sweet lyric effu-
sions."

THE KENTISH CORONAL.

" The volume now before us proves Mr. Mackay to be a man of genius, a
poet, and a sincere christian. ' The Hope of the World' is a POEM, (we speak
emphatically,) smooth and flowing in its versification, and abounding in fine imagery and pure and exalted sentiments ; in it are forcibly pointed out the benefits
which have, and must result from a right appreciation of the doctrines of true
Christianity, and an unfailing adherence to those principles of universal love, and
active benevolence inculcated by their Divine Founder ; the evils resulting from
an opposite course of procedure, and a misunderstanding, wilful or otherwise, of
those gentle precepts, are also delineated with the pencil of a master. Bigotry,
Superstition, Pride, Avarice, Ambition, with their concomitant ills, are here
divested of their gorgeous trapping, and held up in all their naked deformity
to abhorrence and detestation. The ' Sacred Melodies,' the ' Reveries,' the
' Songs for Music,' and the ' Ballads,' which make up the contents of the
volume, are most of them sweet specimens of lyrical composition, some soft
and musical, as a chime of bells mellowed by distance ; some energetic and
spirit-stirring, as a trumpet-peal. ' Count Cask-o'-Whiskey and his three
Houses,' is a fine specimen of the horribly grotesque in composition, and em-
bodies a fearful picture of the evils of intemperance. We perfectly agree with
Mr. Mackay, who says in his preface that ' the age of poetry never will, and
never can pass away,' and sincerely hope, that the apathy felt by the world
towards new aspirants, may in his case, yield to admiration. At all events,
sure we are of this, that if he pleaseth not the many, he will find, among the
tuneful brethren of the lyre, ' fit audience, though few.'

Lightning Source UK Ltd.
Milton Keynes UK
UKOW06f1852221015

261210UK00015B/414/P

9 781331 734789